AF663525

Distance Education

Preface

The work at hand on 'Distance Education' is the result of the appreciation and admiration of my many works on various aspects of education and publisher's desire that I should present this work to the learned scholars and students, hence, I feel duty-bound to express my heart-felt thanks, gratitude and indebtedness to the readers of my earlier works and the publisher alike.

I trust that work on 'Distance Education' will fulfil a national need because it not only spells out the theory and practice of distance education but also attempts to establish that distance learning is in no way inferior in quality and variety. The degrees and diplomas awarded by the recognised universities and institutions are at par with such degrees and diplomas awarded by the universities and institutions imparting education through formal system of education. This has been done through Chapter 19 captioned as 'The Truth About Distance Education', thus it is an unique feature of this book.

This book also stresses that distance education democratises education and attempts to take the education to people's doorsteps and this system is most cost effective for both the nation as well as the learner. This contains two chapters on these aspects captioned as follows:

1. Chapter 16—"Distance Learning—A Cost Effective System of Education".
2. Chapter 17—"Distance Education—A Boon for Neglected Sections of Society—SC, ST, BC, Physically Disabled, Women and Marginal Farmers etc."

The book contains point analysis and description of the subject in Indian context and claims to be most comprehensive among several books published so far. The book contains twenty chapters and lays down the basic concepts of the subject as required to be understood by every specialist of the subject and the common people in general.

I have tried my best to make the study of the subject interesting through simple language and through illustrations and examples from actual life situations which will help the readers to understand the concept of distance education and its utility for everyone because education is a life long process and distance education is the pathway for the same.

Despite my best efforts, to present this work on 'Distance Education' as useful as possible, I feel that the readers are the best judge of its merit, therefore, suggestions for improvement, if any, are cordially invited.

Madhulika Sharma

DISTANCE EDUCATION
Concepts and Principles

MADHULIKA SHARMA

KANISHKA PUBLISHERS, DISTRIBUTORS
NEW DELHI-110 002

KANISHKA PUBLISHERS, DISTRIBUTORS
4697/5-21A, Ansari Road, Daryaganj
New Delhi -110 002
Phones : 2327 0497, 2328 8285
Fax : 011-2328 8285
E-mail : kanishka_publishing@yahoo.co.in

Distance Education: Concepts and Principles
First Published-2006
Edition-2016

PRINTED IN INDIA

Published by Madan Sachdeva for Kanishka Publishers, Distributors, 4697/5-21A, Ansari Road, Daryaganj, New Delhi-110 002, Typeset by Sunshine Graphics, Delhi, and Printed at Rajdhani Printers, Delhi.

Contents

1

Emergence of Distance Education as an Educational Concept

INTRODUCTION

Though distance education is a new concept in educational system but it has been catching up very fast in all countries—developed, developing or underdeveloped, socialist or capitalist, western or non-western, hence, its importance is being realised all over the world and certainly in developing countries. Its significance, utility and importance is more recognised by policy makers than by the educationists, because it is a well known fact that campus-based traditional higher education is a big strain on the public exchequers, which developing countries cannot easily manage.

MEANING OF DISTANCE EDUCATION

The concept of distance education has emerged as a result of man's search for an education which could be provided to a person at home. 'Necessity is the mother of invention' is too well known a proverb to be elicited. In the days gone by; education from a distance was never thought of, because teachers were available to teach those who wanted to quench their thirst for knowledge. Not everybody was interested in higher education or education for leisure or for that matter enhancing his knowledge for further promotion in his job.

But the situation is quite different at present. Time never ran so fast as today. Competition in life was never so hard as we find at this juncture. Knowledge of man never became obsolete in such a short time as we find today.

Ambitions are going higher and higher. Every country has realised the need of educating its population in the real sense of the term. Every man or woman wants to improve his/her life style and living standard. Continuing education is becoming a part of educational system. As such it was increasingly realised that formal system of education as has been prevailing till now was not sufficient enough to meet the demands of the coming century.

Constraints in terms of man power and money to build educational institutions, appoint teachers, provide other infrastructure and the distance of student from the schools/colleges led to the search of a via media which could be alternatively, use to expand education and fulfil educational needs of all. Instead of bringing students to the schools/colleges it was proposed to take school to the student and hence this concept of distance education came into existence.

What, then, is distance education? There is no one meaning of the term 'distance education'. It is known by a variety of names, viz. 'Correspondence Education', 'Home Study', 'Independent Study', 'External Study', 'Off-campus Study', 'Open Learning', 'Open Education', etc. There is what Fred Jevons calls: "A bewildering nomenclature".

In Australia, its official name is External System. "This description is now very much appreciated because it carries vibes of old London external system which usually provides examination but not teaching."

This system is very prevalent in India also. In some countries, the term 'Correspondence Education' is widely used. But it has increasingly been replaced by the term 'Independent Study' in North America. 'Home Study' is sometimes used to describe correspondence programmes of private schools both in North America and Europe.

This is also disliked by many mainly because some of the correspondence institutions have only profit motive, particularly the private ones. No doubt, some of them enjoy very good reputation, but several of them are far from it. Further, several correspondence institutions depend only on one medium, viz. the print material. The distance education today lays emphasis not only on print medium but also on other media.

In fact, multi-media approach is the corner-stone of distance education systems. In France, it is known as 'tele-enseignement'. In Germany, it is described as 'Frenstudium' or 'Fernunterricht'. In Spanish speaking countries, it is described as 'education a distancia'. 'Off-campus' is a term which is popularly used for distance education in Australia. 'Extra-mural' refers to distance education in New Zealand.

These terms have come into vogue because of the historical circumstances in various countries. They have peculiar characteristics of their own, most of which are similar to distance education. For instance, all of them emphasise separation of the student from the teacher.

In India, we have been using three terms: 'External Appearance' (private appearance), 'Correspondence Education', and 'Distance Education'. I would not regard the first as distance education, because, here a university permits a student to take the examination as a private candidate, and if he passes, he is given the degree.

The university does not take any responsibility to impart education to the student. As a result, he is on his own and very often at the mercy of the mercenary tutorial institutions. Since university does not give any education, what is being done under external appearance can best be called 'private study' but not distance education. The second, correspondence education, has been quite popular in this country. Lately some of them have designated themselves as Distance Education and open University System. Thus, in India, two terms are being used: Correspondence Education and Distance Education.

Distance Education (DE) implies education being imparted to a student by the teacher despite physical distance. Of late, many more interpretations have been given in the analysis of DE.

The most popular analysis of Keegan (1986) projects seven principal characteristics of DE such as: the teacher-student distance; the influence of an educational organisation; used of technical media; the provision of two-way communication; the absence of group learning, with students taught largely as individuals (while retaining the possibility of occasional seminars); participation in the most industrialised form of education; and the privatisation of learning (in that learning occurs away from the group).

Moreover there has been a clear-cut basis of understanding the meaning of DE in terms of learning taking place in separation of teacher and student through uses of print based materials, mechanical and electronic media and occasional interactions between tutor and student. DE is identified in different forms existing inside and outside the formal traditional structures of education.

Since the sixties, DE has been gaining ground throughout the world in the forms of Correspondence Courses, Home Study programmes, Universities of the Air, Radio and Television University, Every Man's University, Free University and Open University. Of course, the origin of Distance Education, in the form of correspondence education goes back to the mid-nineteenth century.

BRIEF HISTORY OF THE CONCEPT

Correspondence studies took formal shape in Bath, England, in 1840, through Isaac Pitman who conducted his course in shorthand via the new Penny Post (Sivatko, 1969). It became more systematic in the UK in the last decade of the nineteenth century. Many of the better colleges, viz. Skerry's (1880), Foulks Wynch (1884), International Correspondence College (1894) introduced examination-oriented courses.

In the twentieth century the distance education movement underwent several changes. By 1970, nearly all correspondence institutions in the UK were conducting commercially financed professional courses, university and school subjects, technical studies, general and recreational studies, etc. Also, it is said that the Swedish system of correspondence courses opened a new chapter in systematizing the correspondence instruction, when Hermodes was founded in Malmo in 1896.

Following this, creation of institutions like ABF (1912) and the Brevskolan strengthened the correspondence movement. During the early 1970s, there were nearly a million students opting for correspondence courses. It has been found that one out of every eight Swede was engaged in some form of correspondence study.

In the United States, the first effort to organise correspondence education came in 1873, with the formation of the Society for House Studies. This was followed by the setting up of correspondence institutions like Illinois Western University (1874) and Correspondence University at Ithaca, New York (1883).

However, those initial efforts were shortlived. Subsequently, other institutions like the Institute of Correspondence Schools (1890), American Society for Extension of University Teaching (1890) and National University Extension Associations (NUEA) made considerable headway in the sphere of distance education in the USA.

In the early part of the twentieth century (1926) a non-profit educational association, viz. National Home Study Council (NHSC), was established for setting standards for correspondence schools. By 1967, there were around 70 correspondence institutions which had joined the NUEA and some hundred institutions had become members of the NHSC.

In the USSR, in 1926, a correspondence study department was established at one of the institutions of higher learning. During 1929-30, in response to the demand for specialists with higher education and qualified workers, special attention was given to correspondence studies.

The first legal act dealing with correspondence study (1931), the approval of graduate correspondence work (1939), and the educational reform (1958) have strengthened the base of correspondence education throughout. By 1961, the institutions of correspondence study had become an organic part of the whole educational system of the USSR and encompassed the elementary high school as well as undergraduate and postgraduate courses.

The vast geographic size and the sparse population of Australia were particularly conducive for the growth of correspondence education. Correspondence courses were first started in Australia in the University of Queensland with teacher training programmes and were later extended to the other universities. Also, almost from their foundation days, several of the Australian universities have been providing external tuition for matriculate students along with university level courses.

In addition, many private agencies have established themselves over a period of many years and are offering correspondence courses in a wide range of subjects. From 1970 onwards, a fast and progressive movement could be marked at world level in terms of expansion of distance education institutions, changes in governance models, application of educational technology, improved evaluation system, etc.

The creation of institutes like Open University in UK (1971), Community College of Vermount, USA (1971), State University of Nebraska, USA (1971), Empire State College, USA (1971), New York Regents External Degree Programme (1972), the *Ferm Universitat* in West Germany (1975), the *Universidad Estatal a Distancia*, in Costa Rica (1977), *Centre National de Tale-Ensignement*, in France (1981), etc: seem to have enhanced the popularity of distance study.

This period has also been remarkable for the expansion of distance education system in Asian and the Pacific regions.

Countries like Australia, Bangladesh, China, India, Iran, New Zealand, Pakistan, Republic of Korea, Thailand, etc. have advanced further in this field. This can be marked through creation of institutions like Brisbane College of Advanced Education (1974), Capricoria Institute of Advanced Education (1974), Deakin University (1978), Gippsland Institute of Advanced Education (1972), Hawkesbury Agricultural College (1947), Mibchell College of Advanced Education (1971), Meopoch University (1975), New Castle College of Advanced Education (1974), Orange Agricultural College (1978), Queensland Institute of Technology (1978), University of Wollongang (1974), Victoria College (1976), Victorian Tafe Off-Campus Network (1978), Western Australian College of Advanced Education (1980), etc. in Australia; Directorate of Secondary and Higher Education School Broadcasting Programme (1980), in Bangladesh; Central Broadcasting and Television University of China (1979), Correspondence School in New Zealand (1976), Allama Iqbal Open University (1974), in Pakistan; Korea Correspondence College (1972), in Republic of Korea; Bansomdej Chaopraya Teacher's College (1980), Chulalongkarn University (1983), Mahasarakam Teachers' College (1981), Suknothai Thammathirat Open University (1979), etc. in Thailand. Establishment of these institutions indicate a wide scope of DE in developed as well as developing countries since 1960.

DISTINCTION BETWEEN 'OPEN LEARNING' AND 'DISTANCE EDUCATION'

The two terms which are used inter-changeably and about which there has been some controversy are 'Open Learning' and 'Distance Education'. 'Open Learning' covers "a wide range of innovations and reforms in the educational sector." Included are changes that aim to improve such things as the participation of learners, instructional design, methods of transmitting information and support to learners.

A very comprehensive document entitled "Open Learning" by Mackenzie, Postgate and Scupham which was brought out by the UNESCO in 1975 describes open learning as follows: "Such systems are designed to offer opportunities for part-time study, for learning at a distance and for innovations in the curriculum. They are intended to allow access to wider section of adult population, to enable students to compensate for lost opportunities in the past or to acquire new skills and qualifications for the future. Open learning systems aim to redress social or educational inequality and to offer opportunities not provided by conventional colleges or universities.

In this system, restrictions on learning are few than those in formal educational institutions. Educational opportunities are planned deliberately so that access to knowledge is available to individuals in spite of barriers such as geographical distance. It is argued by some that while distance education is accommodated by an open learning system, the opposite premise may not be true.

As Ruggles and his associates argue: "Not all the distance education programmes have the characteristics of an open learning system. Some are very rigid and inflexible." In their view, this term may symbolise a new and emerging philosophy that will become more closely associated with learning at a distance.

The term 'open' generally refers to four aspects: (*i*) People, where it would not debar applicants on account of their lack of educational qualifications; (*ii*) Place, in the sense that learning would be home-based and not restricted to class rooms or a campus; (*iii*) The use of new methods of teaching; and (*iv*) Ideas. However, writers on the subject find the term 'open learning' or 'distance education' unsatisfactory.

There are several similarities between 'open learning' and 'distance education'. However the term 'open learning' conveys certain amount of vagueness about it. Moreover, when we look at the open universities and open learning institutions, we find that all that is conveyed by 'openness' is not to be found in quite a few of these institutions. Open learning, therefore, is always synonymous with open university or distance education. Several open universities and open learning institutions prescribe certain entry qualifications and they debar those who do not fulfil the conditions laid down by them.

Therefore, if the idea is to provide educational facilities to larger number of people scattered all over, i.e. providing greater access to education, the term 'distance education' would be more appropriate. This term basically emphasises separation of the teacher and the learner, and planning of educational programmes and material by an educational organisation and use of technical media on a large scale.

Distance education has been defined by several writers like Wedemeyer, Holmberg, Moore, Peters and Keegan, each emphasising certain aspects of the system. It is, however, to the credit of Desmond Keegan that he has attempted a synthesis of most of the definitions. On the basis of this, he finds that distance education has the following important characteristics:

- The quasi-permanent separation of teacher and learner throughout the length of the learning process; this distinguishes it from conventional face-to-face education.
- The influence of an educational organisation both in planning and preparation of learning materials and in the provision of student support services; this distinguishes it from private study and teach-yourself programmes.
- The use of technical media; print, audio, video or computer, to unite teachers and learners and carry the content of the course.
- The provision of two-way communication so that the student may benefit from or even initiate a dialogue; this distinguishes it from other uses of technology in education.
- The quasi-permanent absence of a learning group throughout the length of the learning process so that people are usually taught as individuals and not in groups, with the possibility of occasional meetings for both didactic and socialization purposes.

In addition, he finds that there are two other socio-cultural determinants which are necessary pre-conditions and necessary consequence of distance education. They are: (1) the presence of more industrialised features than in conventional oral education; and (2) privatisation of institutional learning.

The characteristics enumerated by Keegan are basic to the concepts of distance education. They provide operational facility for the use of distance education. Separation of teacher and learner emphasises that the latter can learn autonomously. While he can learn on his own, there is the educational organisation which does the planning for him.

A variety of media are used to teach the students. Efforts are also made to provide interaction between the teacher and the student. There may be an occasional peer group interaction. On the whole, the student learns on his own which may be described as privatisation of institutional learning.

A noteworthy feature of distance education is that it needs massive organisational effort which is similar to industrial organisations. Thus, we see that distance education institutions have two distinct characteristics—academic and industrial.

The 'academic' represents the development and preparation of course material, whereas 'industrial' refers to production and distribution of educational material. Those who are familiar with open universities would know that the latter are the largest publishers in the world today.

Distance education thus represents distance teaching plus distance learning. Anthony Kaye presents a systems view of distance education. They are 'operating activities' to describe the activities that contribute to imparting, evaluation and expert perceptions which define the nature of the enterprise and differentiate it from other enterprises.

The operating activities are split into two: (*a*) course sub-system, and (*b*) student sub-system.

The second, logistical (maintenance) activities which procure and replenish the resources required by the enterprises. The activities include purchasing, maintenance and repair of buildings and equipment, staff recruitment, training, motivation, etc.

The third refers to regulatory activities which relate to operating activities and activities of the organisation to its environment. These activities include decision making and higher management functions of planning, financial management, project control and evaluation.

WHY DO WE NEED DISTANCE EDUCATION IN INDIA?

It has been stated earlier that traditional system of campus based higher education is a big strain on the public exchequers. It is a matter of vital importance for developing countries, especially for a most populous country like India, because higher education sets a lion's share of the total allocation of educational budget at the cost of elementary and secondary education.

Distance education with its low cost of instruction is more popular than the costly conventional system of education. Moreover, discipline is a major problem in so far as University Campus hostels are concerned. Distance Education keeps students away from activities which can otherwise create problems for the establishment. Distance Education therefore has gained more popularity among the masses, even though it veers away from the traditional education system.

If we look at the educational scene in this country certain trends are clearly visible and the need for distance education arises as a result of the consequence of these trends. Broadly, the trends are:

(*a*) Inequalities in education, i.e. the question of access to education;
(*b*) Quality of education; and
(*c*) Relevance.

Access to Education

Let us examine the issue of access to education first. It is true that there has been a remarkable expansion in education, particularly at the tertiary level. I do not think that in any other walk of life such a large scale expansion has taken place. For instance, in 1951, there were only 22 universities in this country; today, there are about 200. Similarly, the number of colleges has gone up from 695 to more than 700.

We do need more educational facilities in the country, what should be the approach to meet such demands? Obviously, one approach is to start more and more institutions of higher learning and that is how the governments have been responding to this demand up to 1990 in this country. Now we see that even this phenomenal expansion has not met the demands and inequalities continue to exist. This is mainly because of our approach to education. All along, expansion meant increasing the number of formal educational institutions which suffer from certain rigidities. For instance, formal systems have the following four characteristics:

(*a*) Teachers–full–time teachers to teach.
(*b*) Students–full–time learners to learn.
(*c*) Place–classrooms, where alone learning can take place, and
(*d*) Interaction–face – to – face interaction between the teacher and the taught.

All these are considered essential attributes for imparting education and if these attributes are not there, education cannot take place. There are many in the population who cannot afford to be full-time learners. At the same time, there are governments which cannot afford to employ full-time teachers all the time and provide costly infrastructure in the form of buildings.

Formal education is very costly. As a result, expansion on a large scale becomes very difficult. Even if the society is prepared to provide these, there are sections in the population who cannot take advantage of it. The inevitable conclusion one draws from this is that, if large and varied sections of population are to have access to education, our approach to it must change. We have to think of alternative systems which can supplement the existing system. Distance education is one such alternative and it has the potential to transcend the barriers of time and space.

It is true that since independence our population growth is in the ratio of 1:3 while educational facilities in general and technical higher education growth is more than ten times. Yet it is much less than the actual demand on one hand and requirement of quality on the other hand.

Quality of Education

Several observers in the country have referred to the deterioration of standards in the quality of education year after year. It varies from institution to institution and from urban to rural areas. There are certain prestigious institutions in the country which are as good as any other international institutions. But very few people have access to them.

Similarly, high quality education is by and large confined to certain pockets in urban areas, and rural areas have to be content with substandard institutions. As a result, we find that quality of education, say, in 160 universities of this country is not even; some are very good and some others not so good. Even within the same university, not all departments are of high calibre.

Variations in the quality of education are mainly because of proliferation which has taken place without reference to quality. Secondly, resource allocation for education has been going down. Annual public expenditure per student has declined since 1950-51. For instance, it was Rs. 4011 in 1950-51, which came down to 3664 in 1975-76. This is the position in the universities and institutions of higher education. In the case of general education colleges, it came down from Rs. 486 to Rs. 330 per student per annum. Professional courses where high inputs are imperative for quality education, per student resource allocation came down by half of what it was in 1950-51.

The net result has been that while the nation is spending more on education, the per capita expenditure has really been going down. Within the institutions, there have been glaring inequalities. There are universities and other institutions of higher education (IITs) where per capita expenditure is much more than the others. Therefore, the need is to improve the average quality of education. Most students need to have access to good quality education.

Presently, in some states in particular, per student expenditure is not even fifty per cent of what it was in 1975-76, whereas expenditure on account of pay and allowances of teachers and employees has gone up many times, for example during 1975-76 basic salary of a college or university lecturer was Rs. 400 which at present is Rs. 8000. Similarly the cost of books, equipment and chemicals etc. required in teaching have gone up many times. All this has lowered the standard of higher education in India.

Thus, we feel that there is a need for qualitative higher education for great number of students and we feel that this can not be done even if we double the present expenditure in one year, which is not possible as per financial capabilities of the nation, hence, need for qualitative distance education at present is much more than even before because of its cost effectiveness.

EMERGENCE OF DISTANCE EDUCATION IN INDIA

Towards the sixties the increasing rate of enrolment at the higher stage had posed a threat to the public exchequer and the employment market. It was also apprehended that quantitative expansion would affect the maintenance of the standards of formal system of higher education negatively. The above forecasted consequences of further expansion of higher education had influenced the planners of the country to divert the expected pressure groups of formal institutions to alternative channels of higher education, which might be more economical and non-formal in nature.

Moreover, in the democratic republic the increased rate of students participation in campus politics had started intensifying altogether in different forms than those of pre-independence era. The growing consciousness about youths' participation in national politics and patronisation by different political groups became gradually complex in terms of management of educational institutions.

The campus-based students' movements with the support of millions of students started becoming a headache for the establishments at State and Central levels. Because of this there might have been apprehensions on the part of establishments to divert the overflow of entrance through the creation of non-residential studies like correspondence courses at university stage.

Educationalists of DE are of the opinion that "since distant learners never come together on a permanent campus, student indiscipline and campus violence, which are a common feature of educational scene in this country, are not to be found in the institutes of correspondence courses. These maladies plague the general educational institutions of this country to such an extent that often public properties worth crores of rupees are destroyed by an angry mob of students.

Keeping students away from campus studies through DE can perhaps be used as a major tool to curb students politics in traditional system of education". It was also realised that the traditional classroom based higher education had its limitations. These limitations paved the way for alternative channels of higher education, i.e., via DE in the country.

Further, keeping in view the heavy pressure on the formal system of higher education, for the first time emphasis was laid on distance education in the form of correspondence courses in the Third Plan. In this context, the Planning Commission of India (1960) had pointed out, "in addition to provision in the plan for expansion of facilities for higher education, proposals for evening colleges, correspondence courses and the award of external degrees are at present under consideration".

On the basis of observation made by the Planning Commission of India (1960) the matter was referred to the Central Advisory Board of Education (CABE). The CABE in this 28th meeting held on January 16 and 17, 1961 accepted the following resolution, "for the correspondence courses, the Board suggested further detailed studies by a small committee before a firm decision could be taken" (CABE, 1961). Accordingly the Ministry of Education appointed an Expert Committee in March 1961, constituting 10 members from different organisations like UGC, Ministry of Education and Universities of India.

The committee recommended for introduction of correspondence courses at university level leading to a degree or equivalent qualifications. It had remarked that lack of Indian experience in the use of correspondence method demanded action and the need to proceed slowly so as to ensure that in the absence of regular classroom contact between the teacher and the students, it would still be possible to maintain high educational standards.

The Committee had made the following suggestions with regard to the nature of courses, instructional processes, course development, use of media, students fee, etc. They are as under:

Correspondence courses leading to a degree or equivalent qualifications should be administered by universities only.

That, for the present, correspondence courses should be confined to a first university degree.

For part of the course there should be personal contact between the teacher and the taught, "contact" classes being organised through a tutorial in preference to a lecture based mode.

To maintain educational standards, it is necessary to associate top ranking scholars and experienced teachers in the preparation of courses and the selection of text books. Some arrangement should be made to ensure continuing improvement in the quality of work.

The Committee recommended that the courses be started only in the faculties of Arts and Commerce. And that Science subjects would be incorporated as early as possible.

For a first degree, correspondence courses should normally take a longer period than a degree at a regular college, say, four years instead of the usual three. Outstanding students, may, however, be able to complete this in a period of three years. Flexibility in all matters relating to the application of the system in varying needs is strongly recommended.

Fees for students applying for these courses should be reasonably high in the first year but should be progressively lower in the second and third years and perhaps, if possible be eliminated altogether in the fourth year.

Two supplementary aids (*a*) refresher courses and (*b*) use of radio and television are recommended in order to raise standards in spoken languages and to correct a too easy reliance on the written word.

Correspondence course should be run in the first instance by one university, i.e., University of Delhi and the subjects to be included in the course as well as the details of administration should be as suggested by the working group.

It is important to ensure that the scheme is administered so as to achieve economy. This will be possible in view of the fact that items of expenditure normal at regular colleges can be eliminated under the correspondence system.

Creation of Correspondence Institution in the University of Delhi

As per suggestions of the expert committee, the University of Delhi agreed to the proposal of a pilot project on the introduction of correspondence courses. The University of Delhi appointed a sub-committee to prepare a programme of action of correspondence courses. The sub-committee recommended the introduction of different courses at the first degree level, the subjects being restricted to English, Modern Indian Languages, Mathematics, Economics, Political Science, History and Commerce. And, for the first time in the country, the University of Delhi established its School of Correspondence Courses and Continuing Education in 1962.

Views of the Education Commission (1964-66) and the National Education Policy, 1968 on Distance Education

With a view to maintenance of standards of full-time based higher studies and reducing the heavy influx into this system, the Education Commission (1964-66) had supported the idea of encouraging correspondence courses. According to the Education Commission," one solution to this is to keep full-time seats strictly limited on the basis of resources available and to institute correspondence courses, part-time courses, evening courses, etc., for those who aspire for a university degree but are not able to get admission to the regular courses."

Of course, the Education Commission recommended the promotion of correspondence courses on the basis of other reasons like social responsiveness, economy of the system, and continuing nature of education. It was optimistic about the qualitative and quantitative development of correspondence courses.

As per its recommendation "the opportunities for part-time education through programmes like evening colleges, and correspondence courses, should be extended as widely as possible and should also include courses in science and technology (either at the degree or diploma level). This will help to reduce the capital costs of expanding higher education and cut down the recurring costs to a substantial extent, especially as enrolments grow. And also make accessible higher education to those who desire to study further but are compelled, on economic grounds, to take up employment after schooling. There need be no fear that this will lead to a deterioration of standards, especially if due care is taken to maintain personal contacts with the students receiving correspondence education by organising academic programmes during vacations and holidays.

In fact, it would be correct to say that, by and large, the students in such courses, tend to be better because of the more intensive motivation on the part of the students. We are of the conviction that by 1986 at least a third of the total enrolment in higher education could with advantage be provided through a system of correspondence courses and evening colleges."

The Education Commission was not only optimistic about the role of correspondence education in general courses but also it suggested the promotion of correspondence courses in technical and vocational fields. The Commission stressed that, "a greater use could be made in technical education of correspondence courses for home study.... For areas requiring workshop and laboratory training, institutions can be opened during the weekends and the vacation periods for providing this to correspondence students."

In its report, the Education Commission justified the relevance of correspondence courses as a method of taking education to all those who make a deliberate effort to study whether at home or at the place of work. Quoting the success of University of Delhi in running correspondence courses, it recommended the introduction of correspondence courses on a large scale.

The National Policy of Education (1968) highlighted the idea of introducing correspondence courses on a large scale at the university stage. Of course, looking at the socio-political influences, the policy statements kept silent over the issue of selective admission policy which was recommended by the Education Commission (1964-66). Rather, the policy statements (1968) made it clear that, "education through part-time and correspondence courses should be given the same status as full-time education."

In the meanwhile, the Planning Commission while drafting the Fourth Five Year Plan (1966-71) took a note of the expansion of higher education. The Commission had estimated a further growth of one million in the enrolment of higher education during the Fourth Plan period. The Planning Commission was of the opinion that out of the total increase of one million "0.15 million students will be provided education through correspondence courses, evening colleges and part-time classes" (Planning Commission, 1966).

UGC'S GUIDELINES

Keeping in view the recommendations of the Education Commission and the Planning Commission, the UGC appointed a committee in 1967 to streamline the introduction of correspondence courses at the university stage. During this year, the Government of India sent its first delegation to USSR to study the scheme of correspondence education in USSR and, to recommend suitable measures for improvement of DE in India.

The delegation had come out with supportive statements for encouraging teacher education programmes through DE to clear the backlog of trained teachers. Subsequently the second and third delegations were also sent to the USSR by the Union Government during 1968 and 1971 subsequently to study in detail the system of correspondence courses in the USSR.

On the basis of observations made by these delegations, the UGC formulated a set of guidelines to strengthen qualitative improvements of correspondence courses in the country. These guidelines were modified during 1983. They highlighted the objectives of DE, nature of courses, criteria for admission, norms for establishment of DE institutions, preparation of instructional materials, despatch of course materials, students' response sheets, study centres, personal contact programmes, library services, staff management, norms of work and finances. As per guidelines of the UGC, Distance Education course aims at providing educational opportunities to:

— students who had to discontinue their formal education owing to pecuniary and other circumstances;
— students in geographically remote areas;
— students who had to discontinue education because of lack of aptitude and motivation, but who may later on become motivated;
— students who cannot find a seat or do not wish to join a regular college or university department, although they

have the necessary qualification to pursue higher education;

— individuals who look upon education as a life-time activity and may either to refresh their knowledge in an existing discipline or acquire knowledge in a new area (UGC, 1983).

The guidelines of UGC have been treated as the major tools of coordination and promotion of qualitative aspects of DE, especially correspondence courses in the country. However, the concerned universities having DE programmes have evoled their own practices of management of DE. Scrutinisation of activities and achievements of DE institutes would reveal the extent to which such guidelines have practical implications in the country.

Seminar on Open University in India (1970)

By the end of 1970, in addition to the University of Delhi (1962), Universities like Punjab (1968), Rajasthan (1968), Mysore (1969), and Meerut (1969) had started introducing correspondence courses through their respective directorates/institutes of correspondence courses. Positive reason to these institutions had encouraged the UGC to take further steps for strengthening DE at the university level.

In the meanwhile the popularity of the Open University of the UK which had just started functioning (1970), worked as an eyeopener for the UGC policy makers to look at the possibility of strengthening DE through the open university system. During the International Education Year (1970) the Ministry of Education and Social Welfare in collaboration with the Ministry of Information and Broadcasting, the UGC, and the Indian National Commission for Cooperation with UNESCO, organised a seminar on 'Open University' in December 1970.

The seminar recommended the establishment of an Open University in India on an experimental basis. The open university should be conceived or designed as a quality institution, with the objective of making higher education available to those who have the capacity and motivation for it but are unable to avail of the existing facilities for higher education.

Moreover, the seminar made several suggestions relating to the organisation, finances and modes of functioning of the open university. It also recommended the constitution of a committee to work out the details of the open university in India.

Working Group on Open University (1974)

As per recommendation of the seminar on 'Open University' in 1970, the Government of India appointed eight member working group on open university in 1974 with G. Parthasarathi, the then Vice-Chancellor of the Jawaharlal Nehru University. The group had studied thoroughly the pattern of Open University of the UK and discussed the possibility of creating an Open University in India.

Moreover, the working group considered seriously the problem of expansion of traditional university system and qualitative improvements of the proposed open university with open door admission policies.

On the problems of high rate of expansion of traditional university system with limited physical and manpower resources, the group observed that "in a situation of this type, with the expansion of enrolments in higher education and to continue at a terrific pace where available resources in terms of men and money are limited, one obvious solution, if proper standards are to be maintained and the demand for higher education for different sections of the people is to be met, is to adopt the open university system with its provision of higher education on a part-time or own time basis. The group, therefore, recommends that the Government of India establish, as early as possible, an Open University by an act of the Parliament. The university should have jurisdiction over the entire country so that, when it is fully developed, any student, even in the remotest corner of the country, can have access to its instruction and degrees". Working Group Report, 1947 suggested the following steps:

(*a*) The most crucial input, on which everything else would largely depend, is the preparation of proper reading material, while the contribution of audio-visual aids is not being denied, the written word continues to be the most potent instrument of education... It is, therefore, recommended that the single most important step in setting up an open university in India should be the preparation of reading material of high standards which may be innovative on the one hand, on the other, should be written with a view to meeting the requirement of students.

(*b*) Following from the above, it is necessary to set up a core group of about a dozen scholars of merit not only in the selected field of scholarship, but also in that of preparing reading material suitable for different levels of educational endeavour which would be covered in the early stages of the open university.

(*c*) In the light of the insurmountable difficulties involved in making audio-visual aids and other infrastructure facilities available to each student individually, it is suggested that a study centre be set up for every 700 students or so where tapes, records, library facilities and faculty guidance should be made available to students of that area.

(*d*) To start with, it is suggested that the open university may set up not less than 8 centres to enrol about 5000 students.

(*e*) While the vehicle of the curricular programmes of the university will be the reading material sent by post, broadcasts and telecasts, the role of the teacher cannot be completely alienated. Some form of live contact with teachers will be a necessity.

(*f*) The organisation of the open university should be located in the Union Territory of Delhi and it should work in close collaboration with the universities and institutions of higher learning already in existence. This would have the obvious advantage of avoiding the creation of library and other facilities separately for the Open University (Working Group on Open University, 1974).

On the basis of the recommendations of the working group a draft bill was prepared by the Union Government in 1982 for the establishment of a National Open University. However, for certain reasons, no progress in this direction could be possible at that time.

Seminars and Conferences at National Level (1972-78)

On the verge of major expansion of Distance Education in the country two national level conferences of Directors of Correspondence Courses were held in Mysore and Patiala during 1972 and 1976, respectively. Moreover, the NCERT sponsored four regional seminars on DE during 1978. Major issues reflected in discussions of these forums were on:

(*i*) Status of DE in India;
(*ii*) Development of instructional materials;
(*iii*) Financial management of DE;
(*iv*) Management of instructional system including course materials and student support services like response sheets, contact programmes and resource centres, radio and TV.

As a result of deliberations in the Directors' conferences, the UGC came out with the policies and pattern for development of DE at PG level in the universities during the Fifth Plan period. Moreover, the UGC stated about the norms regarding the status and working conditions of teachers working in the Directorates/ Institutes of Correspondence Courses.

PROBLEMS OF CORRESPONDENCE INSTITUTIONS/COURSES

In an ideal sense, the correspondence institutions must be free from such positions. They should be given autonomy for framing their own course structures, appointing their own teaching and non-teaching staff and managing their instructional programmes on their own. They should constitute faculties of multi-disciplinary departments having teaching staff of the ranks of Professors, Readers and Lecturers. In this context, further questions may be made regarding the norms and guidelines for selection of appropriate staff, their training, etc. The UGC will have to take a radical step in this direction.

Besides the academic staff, the administrative staff also contribute to the success of distance education system. Till today no serious attention has been paid to the improvement of the efficiency of the administrative staff. Considering their role in production and distribution of materials, coordination of different functional aspects, etc. attention should be given to their selection and training too.

We may conclude that strong regional policies should be streamlined to strengthen the organisation and functioning of the system at the university level. Simultaneously, the UGC will have to come out with modified guidelines keeping in view the autonomous status of distance education institutions. Also, a built-in structure is to be developed for co-ordination between the parent universities and correspondence institutions so that the purpose of distance education system could be attained.

Prof. G. Ram Reddy (1988) commented that, correspondence courses appear to have the following problems:

(*i*) They are treated as appendages to the conventional universities. They do not have freedom either in designing their courses or in incurring expenditure. Decision-making is totally in the hands of others.

(*ii*) Their courses, regulations regarding entry, examinations, etc. are the same as those stipulated for regular students. Their courses suffer from the same rigidities as those of the courses designed for regular students.

(*iii*) In most institutes, the only method of instruction is through correspondence material.

(*iv*) The academics and administrations of the conventional system treat the correspondence education as second-class system.

These positions of correspondence courses demanded more autonomy inside the structure of traditional universities. Moreover, they paved the way for creation of full-fledged open universities to satisfy the objectives of DE in the country.

There were stronger appeals from the experts of correspondence education in favour of establishment of a national institute of distance education or national open university. Such ideas had already received support from the UGC (1982) which had suggested taking necessary steps for the creation of a national open university.

While the efforts for establishment of a national open university was in the process, the Andhra Pradesh state came out with its own state open university in 1982. The Andhra Pradesh Open University in the country followed the pattern of OUUK. The APOU was established with the aim of extending educational opportunities to people from all walks of life without any restriction based on age, sex, occupation or residential situation.

Even though the APOU started functioning from November 1982, actual work started in 1983-84. The university offers several courses at UG and PG levels. As per flexile policy at PG stage the student is allowed to opt from any three faculties—Arts, Science and Commerce but has to have at least two optionals from the faculty from which he wishes to acquire a degree.

The university proposes to use multimedia learning through TV/VCR and Radio/Audio tape recorders. It has no prescribed admission requirements except that student should have completed 20 years of age. It has established a network of 30 study centres in different parts of Andhra Pradesh for augmenting student services.

INDIRA GANDHI NATIONAL OPEN UNIVERSITY

Realising the utility and importance of distance education and with a view to strengthening it, the Government of India decided to set-up a National Open University. It was first announced by the Prime Minister, Shri Rajiv Gandhi in his broadcast to the nation in January 1985. Immediately after that the Ministry of Education initiated action for setting up this university.

A Committee of distinguished educationists was appointed with me as the Convenor. Within six months, not only the Project Report was prepared, but also the Bill relating to its setting up was passed by the Parliament and the University formally came into existence towards the end of September 1985.

The University has two important functions to perform:

(*a*) to function as an Open University, and
(*b*) to maintain and co-ordinate distance education in the country. Its jurisdiction is the whole country.

The Directors of Correspondence Courses outlined following aspects:

(*a*) We should create an open learning system in the country in which all the Open Universities would be partners.
(*b*) Avoid unnecessary duplication of creation and production of courses. If one Open University produces a good course there is no reason why the same course should be produced by another Open University. The course can be adopted by the others.
(*c*) Network of the Open Universities. In this network a student who joins an Open University should be free to take courses, which are not being offered in his University, from other Open Universities. The parent university would take into account the credits earned by the student in the other Open University. The advantage of this is that each

university need not produce all the courses and the student will have a very wide choice of such courses.

(*d*) Establishment of a Resource Centre. This will provide information about distance education to all those who are interested in this.

(*e*) Training. Distance education is a new system of education and there are very few trained personnels available in the country. There is, therefore, a need to organise training programmes on a large scale.

The National Open University is interested in promoting these aspects and has following objectives:

1. The University shall endeavour through education, research, training and extension to play a positive role in the development of the country and based on the rich heritage of the country, to promote and advance the culture of the people of India and its human resources. Towards this end, it shall:

(*a*) strengthen and diversify the degree, certificate and diploma courses related to the needs of employment and necessary for building the economy of the country on the basis of its natural and human resources;

(*b*) provide access to higher education for large segments of the population, and in particular, the groups living in remote and rural areas including working people, housewives and other adults who wish to upgrade or acquire knowledge through studies in various fields;

(*c*) promote acquisition of knowledge in a rapidly developing and changing society and to continually offer opportunities for upgrading knowledge, training and skills in the context of innovations, research and discovery in all fields of human endeavours;

(*d*) provide an innovative system of university level education, flexible and open, in regard to methods and pace of learning, combination of courses, eligibility for enrolment, age of entry, conduct of examination and operation of the programmes with a view to promote learning and encourage excellence in new fields of knowledge;

(*e*) contribute to the improvement of the educational system in India by providing a non-formal channel complementary to the formal system and encouraging transfer of credits and exchange of teaching staff by making wide use of texts and other software developed by the university;

(*f*) provide education and training in the various arts, crafts and skills of the country, raising their quality and improving their availability to the people;

(*g*) provide or arrange training of teachers required for such activities or institutions;

(*h*) provide suitable post-graduate courses of study and promote research;

(*i*) provide the counselling and guidance to tis students; and

(*j*) promote national integration and the integrated development of the human personality through its policies and programmes.

2. The university shall strive to fulfil the above objects by a diversity of means of distance and continuing education, and shall function in cooperation with the existing universities and institutions of higher learning and make full use of the latest scientific knowledge and new educational technology to offer a high quality of education which matches contemporary needs (IGNOU, 1985).

THE NATIONAL POLICY ON EDUCATION, 1986 AND DISTANCE EDUCATION

The new national policy on education, 1986 emphasised on the role of Open University and Distance Education in the process of democratisation of education in the country. The programme of action of the new Policy on Education (1986) on this area reads as:

1. The Open University System augments opportunities for higher education, ensures access, is cost-effective and promotes a flexible and innovative system of education.
2. The Indira Gandhi National Open University has been established with these objectives and came into existence in September, 1985. The university has been assigned the responsibility to coordinate the distance learning system in the country and determine its standards. In order to develop and strengthen the Open University System.

The standards will be prescribed to determine the minimum level of learning at every stage of education and criteria will be evolved to objectively assess this level of attainment so that opportunities can be provided to all, be it housewives, agricultural or industrial workers and professionals to continue with their education.

To strengthen the delivery system of the open university and the media support to its programmes, discussions will be held with the Ministry of Information and Broadcasting for provision of separate Radio and TV channels.

In the discharge of its responsibility to co-ordinate the distance learning system and determine its standards, the National Open University will frame necessary statutes for the guidance/ compliance of the State Governments who either wish to establish their own open universities or want to take advantage of the facilities offered by the National Open University.

Arrangements will be made to develop a network of courses in the open university system. This would mean that a student joining one open university can take courses from another open university. The system will, therefore, offer a wide variety of academic programmes.

It is essential that the quality of the open university programmes and the efficiency of the delivery system are ensured. Since adequate expertise and trained manpower in this area are limited, it will be necessary that the open universities to be established, develop their programmes in close collaboration with the Indira Gandhi National Open University.

State Governments will ensure that open universities are established after very careful planning and that the required resources and facilities are available to them. The National Open University will also give financial assistance to the State Open Universities and departments of correspondence courses for development purposes.

The programme of action of the national policy on education highlighted the use of DE in the process of encouraging in service teacher education programmes, continuing education and the training of management personnel of the educational system. Moreover, with a view to encourage media and technology in educational system, the programme of action insisted on:

— establishment of radio stations in teaching universities/ colleges during the Seventh Plan;
— provision of TV channel by 1991-92;
— creation of dedicated satellite system for educational needs in the long run; and
— integration of computer education modules in professional and general education courses by 1995.

No doubt, these achievements at present are of immense use to the spread of DE in the country.

CHARACTERISTICS AND UTILITY OF DISTANCE EDUCATION

In short, distance education is a system of education in which there is no face to face relationship between the teacher and taught but they are linked through correspondence, radio talk or voice and TV appearance. Teacher motivation according to different needs of the learners may not be there, but learner motivation is there.

In our present context distance education is in some ways better than formal direct teaching institutions where motivation factor is absent both in the teacher and learner in most of the cases.

There are no two opinions as to the suitability of distance education at the present juncture when the world population specially in third world countries is growing at a speed not known before. Some of its many advantages may be mentioned:

1. It is most flexible educational system which is not limited by time and place restrictions.
2. Distance education can be used at any level from primary to higher stage.
3. It can supplement the studies of regular students along with being a separate system of education.
4. Under this system learner can progress at his own speed.
5. It is an economical method of teaching as compared to regular formal system. Hosmer compared the costs and results of correspondence study and resident training and found that the cost of correspondence study is but a fraction of the cost of resident study although student achievement is the same for both techniques.

Depending upon the kind of programme and number of students involved correspondence course is often more efficient and economical than any other technique. Teaching can be more efficient and powerful if other media like radio and TV support the system.

It is economical in the sense also that a large and permanent faculty along with equally large infrastructure, at least in proportion to the learner is not needed to run the distance education system.

6. Learner can take advantage of the lectures of the most efficient teachers which is not always possible in all conventional institutions.
7. The best part of the system is that it can reach any remote area through postal service if not through TV.
8. It leads to self-learning, which is education in the real sense and stable and also which is not really encouraged in most of the teaching institutions.
9. It fulfils the need of many learners who either fall out of the conventional stream for different reasons or who are employed and do not find time to go to them howsoever keen they may be.

As regards its relevance to our country along with above considerations, existing education imparting machinery is totally inadequate to the country's need and cannot hope to provide education within the four walls of class rooms to our growing millions in the near future. This inadequacy was realised in the early sixties and the first correspondence course was started at Delhi University in 1962.

The success of the system inspired other Universities also to initiate this programme, with the result that now we have many institutes of correspondence course affiliated to the universities. Radio broadcasting has also been used extensively in our country for formal as well as distance education.

The advent of television gave a very useful new dimension to the programme of distance education.

The opening of Andhra Pradesh Open University, Hyderabad in 1983 was another land-mark in the field of distance education. It started with B.A., B.Com. courses and had about 30,000 students enroll in 1985. Indira Gandhi National Open University inaugurated on 19 November 1985 hopes to meet the requirements of a large number of people. Its educational system would be characterised by innovation and flexibility. The University will make use of the modern communication technology. In the next couple of years a few other states hope to start open universities.

However, looking to the needs of millions of our population which are in need of general as well as professional education, adult and continuing education, these efforts are meagre. Like other third world countries where the challenges to education are greatest and resources to meet them are scarcest, we should take distance education more seriously and expand it to the full.

The growth of universities and institutions opting to impart distance education till 1989 was 48 which is on increase every year. This trend speaks well of the acceptance of the concept of distance education by the Indians because it helps professionals to improve their knowledge and qualification while in profession and as a result of this they get promotions and other benefits which improves their living and social status. Thus we feel that distance education will have much faster growth in the years to come.

2

Philosophy of Distance Education and Its Work Ethics

INTRODUCTION

Every activity particularly the productive activity requires specific modes of behaviour and operation on the part of those involved in it. Distance education like formal education is a productive activity, therefore it is one's perception of distance education that determines the adoption of a particular process of operation to achieve the desired end.

This is discernible in our long association with the system of formal education which has witnessed vicissitudes from the sway of the rod to the rule of the chalk. The system has been viewed in a special way by all—the community, the teacher, the administrator, and so by the learner—and consequently corresponding attitudes have been formed and work ethics adopted.

NATURE OF THE FORMAL SYSTEM

The formal system of education operates on certain premises. It assumes that the learner is not mature enough to decide for himself as to what to learn, when to learn, where to learn, how to learn, etc. The process of education is, therefore, limited to the act of direct teaching by an individual to a group through mainly vocal signals, and it is circumscribed by rules of superintendence, direction and control enforced by an out-side agency.

The product of the system, therefore, needs to be labelled, like one in the assembly line of a factory, by an external examining agency that has nothing to do with the internal process going on in the formal classrooms.

The formal education system being what it is, it imposes certain modes of behaviour and shapes of attitudes on the learners. The system, for example, is centred on the notion of delivery of knowledge, better call it information, that has to be taken in by the student and given out in a set form when asked to do so. It is the delivering agency that prescribes the quantum to be unloaded.

Unfortunately it cannot determine the quantum of the intake by the very nature of the process which is other-directed. An attitude of unquestioning acceptance is formed thereby. It is characterised by intellectual passivity and moral unaccountability for what one does in the process. In extreme cases it generates a fatalistic outlook on life because the system leaves many things to the element of chance as we have been witnessing in the case of the public examinations.

PHILOSOPHY OF DISTANCE EDUCATION

The philosophy of distance education is based on entirely different premises regarding the role of the learner vis-à vis the process of learning, the materials for activating that process and the personnel involved in it. According to it the learner is not a mere subject of certain operations to whom things are made to happen, but he is a generator of forces and currents which he can command and shape as per his initiative and desire.

He is a self-directed, active agent making choices, taking decisions, directing the process quantitatively, and qualitatively, and assuming responsibility for all this. He self-monitors, self-evaluates, self-feedsback and self-improves. In the process, he develops a progressively better competence for self-propulsion.

Thus distance education, for whatever client group it might be intended, whether for the illiterate farmers, farm workers and rural women; or for factory workers and slum-dwellers, focuses on this unconventional perception of the potential of the learner to make wise choices and responsible decisions.

Everyone conversant with the Indian psyche, with the robust commonsense of the Indian masses, would agree to the truth underlying the basic assumptions of distance education.

Everyone that has marked the crippling intellectual effects of the formal teaching by rote in our schools and colleges would appreciate the moral and intellectual value of distance education whose focus is the self-directed individual.

Distance education postulates a design for instruction that is comprehensive in coverage, permanent in nature, multi-level in offerings, multi-media in approach and need-based in focus. It can, thus, be easily distinguished from the delivery model of formal classroom teaching by a teacher on a day-to-day basis. It is a flux rather than an event like formal instruction.

The strategy of formal education is unquickening; whereas that of distance education emphasises the active role and responsibility of the learner in the entire enterprise. It seeks to quicken the very intellectual self of the learner.

There are learning materials and resources of a large variety—print, audio, video etc., requiring him to interact with them. There are processes involving human agents requiring interaction and active involvement in intellectual and creative reinterpretations of reality and experiences. There are moments of moral and epistemological crises requiring a total mobilisation of the self to find new balances.

Distance education perceived thus is a self-renewing exercise for the learner taking place every moment he encounters his life, and its emerging needs with his inadequacies on the one hand and in-built strengths on the other.

LEARNER'S WORK ETHICS FOR DISTANCE EDUCATION

If distance education is a challenging exercise for perennial self-renewal, the learner should be equipped with appropriate work ethics to operate effectively and satisfactorily. He will need materials that should provide him that training as he interacts with them. He will also need training, guidance and support through media, materials and human agents, all of which will be marshalled into a dynamic process of interaction to generate an appropriate mental and emotional climate conducive to self-learning.

Distance education will demand the following work ethics on the part of its students

(1) Goal-setting

The learner should himself set the goal of his learning. For this he may avail of the resource material of the system, the guidance services offered at study and contact centres and information disseminated by the media employed by the system. He must know what he wants to realise progressively in course of time by actively interacting with the programmes of distance education.

(2) Choice of Materials and Methods

Distance education is supposed to be a multi-faceted enterprise involving choice on the part of the learner from out of several alternatives of materials and methods of work. Of course, he will have support services to guide him as to the relative benefits of the available alternatives, but there will be no imposition to accept them. Hence he will have to develop a sense of discriminating choice in keeping with his goals and intellectual equipment.

(3) Self-direction

The distance learner has to undertake a self-directed project all through. He has to take decisions regarding how much to take in, at what speed to move, what and whom to interact with and when to do so, and so on. This requires intellectual alertness, clarity and courage—the qualities that are acquired through conscious nursing.

(4) Self-monitoring and Feedback

Distance education has but remote controls which themselves are recommendatory rather than prescriptive. The system is so designed as to generate in the learner inner monitoring, evaluating and controlling forces. These requires an attitude of accountability and seriousness of purpose on the part of the learner.

(5) Interactive Dynamism

Distance education rests on a network of material resources, human support agencies, and media participation. It has an intricate interacting mechanism leading to incremental learning on the part of the participating learner who must be willing and active, in fact aggressive, to interact with various forces and generate knowledge for himself. There is none to deliver him the goods of information and knowledge at his doorstep in this dispensation. He has to be the prime mover with the system to support him in his endeavour.

GUIDELINES FOR EDUCATORS FOR PROMOTION OF DISTANCE EDUCATION

The peculiar work ethics of distance education are likely to administer a powerful shock to the traditional set of behaviour formed by the learner under the formal system of education over the years. The attitudes of intellectual dependence, fatalistic resignation, non-challenging acceptance and passive conformity that have been developed by the average Indian individual because of a peculiar socio-cultural environment on the one hand and because of the patriarchal system of formal education on the other, are likely to be a hindrance to the development of a different set of attitudes and work ethics required by distance education. It is obvious that adequate steps will have to be taken to build up a climate for this purpose on the following lines:

(*a*) Clarifying the Concept of Distance Education

Mass media, print-materials and institutional infrastructures like schools, colleges, social clubs, organisations of youth, women, and professionals will join in making the idea, the nature and the value of distance education clear in the community. It should be brought home to all that distance education is not a pale replica of formal education, that it is not an alternative devised out of helplessness to tackle the problem of explosion of numbers flooding the formal system, that it is not some make-do second-rate arrangements for people who cannot join the formal system for want of funds on their part or want of space on the part of formal institutions but that it is an equally sound, valuable and valid system of education, perhaps with greater regard for the learner who is offered to self-manage his educational pursuit.

(*b*) Selling the Idea

It is not enough just to put the idea of distance education across the community; it must be sold to them. It must be vigorously advocated by different agencies with evidences of its worth-whileness found all over the world.

Its academic benefits, its cost-effectiveness in terms of financial resources, time and energy resources and economic gains that accrue as a result and its intellectual and moral gains should be explained to the target groups. Here the human support agencies would be immensely helpful through guidance-oriented discussions. Success models available in the community should be used to supplement guidance and counselling.

There is an indirect way of selling the idea, too. It is done by the government that lays down the policy of education in a state or in the country.

Acceptance in the policy statement of the place of distance education in the whole scheme of national education, say by legitimising the open school and the open university system, gives push to the sale of the idea. In the same way requirement by employers of their employees' continuing education for better job prospects also boosts the sale of distance education.

(*c*) Built-in Training Packages

As seen earlier, work ethics and appropriate habits and styles of work get formed over a period of time through constant, conscious effort both on the part of the learner and the delivery agency. The learning resources in any form should have a built-in component of training for work ethics.

Illustrated material, in print, audio and video forms, should be provided along with learning resources. Similarly interface programmes should be recurrently organised to reinforce learning of work ethics through resources. The agents of interface should be trained in delivering training modules to the learners. They should be well-versed in the art of demonstrations.

(*d*) Contact Mechanism

Distance education inevitably provides for a contact mechanism to reduce anonymity and impersonality involved in the very nature of the system. Correspondence, telephone, personal meetings, review classes etc., are the chief means of doing so. This mechanism should be utilised for developing sound work ethics and effective habits of work.

Guidance on specific issues can concretise a particular line of thinking in the matter. There should be a track-record of a distance learner to be maintained by himself as well as the contact centre and to be shared with the distance educator in order to help the former to be an effective and successful learner.

(*e*) Research

There is no single model of working in any field of productive activity, not the least in respect of human behaviour. With a vast range of heterogeneous learner population in the schemes of distance education, influenced by sociological, psychological and cultural forces of an infinite variety, we should undertake research in the dynamics of behaviour and work.

We should continue to try out various processes and modes and guide the clientele in making their choices and in observing their performance and modifying it by themselves. Distance education then will not remain an isolated endeavour but will grow into a well-shaped discipline with a built-in provision for progressive refinement.

NEED FOR WIDE PUBLICITY

In India most people regard distance and correspondence education as second class, therefore, there is a great need for wide publicity to emphasis the following aspects:

1. Distance education is an avenue of life long education and is a means of making higher education freely accessible to all sections of society.
2. These courses are not merely to satisfy the craze for degrees.
3. The courses are similar to the regular courses, they have no pacing; the students have to adhere to a strict schedule. The courses are a means for much desired accreditation and that they are diluted versions of the courses offered to regular student is the opinion of majority of experts.

3

Forms and Systems of Distance and Open Education

INTRODUCTION

The first chapter gave you basic knowledge about some basic concepts of distance and open system of education, which will help you in understanding the concepts of all the chapters. In this chapter we will try to enhance the knowledge gained through first chapter and discuss the concepts concerning forms and systems of distance education.

With the ongoings of centuries of life and new era of civilisations people have seen and developed new horizons in their attempt to live and lead a comfortable life. The complexities and multiplications of human desires and less and less available resources due to the growing population and the futile attempt to grow in response to the requirements have given rise to our general growth of over all educational and institutional setups.

We acquire knowledge and our inquisitive minds get filled with progress in learning the situation around us and the existing problems stand unsolved till we research to bring it down to be familiar and known.

But education, as a basic necessity for human being is not available in cheap or plenty. All those who need it may not be monetarily well off or availability of institutions may be hindrance.

Talking about universities and graduate level education sufficient institutions are not available though students throw their applications for admissions. Supply does not keep pace with demand.

FORMAL, INFORMAL AND DISTANCE EDUCATION

To the terms formal, non-formal and informal education, the terms distance education and open education have been added. Formal education, it will be recalled, is learning within an organised institution, with time schedules established, curricula and syllabus taught by the teacher and learnt by the student, followed by a system of examinations. As such formal education, at first sight, cannot also be distance education, because the learning in the latter case is not taking place within the institution: but it could in the main part also include distance education, if the latter follows the curricula and syllabus of the formal institution.

Non-formal education is learning that is organised outside the formal system, with emphasis on its organised character, its hours of learning being flexible. Here again non-formal education seems to exclude distance education because distance education does not take place within the non-formal schedule of learning in some forms of non-formal education, such as training on the job, or learning leisure hours, however, distance education can be operative.

Informal education is really incidental education through reading, attending lectures, participating in seminars etc., which can be either distance or non-distance education. Open education cuts across all these forms of education and can be expressed in formal, non-formal, informal and distance learning systems.

In reflecting over the concept of distance education, it is necessary to distinguish between the two senses in which the term education is used. Education first refers to the learning process—that is the mental process of internalising an external event in order to understand it and control it.

Second Education could also refer to the infrastructure which makes possible the learning process—school and college buildings, material and equipment, laboratories, playground etc. The teacher and the book and increasingly today the various forms of audio-visual aids occupy a middle position between the learning process and its infrastructure.

The teacher, the book, the electronic aids are part of the learning process in the sense that they help in the internalising process: in fact the teacher is in many cases a part and hierarchically above the book and the audio-visual aid, because he has to interpret the content of the book and explain the message that the electronic instrument conveys.

On the other hand the teacher is apart from the learner and has to be paid a salary and assured living conditions, the book has to be purchased, as is the audio-visual aid, and in that sense all three are part of the infrastructure.

Conceptually the learning process is the result of the interaction of the teacher and the taught. In this sense, education is a 1:1 relationship. Should this relationship be physically a near close one? That was the ancient Indian tradition—the Guru-Shishya relationship. And that is also the basis on which all systems of education have been developed. The ideal of a literal 1:1 relationship, however, became impossible with both the democratisation of education, and the upsurge in people's desire to learn.

From the point of view that education is the resultant of the personal interaction between the teacher and the taught, conceptually distance education seems to be a contradiction in terms. In distance education, the teacher and taught are separated by distance, and there is no personal element in the teaching and the learning process.

Thus in a geographically separated form, where teaching emanates in a kind of impersonal manner from a centre, and is spread out over varying distances, the educational process is not of the kind and variety that we are used to and have defined earlier. In fact a question can be asked as to whether distance education is education at all.

The concept of education as a learning instrumentality is, however, reinterpreted in distance education. In distance education, learning takes place, that is the external reality is internalised, not through the mediation of a teacher, but through the message and information that he puts out.

Whereas in formal education the learning process of a student is mediated by the physical presence of a teacher, in distance education the learning process is mediated by the books, materials and electronic messages that emanate from the teacher(s). In that sense distance education is conceptually a new form of education.

SPECIAL NATURE OF DISTANCE EDUCATION

Terms like 'Distance Education', 'Distance Learning' and 'Correspondence Education' are being used synonymously. Ripleysims (Holmberg) expresses in UNESCO report that "the unique and distinguishing feature in the correspondence education process is that the learner is at a distance from the teacher for much, most or even all of the time during the teaching-learning process."

Distance Education is an effective alternative to the formal education. It has immense significance for the emerging learning society in general and educational undeveloped or developing society in particular. It has its message both for life-long education as well as for universalisation of education. It is a useful medium for promoting diversified as well as vocational education. It is a source of inspiration for those who have 'dropped out' of it at some stage or other.

In other words, the distance education is an organised provision for learning opportunity on part-time basis, outside the time table of the formal system of education covering a person's life time in his own environment, more or less according to his own perception and at his own time. It is therefore, democratic as well as socialistic in nature.

The Educationists and researchers were attracted to this Distance Education system and felt that it could help in diffusion of education and equalisation of educational opportunities. Besides, cost of such correspondence course would be less in comparison with the formal system of education and its standards would not be lower in any way.

In distance education, there has to be real learning, not the rote repetition of what the teacher says, as in some parts of institutional education. For one thing there must be strong motivation in the case of distance education for a student to enter this area of learning, for not only is he deprived of the usual large infrastructure, the classroom, the library, the laboratories, the teachers and fellow students, available to the student of institutional education, he also has to set aside his free time after his working hours to become a student under the system of distance education.

Comparative studies which have been made of learning acquired under the two systems, show a higher level of learning and individual acquisition of knowledge in the case of students under distance education compared to those under non distance education.

THREE FORMS OF DISTANCE EDUCATION

The first and simplest is what is called correspondence education for undergraduate courses. Here the course of study prescribed by a University for an undergraduate course broken up into a number of modules, which are posted to student, who works on the material sent to him, and can obtain further guidance and clarification through writing back to the diffusing centre, and through attending the periodic contact classes which are organised at or near his place of residence along with other students participating in the correspondence course.

Here some original work is called for in breaking up the course into graded, self-contained learning units which are intelligible and comprehensible to the student who has no other aid. There should be regular posting of the material to the learner and prompt replies to queries on the course posed by him.

The problem with this form of distance education is that it is a unilinear, uniform course, which cannot follow the differing learning ability and path of the individual student, as the system of private tuition does. Also any irregularity in the despatch of lessons to the learner will lead to a deal of confusion and disruption. The advantage of this form of distance education is its unlimited outreach to learners wherever they may be resident. The only requirement is that there should be a postal service servicing him and preferably good public library.

This form of distance education has become very popular in that a large number of universities have organised such courses. The popularity of the course is such that the universities which run them make large sums of money (around Rs. 3-4 crores a year) from it. While this form of education provides education to those living in distant places and who want to pursue learning and upgrade their knowledge and skills, the danger it faces is that it may commercialise the education system, and be regarded merely as a source of income to the university running the course.

The second form of distance education is one which uses not only the posted material, as in the above case, but also the electronic media. The radio has been used in this country to supplement classroom teaching and not as a form of distance education. It is an instrument which can reach distant places, places which even the postal system cannot reach.

So there is need for the radio to be used to broadcast the entire course in a given undergraduate programme as well as to supplement the written material sent to the student. Broadcasting of lessons calls for special skills on the part of the broadcasting teacher, of systematic analysis, clarity of speech and convincing presentation. It is more difficult and complex than the routine lecturing or the writing out the lessons in the course.

Similarly the TV can be used to supplement the written lessons or can be used as a self-contained means of learning. This electronic media is particularly useful in providing science & technology lessons as well as lessons in technical education, the lessons revolving around the scientific equipment in the laboratory or the machinery in a workshop or industry. In the case of science learning, the distance education centre can design and make available science kits around which science lessons can be given.

The advantage of this media is that the very best teachers in each field can be used in providing the TV or radio education. The one limitation of this medium of distance education is that there is no two way exchange possible and learning, as noted earlier, is the result of a dialogue. Even the best of monologues, such as a lecture or a sermon, has its learning limitation. In the use of radio and TV either as a supplement to postal teaching or as a comprehensive self contained form of distance education, there are rich possibilities which should be developed in the country.

The third form of distance education is one which breaks away from the established syllabus and content of the schools and universities, and innovates with new learning content. This new content may relate to television age and stage of learning. For instance research in one of the country's university adult education department has shown that an illiterate adult can reach the literacy level of a child at the end of the second standard of the primary school through 6 weeks of literacy learning, in 72 hours of study.

Similarly the learning of a worker in a leather factory can combine academic study and professional training in a 3-year programme, during which he could be continuously assessed and given a certificate to proficiency, which may enable him to move up to a superintending post.

Again science and technology learning is changing and developing very fast. This is particularly so in high technology areas. Renovating and modernising science and technology modules can be devised to provide scientists, technicians and engineers for updating of their skills and the specialising in the latest in their fields.

SCIENTIFIC BASIS OF DISTANCE EDUCATION

In fact with the traditional view now exploded that persons can only learn before becoming adults which was true in a world where knowledge was fixed or changed very slowly, with fast, rapid and accelerating change in knowledge and information, obsolescence is a greater present reality for every scientist and scholar than what his degree indicates. Studies show that four years after his MA, MSc, or PhD a scientist loses half his usefulness because of obsolescence. One answer to this fact of obsolescence is for the working scientist to return to the university as a full time student, or opting or being forced to early retirement.

What has recently emerged as an answer to technological obsolescence is the programme of distance education, which is the means of continuing education and updating of knowledge. The world of today faces a rapidly changing environment, arising from shortages of energy and raw materials, sociological and technological breakthrough and changes, so that the very survival of the scientist and the worker depends on his adaptability to the changes and his being able to continue learning, which distance education makes possible.

Studies show a correlation between those undergoing such distance education courses and their job satisfaction, or increase in salary or promotion. With the fast changing society for the worker, working scientist and the specialist, distance education is the means of keeping himself up-to-date and surviving.

It is in this area of the devising special updated curricula and modernising learning programmes to meet specific learning needs that distance education merges with open learning system. Such open learning systems can and should operate at the equivalent of the secondary and higher secondary school, the polytechnic, the university, the engineering, agriculture and medical institutions and the centres of research.

In this third type, distance education will operate the open learning system at the equivalent of every level of learning and skill. This will call for persons who can devise such courses on the basis of what people joining the open learning system want. The system can and should use all media—the printed as well as electronic media. This is the next stage to which our distance education in the country should move.

The use of the fast growing communication technologies open up further larger vistas for distance education. The proliferation of computers and their development through their peripherals, the growing use of cable television, information technology, communication satellites and the development of micrc computers which free the user from the need to be linked to a network or a main frame computer centre are a pointer to the endless learning techniques and methodologies that are at the disposal of distance education in the near future.

Further, one teaching and learning tool of distance education, informatics, is of particular interest to us in India as it can be used in the management of our educational services which are facing a crisis of numbers and complexity.

The problems faced in the use of these new forms of communication technology in distance education are: (*a*) the determination of priority areas for their application (as they cannot be applied over the whole field to start with), (*b*) development of teaching software, and (*c*) above all the training of teachers in their use and development. In fact if teachers learn how to use this technology and how to interpret the message they transmit, distance education too, like non distant education, can become a two way traffic.

DISTANCE EDUCATION SYSTEMS

Life long education is wider concept which may be in the form of distance education or human interaction with his surrounding environment. The UK experiment of Open University based on their national need has been quite successful to impart educational opportunity to their citizens on the principle of distance education.

At present postal coaching systems are predominantly working in the name of correspondence directorates in different universities. But distance education systems of tomorrow are expected to use multi-dimensional methods to cater to their student population. Multi-dimensional methods may cover hardwares—Computers, Films, Television, Radio, VCR, Tape-Recorders, Teaching machines—self instructional texts and manuals, seminars, group discussions, case study methods, assignments, tutorials, directed discovery strategies, laboratory experiences, library guidance services. Student population should be provided opportunity to select their strategy for various types of courses according to their needs and capacities.

Distance Education Systems and Computers

Development of computers is an important contribution of the bionics science where methods of creating mechanical systems are investigated and computers are going to be common market products in our technologically advanced society. With the changing socio-economic structure and increasing consciousness for quality of education, there comes an era of automation and computers in education (Sharma and Garg, 1979).

It has been observed that Computer Assisted Instruction (CAI) permits many pupils to interact on an individual basis with teaching material stored in the computer. It is possible that students may have teaching and advice and designed schedule while solving problems or working through practical task. Even it is possible to design strategy based on inquiry guided discovery or laboratory mode. Various peripheral devices like slides, film projectors, tape recorders can be easily controlled by computer.

There are some important systematic studies which have been conducted in some of the developed and developing countries to use computer for educational purposes. Gilligan (1973) used computer to teach 33 pupils of the first year biology class successfully, whereas an experimental investigation was conducted by Wood, Hartley, Lovell and others (1973) to use computer for special functions. Sharma and Garg (1979) designed the two strategies of computer assisted instruction and studied their relative effectiveness.

It was concluded that there was no significant difference in achievements of students taught by strategy-I (using tele-writer) and strategy-II (using key-punch machines). Computer aided learning can handle many students individually and allow them to proceed at their own pace and level of achievement.

Computer assisted instruction can be used in the distance education system where provision of learning centre or resource centre exists. Computer controlled telecommunication and television project can be used for the computer assisted instruction on various topics selected on the basis of interest and importance. Even popular learning packages could be prepared for the learner which could be used for education purposes on computer terminal of computer centre.

Production of mini-computers and micro-processors on a large scale may be helpful for computer assisted instruction imparted for the sake of distance education. It is possible for computer manufacturing firms to design special computers for distance education systems with suitable cost which could be afforded by the community residing in rural and remote regions.

In future it would be possible to have a common computer terminal for the number of Resource centres working under the distance education systems. Even faculty members working in the management (Trivedi 1983) pointed out that computers' application in management and administration got momentum with fastest speed due to advancement in computer hardware and software technology.

Distance education systems can use computer centre for professional development, education administration functions involving data analysis relating to admissions, examinations, facilities, inventory (Shankar Narayan, 1979-1982). Computerised management system could be developed for the effective planning and management of Distance Education Systems.

Management information system thus developed should be useful for group members as well as group leaders which would be helping them to take appropriate decisions for the various problems they come across in context of policy framing situations and routine matters. Proper communication channels should be developed to provide up-to-date and exact information to the group members (policy makers, top managers, middle managers, etc.).

This requires flow of information about resources (time, finances, manpower), rules, regulations, job performance and various types of records (Darji and Sharma, 1983). Computerised management system will be a great asset for distance education systems to be used effectively to maintain managerial harmony.

Satellite Communication and Distance Education Systems

Distance Education systems can work efficiently with the help of the satellite communication. This was suggested by late Dr. Vikram Sarabhai who realized the importance of satellite television as a means of communication and education relevant of India's developmental needs. It is a well known fact that hundreds of crores of rupees are needed for space programme. It is possible to justify the accountability aspect of this considerable amount if we consider educational, public awareness and social consciousness programmes by this noble means for social and economic development of our country, keeping in view its size, population and area.

The Satellite Instructional Television Experiment (SITE) was launched during August 1975-July 1976 using the American satellite ATS-6. The success of the SITE project inspired the space scientists to build INSAT-TV broadcast system. For the same purpose INSAT-IA (launched from USA on 10th April 1982 by NASA) and INSAT-1B (launched from USA on 30th August 1983) were launched in the orbit.

On the basis of the various tests INSAT-1B could be called operational on 15th October, 1983. Now the space communication has become a billion dollar (per year) industry and still growing. The direct broadcast satellites have proved to be cheaper than the present conventional system for communication (Ramnath, 1983).

Distance education systems can make use of the television for providing education to the masses. This requires careful planning and management. It is better to have preliminary survey of the needs of the society on the basis of region and their socio-economic balance. Social set up of the people living on high altitudes is quite different from the people living in plains or coastal belts of the country.

Of course certain programmes may be useful to whole of the society. Teams of planners for these types of programmes will consist of educationists, psychologists, sociologists and communication experts who have wider outlook about the regions of this country and their problems. Interested educational and research organisations could be invited for this noble task.

Unplanned and ill-organised programmes selected randomly may damage the whole cause. Unfortunately the present TV programmes regarding information and education are not attracting the masses and day by day motion pictures made for commercial purposes are becoming sole basis to justify Doordarshan.

The whole TV system should be reorganised so that distance education systems can work efficiently. Space Application Centre (SAC), Ahmedabad is one of the important agencies working under the set-up of India Space Research Organisation (ISRO) for telecommunication and TV broadcasting. SAC should take pioneering steps for distance education activities in collaboration with various universities and good institutions.

It should work for effective planning and implementation of distance education programmes. It can also be a coordnating machinery for different agencies working in this direction. Important organizations working for the cause of expansion of education and having much workload in their respective fields are expected to coordinate and provide co-operation for developing distance education systems.

It is better to start a National Institute of Research and Training for Distance Education. This institute will be doing research work for distance education along with training the human resources for distance education systems, UGC, SAC Ahmedabad, Department of Science and Technology (DST) and the Association of Indian Universities (AIU) can provide assistance to this national body in various ways. It will provide guidance to various distance education systems of tomorrow. This institute may have following departments and centres:

1. Human Resource Development for distance education systems,
2. Mass-Media Research Department.
3. Library and Documentation Development Centre,
4. Centre for Development of Self Instructional Text Materials,
5. Computer Application Centre for Distance Education Systems,
6. Research and Survey Department for Distance Education Systems,
7. Constancy Centre, and
8. Evaluation Unit.

Distance education systems of the future are expected to cater to television needs and aspirations of various categories of learners with varying attitudes, aptitudes and interests on a reasonable cost with appropriate time adjustment strategies.

They should be in a position to produce quality and excellence in our human resource development programmes. Careful planning and effective management strategies are required to design workable distance education systems for the future.

4

Dimensions of Distance Education

INTRODUCTION

The last century is widely known for scientific and technological as well as for industrial development, but the real fact relates to educational development during this period. During this period formal education encompassed large number of new subjects as independent disciplines of study as well as the development and growth of informal and non-formal forms of education. Distance education is one of such developments which has earned social acceptance alike the formal education.

Concept of Distance Education (DE) is a relatively new one and arose out of the development of modern communication technologies. In order to explore the dimensions and extensions of the new concept, it is necessary to consider the factors that created the concept and the social and technological imperatives that are creating diverse and extensive applications of DE.

Modern communication technologies such as satellite, radio, TV, audio-visual tapes and equipment, computers, cable TV, etc. are finding their wider applications and slowly national and international communication networks are getting established.

The printing technology gave boost to the whole educational field by creating many colleges and universities and establishing an education system that fulfils the needs and requirements of the industrial society. Micro-electronic revolution is offering new electronic media of storing and retrieving information, not only in print but also in audio-visual forms, which are far more economical and accessible to larger sections of the society. The new media are using besides reading and writing, wider human faculties and abilities, and are, therefore, more versatile and widely applicable.

FACTORS LEADING TO THE GROWTH AND DEVELOPMENT OF DISTANCE EDUCATION

Though a reference to this aspect has been made in earlier chapters, yet vital details for the development are as follows:

1. Emergence of Post-industrial Society

Agrarian society gave way to the industrial society which has been developing during the last two-three centuries. During the last couple of decades micro-electronics and development of computers are leading to automation and mechanization, which are likely to perform all routine mechanical tasks.

The transformations of processes of production, management, entertainment, culture, etc. are entering into every walk of life and it is expected that within a period of one or two generations the present industrial society may get transformed into a radically different post-industrial society.

The quantum and quality of knowledge required by an individual to live and function in the society always increases as the society develops into higher and more complex forms. The nature and content of knowledge, higher abilities and skills, and appropriate attitudes required also change with the changing society. The urge for higher education is well expressed in the report on the 'Open University' submitted to the Secretary of State for Education and Science (1969) of the United Kingdom. It says:

> "It is... unjust to the individual and unwise for the society to deny the greatest educational opportunity to the greatest number of its citizens. For long regarded as the privilege of the few, the opportunity to engage in higher education is at least becoming widely accepted as a basic individual right. Moreover, education in general, and higher education in particular is, at one and the same time, a necessary condition of a modern technological society and defence against its abuse".

Industrial and post-industrial societies will require to have educational opportunities for every one, and the future educational system has to be appropriate to fulfil the needs of a 'learning society'.

2. Limitations of Formal Education System

Formal system of education offering education through a large number of colleges and universities is essentially developed to educate younger generation mostly of the age group of 17-24 for various technical, vocational and professional activities. It also contains substantial component of general and liberal education. It operates through full-time, specialised institutions with mostly face-to-face teaching done by full-time professional teachers. Over the decades, it has developed its own formalism, structures and culture and has been serving its purpose fairly well, in so far as the task is that of educating a selected and limited number of students.

With the demand for democratization of education, for access to education for those sections of society hitherto neglected, the age-old formal structure cannot change its structure and functions to accommodate the pressure of large enrolment and diversity of knowledge and skills required for social development and progress. The major constraining factors of the formal educational system are:

(*a*) full-time and long study periods leading often to uncertain achievements;
(*b*) limited places for enrolments;
(*c*) requirements of formal degrees for admissions, linear study programmes, yearly promotions, limited choice for combination of subjects, faculty-wise channelization, over crowded curricula, instruction from full-time teachers along with their formalism of teaching and limitations of teacher expertise etc.;
(*d*) no relationship of courses to the needs and requirements of students and also to the socio-economic environment;
(*e*) limitations on studies due to formalism and pressures of examinations; and
(*f*) high per capita cost of education.

All these constraints make virtually impossible to expand the formal system beyond a certain limit to serve the needs of larger enrolments and of learning society. It is, therefore, necessary to evolve non-formal educational systems by establishing educational networks by using Distance Education methods.

The use of communication technologies should ensure *equality* of educational opportunity, serve larger *quantity* with higher *quality* of education and *diversity* of courses that are relevant to the individual and societal needs, and in the process, achieve *economies* of scale.

It should be realised that the non-formal system will offer alternative and complementary channels and will never replace the formal system which has specific target groups of students, definite nature of full-time face-to-face education offering learning and development opportunities.

However, the modern communication technologies and certain aspects of DE methods will enter into the formal system also changing in future its objects, nature and functions.

3. Explosion of Knowledge

With the rapid scientific and technological developments, there is explosion of knowledge, which, it is estimated, doubles in volume after every 7/8 years. This has created a high rate of obsolescence and the need for rapid changes in courses to offer learning opportunities in new knowledge and skills. Rigidity and high cost of formal system are making the changes rather difficult.

4. Information Communication Network

New communication technologies are helping in building up national and international Information Communication Networks and a new information order is getting developed. The Network has great capacity of storing, processing and transmitting information electronically, and any one having access to the network can receive any information from anywhere stored in the network.

Versatility and capabilities of the network are expanding with unimaginable rapidity. With the fifth generation computers round the corner, and such technological change in the offing, in which TV electronic tube may be replaced by liquid crystal screens thereby reducing the size and cost of the television and increasing its portability and convenience, and the availability of more versatile satellites that would offer larger number of channels and would link any two locations on the surface of the earth, the stage is well set for revolutionary changes, which even the best experts in the field fear to forecast.

The new information technologies have, on the whole, very specialised and centralized needs for the development of their hardware. However, its mass-production has made the product very economical. Further, the software developments, appropriate to local situations and requirements, necessary to use new technologies have given the technologies, the common features of being *economical, versatile*, having wider *accessibility* and *decentralised* nature. The new communication technologies, with the above characteristics, will generate creative processes and activities at various localities and will effectively contribute to the creation of knowledge, which itself will become decentralised in future.

Broadcasting (radio, television) and non-broadcasting (audio and video cassettes, computers, etc.) channels of communication network offer an excellent opportunity of creating an Educational Network. Television educational network will essentially consist of storage of learning material in audio-visual and textual forms with linkages through terminals with the receiver, the students, study-centres, and other groups or institutional centres. It should have teaching and counselling facilities which should be made available to every student linked with the educational network.

The network is likely to change not only the nature and functions of the library but the whole teaching-learning process, both in formal and non-formal education. During the transitional stage, the educational network will use both broadcasting and non-broadcasting channels and will have face-to-face teaching-learning component characteristic of the formal educational system. As the DE technologies become interactive and distance communicative, the face-to-face component may get reduced.

5. Features of the New System

Discussions of the above factors lead to the conclusion that it is necessary to evolve an education system, alternative and complimentary to the formal system, that should be:

- (*a*) non-formal in nature;
- (*b*) capable of serving educational needs of every adult learner;
- (*c*) capable of offering learning facilities at or near home; and
- (*d*) open in its approach.

Modern communication technologies can be used effectively to develop a non-formal open distance education system that will have all the features mentioned above. Development of Open University systems is an attempt to evolve such a system of education.

BASIC INGREDIENTS OF DISTANCE EDUCATION

Though a reference to this aspect has been made in the first chapter, yet for better understanding some details are given hereunder:

(1) Definition

Emergence of DE is described by Henri Dieuzeide as the "Copernican Revolution", changing the centre of gravity from *teacher centred mentality* to the *student centred approach*. DE has been defined by many, and most of the definitions describe it through two parameters; *distance* between the learner and the teacher and *structure* of the teaching-learning programmes.

One of the well accepted definitions is by Otto Peters who compares the structure of the teaching-learning process with the industrial structure. Otto Peters defines DE as:

> "The distance teaching/education (Fernunterricht) is a method of imparting knowledge, skills and attitudes which is rationalised by the application of division of labour and organisational principles as well as the extensive use of technical media, especially for the purpose of reproducing high quality teaching material which makes it possible to instruct great number of students at the same time wherever they live. It is an industrialised form of teaching and learning."

Desmond Keegan has considered some definitions of DE and given the following main elements in the definitions:

- the separation of teacher and learner which distinguishes it from face-to-face study;
- the influence of educational organisation which distinguishes it from private study;
- the use of technical media, usually print, to unite teachers and learners to carry the educational content;
- the provision of two-way communication so that students may benefit from or even initiate dialogue;
- the possibility of occasional meetings for both didactic and socialisation purpose; and
- the participation in an industrialised form of education which, if accepted, contains genus of radical separation of distance education from other forms.

(2) Distance

Distance between the learner and the teacher, who may lose his identity and become one with the structure or institution, could be *high* or *low* depending on the extent of dialogue or face-to-face contact allowed in the teaching-learning process.

High distance or *low dialogue* could be reduced through the extensive use of audio-visual and interactive media compensating for the face-to-face contact characteristic of *low distance* or *high dialogue.*

(3) Structure

Structure of the educational institution resembling industrial form should carry out the following functions:

(*i*) *Course Creation:* After studies and 'market' survey develop courses and learning programmes that would serve the needs and requirements of the target groups. This resembles R&D work of the industry to develop the required product.

(*ii*) *Course Production:* To multiply the learning material in print and audio-visual forms to fulfil the needs of students enrolled.

(*iii*) *Course transmission:* Through the educational network carry the contents to the students.

(*iv*) *Evaluation:* To carry out continuous evaluation to help the learner in his studies and the end-of-the-term evaluation to assess achievements of the student and for certification.

The structure should enable us to develop *'knowledge or educational industry'* to serve large scale needs of the learning society.

(4) Features of Distance Education

Educational systems highly dependent on distance teaching methods have to adopt radical changes in order to make them student centred. The major approaches for the changes are:

(*i*) *Self-instructional:* The learning material has to be developed in such a way that an average student can study it in his home situations.

(*ii*) *Experimental learning:* The approach in developing material for a particular target group is to relate the textual and audio-visual material with the life experiences of the group or with the observations the student can make in the community or in the field or laboratory work. This will link the elements of knowledge with the reality and would lead to the appreciation of knowledge in general.

(*iii*) *Relevance of Courses:* The course contents should be related to the most vital and useful areas of knowledge, skills and attitudes required by various segments of society in their economic and socio-cultural development.

It should also be related to the felt-needs in life situations or perceived needs that are or will be created with the onset of new technologies and social transformations. The diversity of the courses has to be so large as to offer every one courses of his need and interest.

(*iv*) *Freedom of Learner:* Central to all the teaching-learning system through non-formal and open educational system is the freedom of learner to choose objects of his learning, contents, course combinations, study methods, pace of learning, etc. The open learning system should offer maximum freedom to the student in his learning process.

With the above features, levels of the learning materials should be so arranged that at higher levels more emphasis be given on the development of critical thinking, higher cognitive and affective abilities.

Many programmes have been evolved which incorporate some features of non-formal and open learning systems. They are extension programmes, correspondence courses, external degree programmes, open university programmes of the formal universities, university without walls, off-campus studies, etc. Some are open in spatial sense, some remove admission constraints, but few offer freedom in more significant dimensions such as selection of subjects, of courses, their contents, adaptation of the curriculum, pace of learning, etc. The Open University should offer complete openness, non-formality and true distance education.

FEATURES OF STUDENT CENTRED DISTANCE EDUCATION

In order to make the non-formal system of distance education student centred, many of the concepts, methods and approaches of the existing formal system are to be discarded or adopted with appropriate changes.

(1) Levels of Education

In the formal system, education has been divided into various stages or levels. The usual levels are primary (7/8 years), secondary (2/3 years), higher secondary (2 years), first degree (3-5 years), second degree or master's level (2 years), and research level (1-4 years). The levels of education are characteristic of formal structure that caters to the various age groups starting from childhood. They often relate lower level knowledge and skills to those at higher levels, as decided by educationists.

These levels, even at the level of higher education need not be taken-up as they are n the non-formal system. In fact it is essential to have some objective criteria to decide the levels of education for adults learning through DE methods.

If we assume that application of education is in various life and work situations, we may be able to divide the entire knowledge field in various levels appropriate to its use. Since wider application of science and technology is developing industrial society, it would be appropriate to use industrial terminology with its broader meaning to categorise various levels of education. The following levels may clearly be distinguished:

— *Layman's Level:* It should contain the knowledge, skills and attitudes required in every day personal and community life. It will rise as the nature of society becomes more complex and technologically oriented.

— *Technician's Level:* It should be the education required in various vocational and job situations, such as those of electronic repairers, mechanics, secretaries, nurses, etc. Emphasis is more on skills and their practical uses.

(*a*) *Diploma level* (*Lower*): It should contain, besides skills, the knowledge required to understand why and how of the skills. The person would be a lower level specialist in a particular vocation or profession.

(*b*) *Diploma Level* (*Higher*): Higher level specialist who can manipulate knowledge elements in practical situations to a limited extent.

— *First Degree Level:* Emphasis should be on development of total personality by developing comprehensive background in certain groups of subjects along with the development of higher level abilities through extensive course work.

— *Second Degree Level:* It should develop specialists required in design and development work leading to contribution in knowledge and should clearly be based on the first degree programme.

— *Research Level:* It should enable one to make sustained contribution to knowledge.

(1) The course contents at various levels should be decided on the basis of the knowledge, skills and attitudes required for a particular profession/vocation. This may make various certificate and diploma courses of different durations and sizes. However, successful completion of the course work should make one competent to work successfully in the chosen vocation.

The levels decided this way may or may not have comparable levels in the formal system. However, they might find greater acceptance and relevance in real life situations. At the lower levels of certificate and lower diploma, the courses could be decided more on the basis of relevance to practical fields.

However, higher level courses of higher diploma, first and second degree could be more related to the knowledge and intellectual skills and abilities to be developed and, therefore, should find comparability with honours or first degree and master's level in the formal system.

In order to offer freedom in the choice of courses and their combinations, it is necessary to arrange courses at various levels in modules, so that various combinations may lead to certificates, diplomas, degrees, etc. in different subject areas. Freedom should be given to develop oneself in certain narrow areas, say electronics, by going ahead through courses to the highest level available. Simultaneously, combinations of some diplomas and other specified requirements should enable one to take a first and second degree in any faculty.

(2) In the formal system, teacher work-load and student contact periods are measured in terms of lecturing or lab. hours or proportionate credit points. In non-formal system, we have to introduce *learning period* which usually will not be a fixed period in the home-based study and may depend on various learning

activities such as reading texts, viewing video/TV lessons, listening radio and audio tapes, working through tutorials, etc. Under the circumstances it is better to accept the weekly learning period as a unit for measurement. As estimated by the UKOU, a working adult would be normally able to study about 12-16 hours or average 15 hours per week. This may be taken as the basic unit and credit-points to measure course work/study could be developed in terms of this unit.

Academic terms or year could be fixed to arrange study periods conveniently for the learners. However, there could be many courses for which starting and end points in time could be kept flexible to suit the convenience of learners and their pace of learning.

(3) The practice of separating theory and laboratory courses, uniform examination for all students of the course, etc. are typical practices of the formal system and they could be changed in the non-formal system. It is possible to develop *evaluation technology* that would offer frequent opportunity to students to take their end-examinations.

ANALYSIS OF INDIAN SITUATION

Dr. S. Balasubramaniam in his dissertion for Ph.D. from the Osmania University recorded following conclusions regarding the status of distance education in India. It is true that much has been done, since then, to overcome these aspects but still much needs to be done, therefore, hereunder we are giving conclusions of Dr. S. Balasubramaniam's study:

The responses clearly indicate that there is preponderance of arts and humanities courses and they cater to various segments of society. The courses are still conducted mainly in English—especially the postgraduate courses.

The contact courses are still mainly conducted in cities and sometimes in district centres. The library facilities are still inadequate. There are no book banks and reference materials. There are no study centres and no laboratory facilities.

In the organisation of the courses the responses indicated that extensive written material is provided but this is supplemented very little by radio broadcasts and none by TV (except in one or two cases). There are not enough coordinators to look into the problems of individual studies. The lectures given in the contact programmes are a repetition of the instruction material provided.

At the same time the responses indicated that students found it useful to attend to lectures to clear their doubts.

The preparation of the written material which is provided to the students and is the backbone of correspondence courses brought out mixed reactions. There are no permanent members to prepare the course material. The responses indicated that a course team is not always utilised as this item brought an outright negative reply. The names of the authors are seldom mentioned in the written material provided and most of the time the bibliography for the material is not included. The item concerning the periodic review of the scripts also brought a negative reply.

The personnel opined that enough number of assignments are not given and most often model answers are not included. The treatment of response sheets is found out as this is the only way by which a link between the pupil and the teacher is established. The authorities are comparatively strict about receiving the response sheets but the sheets are not returned with corrections or comments. The response for feed-back is negative.

The final section of the questionnaire dealt with the contact programmes as this was occasion when students came into contact with teachers and also with like-minded people who were taking similar courses. Attendance is satisfactory and the students enjoy the courses but different types of activities are not held.

The conclusions drawn from this study are that correspondence courses make higher education accessible to all sections of society. They provide scope for self-study which in turn gives self-fulfilment to the students.

The other conclusions that can be drawn are that these courses are not fulfilling the objectives of making people aware of social change and cultural development. It is clear that new skills are not taught. The courses are impersonal and not different from the mass media of the present day.

The correspondence courses are similar to regular courses, rather diluted versions of the regular courses, and stereotyped with no innovation, are brought out clearly in this study. Another interesting conclusion is that even though flexibility and diversity are part of the aims of correspondence education, these features do not find a place in the correspondence education which is conducted. The scope for practical experience is almost negligible. The courses are not in any way related to the socio-economic needs of the people.

The evidence shows that there are no adequate study-centres or book banks and in general physical facilities like libraries are lacking.

The students are given extensive written material but it is not supplemented by discussions on radio or TV. The experts are not sure whether the students are entirely satisfied with the material given. The lectures in the contact programmes are a repetition of written material but provides an opportunity for the students to clear their doubts. The lectures are however chosen with care and thought before the courses start.

There are permanent members of staff for preparation of material in some institutes. But the number is few and hence help is taken from outside and there are no meetings between various members who make a course team.

Authors' names and bibliography are not mentioned in the written material and suggestions are not invited from the students about the material—an important feature of teaching-learning process is sadly lacking. A mixed reply about the periodic review of scripts shows that it is done in a few institutions and is not frequent enough.

Sufficient number of assignments are given but there is no monitoring of corrections—rarely written comments are written when the assignment sheets are returned (CIEFL, Hyderabad does it.).

There is no provision for different types of activities during contact programmes except listening to lectures. But still the students seem to enjoy the courses.

The conclusions to be drawn from the above discussions are that some of the elements of correspondence courses are weak. The courses have to be strengthened by introducing new types with flexibility, diversity and innovation; above all, varied experiences have to be introduced.

The courses should be tailored only to meet the needs of acquiring degrees. In this context the role of open universities might bring forth new vistas in providing higher education. Not only should the planning be done meticulously, but care has to be taken in executing innovative methods.

MAJOR FACTORS LIMITING GROWTH OF DISTANCE EDUCATION

Various factors would limit the growth of enrolment of students in the Open Learning System. The major factors may be identified as:

(*i*) limited financial resources available either from the Government or through tuition fees and the cost of creation, production, transmission, etc. of the course;

(*ii*) requirements of maintenance, i.e. changes or reforms to keep the courses relevant and useful to the learners;

(*iii*) limited expertise available for the creation of courses, and for teaching/counselling in certain subject areas, wherein utility and cost considerations may limit the number of courses;

(*iv*) man-power requirement in certain specialised and vocational areas would also limit the enrolment;

(*v*) limitations of knowledge in its basic form to be taught through Open University System on a large scale; and

(*vi*) limitations of the University structure and its management system to deal with student enrolment effectively beyond a certain limit through distance and non-formal education methods.

If it is aimed to develop an Open University to cater to the needs of learning society, i.e. to develop a *Mass-Varsity* or a *Lok Vidyapeeth,* the above factors need to be considered while designing and developing the structure of the University. By disregarding these factors, the University is likely to reach, within a finite period, its limited size and activities.

AN EVALUATION

(*i*) Distance Education is essentially an outcome of the developments in modern communication technologies. Emergence of industrial and post-industrial societies have created, even at the higher level, great demand on education appropriate to the learning and fast changing society. Development of the national and international communication network has made it possible to develop an educational network that would be accessible to every adult.

It is, therefore, possible and essential to develop non-formal open educational systems by using distance education methods that would ensure *equality* of educational opportunity, serve larger *quantity* with higher *quality* education with *diversity* of courses that are relevant to the individual and societal needs and at the same time achieve *economies of scale.*

(*ii*) Distance education methods require the form and structure of an educational institution resembling industrialised forms. DE should develop a system with low distance or high dialogue and a structure that would carry out functions of course creation, course production and transmission, and evaluation. The structure should enable us to develop 'knowledge or educational industry'.

(*iii*) DE should offer relevant courses that are self-instructional, offer experiential learning and freedom to learners. At higher levels of knowledge, development of knowledge, critical thinking and higher cognitive and affective abilities need to be emphasised.

(*iv*) The non-formal distance education system for adult learners would need radical departures from many of the concepts, approaches and methods of the formal educational system. In particular, levels of education need to be redefined by considering their relevance and applicability.

(*v*) There are many factors that limit the growth of an Open University. Any design and structure of an Open University that aims at serving the learning society, i.e. becoming a mass-varsity or a Lok Vidyapeeth has to consider the limiting factors and avoid their influence while designing the structure of the Open Learning System.

5

Evaluation in Distance Education—Approaches and Process

INTRODUCTION

The effectiveness of educational systems is determined to a large extent by the evaluation machinery inbuilt in them. The conventional system of education has been castigated for its overemphasis on achievement and examinations. Passing examinations and acquiring paper qualifications have become major objectives of education at the cost of other worthwhile educational outcomes.

Distance education, which is fast emerging as a worthy alternative to conventional education and which has to its credit several innovative features and advantages, must avoid the pitfalls in which the traditional education has fallen. Distance educators and researchers must, therefore, direct their efforts to the task of evolving a suitable evaluation machinery for the distance learning systems keeping in view their characteristics, diversity, potential and promise.

THE CONCEPT OF EVALUATION

Evaluation is a continuous process contributing to the process of learning by enabling the learner to appreciate the strong and weak points of his own learning, through the process of learning itself and the instructional process by enabling the teacher to understand the strengths and weaknesses of his own institution through an appreciation of student responses to the same.

Ebel defined evaluation as a judgement of merit based solely on measurement provided by test scores but frequently involving the synthesis of various measurements and kinds of evidence. Tyler (1950) points out that the process of evaluation is essentially the process of determining to what extent the educational objectives are being realised by the programme.

Any educational system can be conceived as comprising three conceptually distinct components—inputs, operations or processes and outputs (Austin 1965, Austin and Panos 1960) or antecedents, transactions and outcomes (Stake, 1967).

To be maximally fruitful in decision-making, evaluation should provide information concerning all the three components and their inter-relationships. In fact, evaluation spans time and connotes some change in state occurring between the input and the output, referred to as the process as shown schematically.

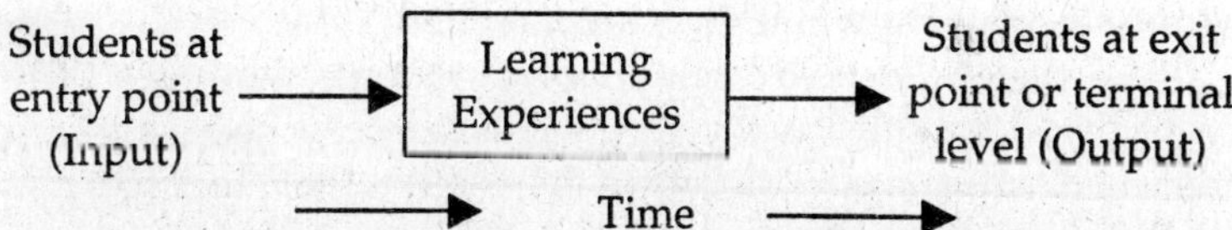

Input includes students described by age, sex, attitude, aptitude, previous learning, motivation, staff, curriculum etc., and other resources. Process denotes changes or learning that occurs during the period between the input and the output. Evaluation to be acceptable, must conform to certain scientific criteria such as validity, reliability, objectivity and timeliness.

The first step in the evaluation process is the identification of the programme goals and objective, which should be definite, specific and stated in observable, measurable behavioural terms. Next the manner in which the learning experiences are provided to realise the stated objectives should be assessed, as evaluation does not confine itself to the assessment of results alone but also extends to the means adopted to reach the ends. The third step deals with the determination of the indicators which will reveal, when the programme objectives have been achieved. These steps are followed in order, by data collection, analysis, interpretations and conclusions.

NEED AND SIGNIFICANCE OF EVALUATION

The concept that education is for all and can continue through adult like is being accepted more and more widely. Learning is no longer a privilege of a wealthy aristocracy. It has become the birth right of each individual to acquire as much education as one is capable of absorbing. The development of literacy, greater opportunity of leisure due to advances in technology and the change in attitude that education is a life long affair have increased the demand for continuing education.

To meet this demand distance education is being used to solve educational problems of both quantity and quality, extending education beyond the limits of the school and college system. If it is to serve as a valuable tool in any educational crisis and play a permanent part as a parallel strategy to the regular system, it should have an in-built feed-back system, both formative and summative. No matter how carefully the educational materials are prepared, they will not meet the needs or clear the doubts of all the students for whom they are intended.

The system of feed-back enables students who face some problems with the instructional materials to receive necessary help. Also it provides an opportunity to the lesson writers to assess how far they have been effective in what they were trying to achieve. Thus, in-built feed-back is a must both for the students who cannot otherwise overcome their learning difficulties and for the instructors who cannot otherwise see how effective their 'teaching' has been.

Beyond that, there are ideological reasons for stressing the indispensability of feed-back. Unless it is built into the system, the curriculum of distance education system assumes that the teacher is the master of all relevant knowledge and the learner's knowledge and understanding is of no importance to the educator. Feed-back, though difficult to organise is the only way of initiating dialogue between the teacher and the student in a distance education system. The educational effectiveness and the quality of distance education which uses mass-production methods can be maintained only through in-built evaluation systems.

APPROACHES TO PUPIL EVALUATION

Unfortunately, most distance educators, like their brethren in the formal system are ignorant about the basic purposes of evaluation which are (*a*) diagnostic, (*b*) motivational, (*c*) guidance, (*d*) prognostic and certification respectively (Gupta 1975). They are, on the one hand, not properly informed about the repertoire of techniques available to them for multi-dimensional pupil assessment. On the other hand, they are unwilling to use these in their day-to-day work for various reasons—inertia, lack of knowledge and mastery, and lack of faith etc. It seems worthwhile, therefore, to identify the main approaches to pupil evaluation which can be used with advantage in the distance learning systems main characteristics of which are (*a*) separation of teacher and learner, (*b*) influence of an educational organization that distinguishes it from private study, (*c*) use of technical media, usually print, (*d*) provision of two way communication between teachers and learners, (*e*) teaching of people mainly as individuals and rarely in groups, and (*f*) elements of a more industrialized form of education with activities like job scheduling, warehousing, postal and media despatch etc. (Keegan, 1980). Figure 5.1. is illustrative of the three approaches to pupil evaluation.

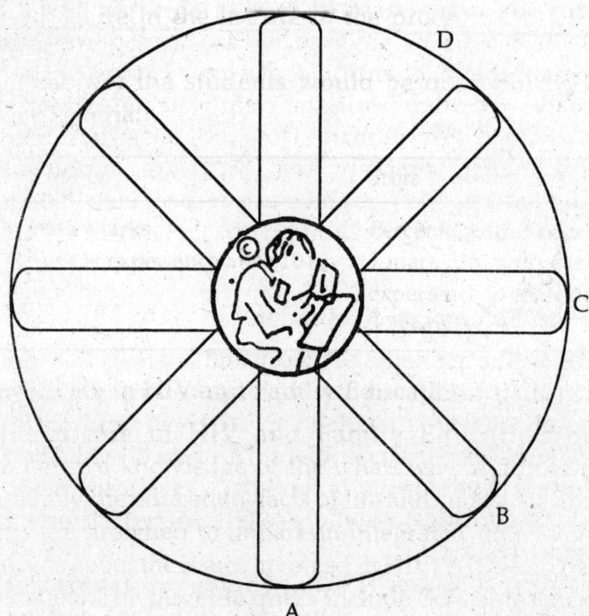

Fig. 5.1: Main Approaches for Pupil Evaluation

© Distance Learners
A Norm Referenced Evaluation
B Criterion Referenced Evaluation
C Individual Referenced Evaluation
D Instructional Programme at a Distance

In Figure 5.1 the core © represents the distance learner, a dynamic entity with definite abilities, experiences readiness, learning capacity, personality and behaviour which are always in a state of flux. Through the instructional programme offered at a distance according to any of the four models outlined by Keegan (1982)—the correspondence school model, and the Integrative model—educational and behavioural changes are to be effected in the individual and mastery over certain skills, concepts/facts ensured. At the same time, development of certain abilities may also be involved. All these have to be assessed effectively. The use of three evaluation strategies becomes important. These are:

1. Norm Referenced Evaluation

It is based on the theory of individual differences and is ideally suited for the assessment of human abilities. Some of the abilities which learners are expected to develop are abilities to think, comprehend, identify, organize, synthesize, perceive, manipulate, articulate, initiate, demonstrate, communicate, classify, interact, discriminate, compare, construct, rearrange, memorise, match, complete, analyze, relate, apply, evaluate, interpret, produce, generate and create respectively (Bloom, 1956; Gallach and Sullivan, 1969; Guilford, 1971; Flanders, 1971, Gagne, 1975).

2. Criterion Referenced Evaluation

It is based on the acceleration theory and assumes that almost all pupils can attain high levels of achievement in terms of appropriate behavioural outcomes provided they are given sufficient time and appropriate instructional conditions. This type of evaluation is best for the testing of attainment of concepts, or skills and behavioural outcomes according to some predetermined criteria i.e. for performance testing.

According to Glaser (1962), performance assessment is the process of measuring the student's auxiliary and terminal performance during and at the end of instruction. According to Carroll (1963, 1965), realisation of educational or instructional objectives depend upon the time spent by the learner to learn a task. The aptitudes, perseverance and ability to comprehend instructions are important ingredients while quality of instruction is vital in ensuring learning.

3. Individual Referenced Evaluation

This type of evaluation is a contribution of humanistic psychology. According to self-theorists namely Maslow (1954); Allport (1961); Coombs & Snygg (1961) and Roges (1969) self-enhancement and self-actualisation of the individual are the ultimate objectives which should be promoted through the discovery of his talents and areas of strength. Personal adequacy, self-esteem, satisfaction and actualization provide motives for learning and good human relations, values, attitudes and adequate personality.

Success and satisfaction should be the outcomes of instructional procedures. Evaluation is to concern itself with an individual's experiences, personality and behavioural changes; it has to be flexible and not imposed on the pupil. The student himself determines what he has and has not learned in the light of his own needs, problems, interests, aptitudes, goals and values, performance assessment and comparisons vis-a-vis others are not important. These really do not matter.

The three approaches to evaluation discussed above, yield different types of information about the individual. While there may be some overlapping in the information yielded by these approaches, yet the significance of obtaining a comprehensive multi-dimensional feedback about the learner based on the combination of the three approaches need to be understood and incorporated suitably in the distance learning system.

KINDS OF EVALUATION

Schematically the process of evaluation may be viewed as follows:

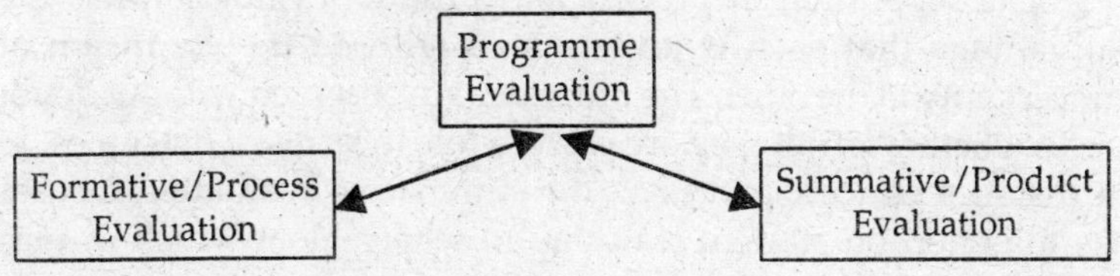

Formative/Process Evaluation

In process evaluation, the evaluator is interested to find out how and why a programme works or does not work or how the different programme inputs can be manipulated to yield desired outcomes. It concentrates on the design and the operational components of the programme in gathering data for assessment and effecting improvement.

As such, it constitutes a picture of input effectiveness which identifies the strength and weakness of the programme in its design and operation during the process of implementation, and suggests ways and means of improving the programme by maximising its strengths and reducing its weaknesses, by the use of appropriate alternatives.

Among the different components of the distance education system, the formative evaluation needs to concentrate on educational needs of the groups and objectives of the programme, curriculum design, learning multi-media packages and the delivery system.

Programme effects are continuous throughout the operation of the programme and formative assessment helps in improving the programme by providing feed-back to persons responsible for its implementation, and identifies the potential sources of failure in the interpersonal relationships among staff and students, communication channels, material and human resources, physical facilities and time schedules.

Summative/Product Evaluation

Summative or product evaluation (post-programme evaluation) is equivalent of outcome or impact evaluation. It is the assessment of programme effects, after the termination of the programme. Seriven (1967) used the terms 'formative' and 'summative' to refer respectively to evaluation mainly intended to help form a new curriculum and evaluation design to give a final judgement on a finished programme.

The separation of process and product evaluation has the advantage that each is investigated without the confusion of uncertainty in the other. The processes are observed without doubt as to whether or not they are worthwhile in terms of outcomes. In a distance education system, the summative evaluation focuses its attention on student learning or achievement which in turn reflects the efficacy of the whole system.

METHODOLOGY AND PROCESS OF EVALUATION

The underlying spirit behind the system of evaluation is just to know the actual standard of the examinee. However, while deciding the evaluation methodology and procedural details various factors should be kept in view. Analysis of these factors may help in having a pragmatic approach to the issue. This is more significant in relation to distance learning system which is itself in the process of evaluation and is yet to take a definite shape.

Establishment of Indira Gandhi National Open University, New Delhi is a forward step towards achievement of the goal of a well established system of distance education and the present analysis is mainly in the context of this University. The factors which may have impact on designing the evaluation methodology are as follows:

DESIGNING OF EVALUATION METHODOLOGY

Following factors effect the designing of evaluation methodology:

(*i*) There is no formal and regular classroom teaching in the distance learning system. The students learn at home in their own way whenever they get time and it is convenient to them. Chances of face to face interaction between the teacher and the taught are very limited in this system. It is, sometimes, arranged through contact programmes but the duration of such programmes is generally very limited, say a fortnight or so.

The students try to learn through recommended textbooks, subject booklets, written lessons, radio and television broadcasts and other audio-visual material. On Indian scene, it is the written lessons which provide the major part of source material. More than 90 per cent course component is covered by such lessons.

(*ii*) Number of students in an open university system may be unlimited. Having its jurisdiction over whole of the country, the Indira Gandhi National Open University has enrolment in lacs.

While talking about evaluation methodology this important factor should be kept in view as regularisation of academic calendar is directly related with a timely commencement of examinations and declaration of results.

(*iii*) Having its jurisdiction over whole of the country an open university while deciding examination system cannot overlook the factor of physical distance. This factor becomes more significant in case of National Open University, New Delhi which has to take the vast geographical area into consideration. Needless to mention evaluation scripts will have to be collected from the examination centres, scattered all over the country.

(*iv*) Infrastructure developed for the purpose of teaching and general administration has a direct bearing on the arrangements made for examination. This is also true in case of formal education system where the colleges and schools are kept as examination centres and the same machinery is used practically for all purposes.

From the angle of administrative arrangements, monitoring and review it is noteworthy that our national open university may have three tier administrative set up as is illustrated below:

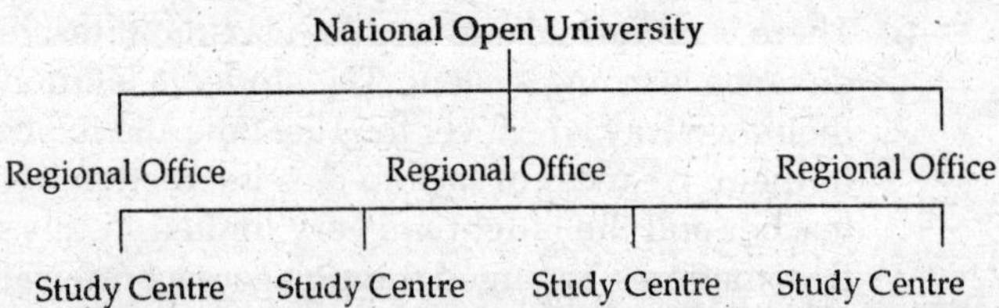

It is expected that the regional offices would be set up at the State capitals. The Study Centres may be established at district or sub-division head-quarters keeping in view the various factors such as number of students, physical distances, availability of transport facility and suitable teaching institutions etc. In big cities there may be more than one Study centre.

(*v*) Linguistic difference is the major factor which should be kept in view. In different parts of the country different languages are in use as medium of instruction upto secondary level. English and/or Hindi are used as link languages. However, there are areas where neither English nor Hindi is understood well.

(*vi*) The open learning system has tremendous flexibility with regard to the admissions and choice of courses and optional papers. The entry regulations may be liberal and flexible so as to enable different sections of the community like employed adults, housewives, dropouts and left over youth and other disadvantaged group to avail of the facilities offered.

Thus a heterogeneous mass of pupils—old, young, persons from cities, rural areas, developed plain areas and underdeveloped tribal areas may get enrolled. No formal qualification or certificate is required at entry point. There may be an entrance test, just to ensure that the applicant has the capacity to understand and follow the courses. Having persons from different cultural background it is desirable to evolve such an evaluation methodology in which only the knowledge gained by the students may be the primary thing for judgement; no other factor may affect the assessment.

Aspects of Evaluation

In the context of education system the term evaluation means to assess or to determine the value or standard of knowledge of the examinee at a particular time i.e. the time when he appears at the examination. Thus the evaluation has two ingredients—student and examiner. The examining body, a university or a board, plays the role of co-ordination in between the two.

The examiner may try to assess the mental standard of the examinee in more than one ways. He may ask him to speak on a given topic, may discuss with him, may watch his action if assignment is that of a practical nature or may ask him/her to write the answer of questions given in question paper. In this regard, three points are worth considering:

(*a*) What are the aspects of assessment? What do we want to assess? We want to assess knowledge, understanding, application, expression or writing power. Needless to mention, the form of enquiry would be determined by this.

(*b*) The form of enquiry or the type of questions aiming to get spontaneous answers from the examinees.

(*c*) The ratio between various aspects of assessment. It generally depends upon the purpose of assessment. May be that reasoning is the main objective of assessment in one examination while the knowledge or expression in the others. Naturally the main aspect will form the major part of enquiry (examination).

Evaluation Scheme

Keeping in view all this and the factors analysed in the foregoing paragraphs the following scheme of assessment may be suggested for the distance education system.

A. For subjects having practicals

(*i*) 25 per cent marks for tutor marked assignments.

(*ii*) 25 per cent marks for testing the capacity of practical application. The examination may be arranged at the local college (study centre) level in the form of practicals, viva-voce, group discussions, interviews etc.

(*iii*) 50 per cent marks for theory papers which may be held at the end of the course. These may be computer marked assignments.

B. For subjects involving no application (practicals)

(*i*) 25 per cent marks for tutor marked assignments.

(*ii*) 75 per cent marks for theory papers which may be held at the end of the course. These may be computer marked assignments.

THE PROCESS OF EVALUATION

In distance education tutor marked assignment form a vital part, which we have discussed in earlier chapter, hence hereunder we will discuss the concept of the main part of evaluation:

Question Paper Setting

While setting question papers for annual examination, it is desirable to keep the following guidelines in view:

(*i*) The questions should be set covering the whole syllabus. For this purpose the course contents may be divided into various units.

(*ii*) The questions should be such that these cannot be answered without a thorough reading and deep knowledge of the subject.

(*iii*) The questions should, as far as possible, be of objective type so that uniformity of assessment may be maintained with the help of a marking-key, prepared for the purpose.

If need be the scripts may be examined by computer also. This is very much relevant in an open university system where the number of students may be in lacs, the examination centres be scattered all over the country, the examiners may be, selected from different universities and the students may have different linguistic backgrounds.

If the questions are to be answered by a long narration it may take longer duration in assessment in addition to the language difficulties faced even at the end of examiners.

(*iv*) There may be one-word answer, multiple-choice, filling in by suitable answer and pair-making type questions. The question paper and blank answer-sheet may be one and the same.

Such scripts may easily, quickly and correctly be assessed by both the examiner as well as the computer. From the view point of timely declaration of result and regularisation of academic calendar it is desirable that the job is done by computer.

(*v*) The question papers should be set in two languages i.e. English and Hindi.

(*vi*) The number of objective type questions to be answered in a given time should be enough so that the examinee may not afford to divert his attention even for a while.

(*vii*) If the scripts are to be assessed manually, short notes, comments and one line answer type questions may also be asked.

In fact, the setting of question papers is important part of the examination. Type of questions directly affect the time consumed in assessment and also the quality of assessment. It has been observed that the variation in awards (for the same answer-book if assessed by more than one examiner) is much more in essay type questions as compared to objective type or short answer type questions.

Thus to minimise the chances of subjectivity, to improve the quality of assessment and to reduce the duration in the process, it is desirable to lay emphasis on the objective type questions. The question paper setting, in fact, is an art and an efficient paper setter can easily judge the standard of actual mental calibre of the examinee through answers very easily.

Concept of Blueprint

Advance planning should be done in regard to setting of question papers. Looking into nature of subject, blueprints should be prepared for each paper. This job could be done at university level by the subject experts. Once the blue-print is prepared for a paper it can be used for more than one year or ever more unless there is a marked change in course content. Such-blueprints may be given to paper setters.

A blueprint is a sort of outline which provides guidance to the paper setter. With that guidance he may set questions to assess the capacity of examinee in the specific areas. Such areas may be the knowledge, understanding, skill or practical application etc. For example, in the paper of language or mathematics, objective type questions may be set to test the capacity of practical application. In the area of skill it may be tested whether the knowledge and understanding of a particular subject has added to the skill of the examinee in that particular field.

A Model Blueprint

Subject........................Paper.................Year...................

Course content	*Knowledge*	*Understanding*	*Application*	*Skill*
Sub-unit	O M F T	O M F T	O M F T	O M F T

O = One word answer, M = Multiple choice, F = Fill in the blanks, T = True-false.

For each sub-unit of the course content percentage and the number of questions to be asked in the areas of knowledge understanding, application and skill may be prescribed. In the same way, the number for each type of objective questions may be mentioned in regard to each area. After completing all the units, the totals for each of the four areas and each of the four types of questions should be calculated. If the totals tally the blueprint may be taken as completed.

For example, the nature of course content in a paper is such that it requires 50 per cent questions on knowledge, 35 per cent on understanding and 15 per cent questions on application. Time given for the examinee is 2 hours and within this duration he has to attempt 200 questions. The number of questions to be asked in each area would be as under:

Knowledge	100
Understanding	70
Application	30
Skill	0
Total	200

The number for each type of questions will also depend upon the nature of course content. In this example, it may be as under:

Area	*Total No. of questions to be asked*	*One word answer*	*Multiple choice*	*Fill in blanks*	*True false*	*Total*
Knowledge	100	15	35	30	20	100
Understanding	70	10	25	20	15	70
Application	30	5	15	5	5	30
Skill	—	—	—	—	—	—
Total	200					200

Practical Examinations

There are certain subjects in which practical exercises are required to develop the capacity of practical application. It is essential in the field of natural sciences. In humanities and fine arts also there are some disciplines where such exercises are desirable. In distance education system where there is no formal teaching, these exercises are arranged in the local colleges in the evening, on Sundays or during the holidays.

The coordinator generally makes such arrangements with the institution situated at the headquarters of Study Centres. Local lecturers are engaged for the purpose. Thus it is a sort of camp coaching where all the practical exercises are got completed within a given time. As far as examination for these practical exercises is concerned it is desirable that:

(*i*) the examiner should be called from outside. He may be from any college situated within the region. This examiner may be called as external examiner;

(*ii*) the local person who actually guides the students during the coaching camps may also be associated in capacity of internal examiner;

(*iii*) the award sheets of these practical examinations may be collected at regional office from where the lot may directly be despatched to the computer firm for tabulation;

(*iv*) the external examiner, in consultation with internal examiner, may set the exercises there on the spot. However, a general frame for the various exercises such as experiments, viva-voce, group discussion and record etc., may be prescribed so that the examiner may fit in his queries within that frame. This is desirable from the view point of uniformity in assessment as well as tabulation of marks; and

(*v*) Practical examination should be held prior to the theory papers. It will help in early declaration of results.

ORGANISATIONAL ASPECTS

Examiners

As the students enrolled in open university system are scattered all over the country and their number may be in lacs, the panel of examiners should be prepared on national level. Applications may be invited through open advertisement. The panel of examiners may be further rearranged subject and region-wise. The names may be ticked as per requirement. For practical examinations the selection may be made on regional basis.

Examination Centres

Like other activities, for examination management also the open university system may be three tier set-up i.e. Central, Regional and the Study Centre level. The examination centres may be decided by the regional office. While finalising the examination centres the following points should be kept in mind:

(*a*) The place is well connected by rail or road transport.

(*b*) No student is required to travel a distance of more than 30 km. to reach the examination centre.

(*c*) It should preferably be a Government or semi-government institution.

(*d*) Each centre may be given a code number. Such numbers should be known to the concerned persons only.

(*e*) The Principal and Vice-Principal of the college (where centre has been made) may be appointed as Centre Superintendent and Additional Centre Superintendent respectively.

(*f*) There may be certain guidelines and norms for invigilators. Only persons fulfilling these norms may be appointed as invigilators by the Centre Superintendent in consultation with the regional office.

(*g*) Examination and subject-wise numerical returns should be prepared for each centre well in advance so that the answer books and question papers are sent accordingly.

Assessment

Initially all the answer books may be collected at the regional offices: further steps will depend upon the mode of assessment. If assessment is to be done by computer, answer-books from all regional centres may be despatched to the university/computer centre.

On the other hand, if the scripts are to be got assessed by the examiners, these may be sent to the examiners directly from the regional office collection centre. Examiner-wise allotment of answer books may be done at University level and accordingly subject-wise lists of examiners may be sent to regional office.

Examiner-wise Allotment of Answer Books

For the Examination..................................(Year)

Name of Exam/Class.............Name of Subject/Paper............

1	2	3	4	5	6
S. No.	Name of Examiner	Address	Code No. of Centre(s) Allotted	Total No. of answer books Allotted	Roll No. from... to......

As a third alternative, if the scripts are to be assessed by examiners centrally at a fixed place, it should be organised at the regional level. For central evaluation which is generally arranged from the view point of early declaration of results, an advance planning is desirable. It should be ensured that roll numbers of a particular region are allotted to the examiners from the colleges situated in the proximity of the regional office so that the expenditure on TA and DA may be minimum. From central evaluation centre awards can be sent to computer firm directly.

Result

For tabulation and working out of results three types of marks would be fed to the computer i.e. marks of tutor marked assignments, practical examinations and theory papers. The first two sets of marks may be fed in advance. For the marks of previous examination, say in case of II Year or III Year, there should be no problem as the computer itself would do the job of reconciliation. We can't expect things like supplementary examinations or revaluation in the distance education system. R. W. (result withheld) cases too should be totally absent in this system as all the requirements and information are completed at the time of registration.

Moreover, requirements like migration certificate, domicile certificate, mark-sheet/degree of qualifying examinations and proof for age which cause withholding of results in the formal system, do not have any relevance in the open learning system. Thus the situations like updation of results can hardly be there. All this may help in early processing and declaration of results.

Percentage for passing an examination and that for awarding divisions may be kept at par with other universities so that the students having a degree from the open university may feel that he is in the mainstream of higher education and in no way inferior who pass out through conventional system.

The result should be communicated to the candidate concerned under registered post along with the marks-sheet. In the same letter it may be asked whether he is interested in further courses. If he is willing he may be advised to send the requisite fee within the prescribed time. No other formality be required to be observed for the purpose of admission to the higher standard or appearance at next examination.

CLOSE MONITORING AND REVIEW

'Man' is the key factor behind all the systems. Unless the persons involved in the system work sincerely, honestly and with utmost dedication no system can reach the stage of perfection. This is specifically true in case of examination management where each step is a time bound programme. It a system like that of distance education the necessity of monitoring becomes manifold.

With a very vast jurisdiction, huge number of students, flexibility in admission and offering of courses, no open university can do successfully unless it has a well developed system of close monitoring. Out of the three tiers, i.e. University, Regional Office and Study Centre, the middle link i.e. the regional office has a vital role to play. It is the regional office, in fact, which regulates the whole scheme.

Right from arrangements for the study centre to declaration of results this level has to activate the whole machinery. Thus a very effective system of a monitoring is required at this level. At university level there should be a separate monitoring cell, always busy with preparation of time schedules, collection of information on prescribed proformas, analysing the progress, identification of weaker areas and suggesting remedial steps.

NEED FOR RESEARCH TO UPGRADE THE SYSTEM OF DISTANCE EDUCATION AND EVALUATION

In the task of delineating sound and functional conceptual framework for evaluation in distance learning situations, the following issues need serious consideration at the hand of theorists and researchers:

1. Place of self-evaluation in the evaluation machinery and the weightage given to self-evaluation vis-à-vis external evaluation.
2. Effective use of evaluation in reducing dropout rates and increasing success.
3. Design of adequate, reliable and valid assessment techniques for measuring changes in disposition, attitudes, values, satisfaction and self-enhancement on the one hand and higher order abilities like creativity, problem solving, resourcefulness, etc. on the other hand.
4. Ensuring comparability of standards in academic programmes utilizing distance learning techniques, engendering confidence in the evaluation of an institution issues related to accreditation on local, national and international planes.
5. Use of multimedia in devising objective, reliable and valid assessment techniques.
6. Establishing relative efficiency of different evaluative techniques and devices for different target groups, different instructional programmes and different situations to highlight intra-individual and inter-individual differences.

Morgan, Taylor and Gibbs (1982) rightly described assessment as the most powerful influence on student experiences of learning in distance education. However much remains to be done to make his assessment theoretically sound, objective, reliable, valid, flexible, mulit-dimensional and useful. The sooner distance educators realize this, the better it would be for the future growth, development, success and utility of distance education.

6

Management of Distance Education—The Concept to Take Education to People's Doorsteps

INTRODUCTION

The present day democratic society for its own good must strive at people's education but in populous societies like India the formal system of education can not meet the educational needs of the whole population. Therefore, it is the need of the hour to accept the utility of distance education and find out ways and means for its better management.

In the developing countries of the world, the concept of distance education is fast catching up. More and more students are seeking admissions to correspondence schools. The knowledge that per capita expenditure on education is constantly increasing puts our educationists on the alert. In the developed countries of the world, distance education is popular, although for different reasons.

These young boys and girls would like to get involved in readily available gainful employment after they attain majority and get their education as a continuing process.

We are looking forward to the day when in India some miracle takes place in either the thinking pattern of our young population or in the economic pattern of our country. To elaborate the former, if our youth takes to the family occupation, whatever it is from astrology to shopkeeping after his matriculation and decides to get higher education through correspondence, it would be an ideal arrangement.

It would be better still if our planning generates more job avenues for our young persons so that they get higher education through correspondence schools. Even now we find more and more persons join postal courses. And that makes us think of how best we can manage our distance education system.

TWO-PRONGED MANAGEMENT STRATEGY

A two-pronged strategy is needed for managing our distance education system: Academic and administrative. Since the focus of attention must be academic, the administrative or the executive staff should ensure promptitude in handling the educational wares.

At the academic level, the first thing should come first. Central to all schemes of things in education is the teacher. No doubt, we have teachers to train pupils in our distance education schools, but we have none to train teachers in this non-formal system of education. It is rather amazing that there are teacher-training colleges for the school teachers but there are none for those who teach in seats of higher learning; and all those who are teaching there drift into that profession by accident and not by design. Straight from on the benches, they get behind the lect.

It is a reversal of roles, a student yesterday, a teacher today. Naturally that obviates a judicious choice of teachers for our centres of distance education, if spoken word is supreme in formal system of education, it is the written word in non-formal system. Only persons with a flair for writing should be recruited. The polarities that separate the two systems, the formal and the non-formal, are characterised by the written and the spoken word. The spoken word has a tendency to get scattered in the air. But the written word is open to public scrutiny, delivered on open-circuit broadcasts. It must carry on it the stamp of authenticity, meticulousness.

Hence in the management of distance education, a team of distinguished scholars with a remarkable command over language and a knack of turning out neat phrases and handling the educational material with care is needed. It is here that idea of making distance education cellular comes in.

Hitherto in most of the universities, correspondence courses departments have been in use as havens for mediocrities who can not make the grade in academic departments. The reason advanced is that centres of distance education are not research oriented. There seems to be no reason why research cannot be incorporated in Correspondence System of education.

To speak just in the parenthesis, Punjabi University, Patiala was the first University in India to launch M.Phil. programme for in-service lecturers. After M. Phil., many of these scholars did their Ph.D. with the faculty of the Directorate. The management of distance education should have research programme in all the disciplines it is servicing.

TRAINING OF DISTANCE EDUCATION TEACHERS

In any case, special arrangements have got to be made for training our teachers before they take up assignments with schools of Distance Education. Simply because this experiment when tried in Kampala by Kyambogo Government Teachers-Training College, the earliest Teacher-Training Programmes for Correspondence Teachers, had just flopped (ICCE's Newsletter, 1983) should be no damper because the failure of the experiment took place way back in 1953 through 1961. The world has by now made rapid strides. New means have emerged so that a greater degree of concentration can be brought to bear on this aspect of Teacher-Training.

As opposed to Kampala, the pattern tried by Uganda can be adopted, 3-week training of 8 Teacher-Training Colleges in Uganda, each college headed by a Course Director and 8 tutors. This kind of exposure is essential for teachers.

The report of ICCE's Newsletter relating to 1981 shows that trained teachers are doing better job in teaching through correspondence. It goes without saying that unless we have professionally trained teachers, distance education cannot be effective.

As a part of the latest revolution in the field of education is the availability of media as an effective vehicle of communication. Teaching through visual aids has an instantaneous appeal on the relatively fresh minds. Whereas the role of media such as radio, television, audio/video cassettes, linguaphone etc. may not be very pronounced or even relevant in a formal classroom system of education, its role in distance education can hardly be underestimated.

In India, our teachers are still teaching with the traditional methods. But may be a switch-over is round the corner. It is a happy augury that the educational administration in India is already thinking of making distance education a multi-media system. Various universities in India are pressing hard to set up Audio Visual Centres/Educational Media Centres (AVC/EMC) as a central facility for purposes of pressing latest technology into educational use. Before this is done we have to ensure that our teachers are properly trained in the art of handling hardware and software. Also, perhaps, more importantly, the man in the teacher has to be saved from being hidden behind the machine.

Media cannot be made effective by the appearance on it of robots. In any scheme of things, the vibrant being of man is more important than television media. The voice whether heard in a face-to-face conversation or through the linguaphone or on the audio cassettes has got to be the twin of man's vision. Such teachers have to be judiciously selected for this job.

THE CONCEPT OF FINANCIAL AND FUNCTIONAL AUTONOMY

If we want Distance Education Centres to be really impactful, it is necessary that complete financial and functional autonomy is given to them. It is a big question as to how these Distance Education Centres should be funded, through the government aids, through the munificence of philanthropic individuals or organisations or through the money coming by way of fees from the students themselves. A mechanism has got to be worked out for getting our Distance Education Centres funded.

Major portion of the finance should come from the beneficiaries of distance education and a certain percentage from beneficient agencies which subscribe to the dictum: *Vidya Daan Mahan Kalyan.* Efforts must be made to make distance education participatory. On the governing bodies of our correspondence schools should be nominated distinguished persons who can, on an assurance of accountability, create special endowments for running Centres of Distance Education—something like in Spain known as the "Patrons of the University".

Distance Education is after all primarily for those who are in-service, as proposed earlier; right in proportion to the enhancement in their financial position, they should contribute to the funds of these centres; the school is the Alma Mater, symbolising the mother and the children's concern for the mother will carry an aura of religiosity about it.

As to the functional autonomy, now when there is a talk about setting up of autonomous colleges, there is no reason why Centres of Distance Education should not be given this autonomy. For another reason too: The exponents of the Formal System who proclaim academic excellence as their ultimate goal are generally either averse to or ignorant of the basic commitment of distance education to also the in-service people with long standing in their profession who just want to improve their qualifications and for whom job-oriented courses are usually launched by the universities.

Our Postgraduate Diploma in Management of Public Enterprises, Public Relations and Advertising, in Library Science or M.Ed. course have on our rolls in-service students who represent a cross-section of society. These courses are self-supporting.

It is amazing that Distance Education Centres have to get a clearance (may be in a few universities) for launching such courses from the Boards of Studies and Academic Councils, packed with 'Sanatanists', advocates of Formal System of Education.

In the words of Vice-Chancellor Sir Walter Petry of Open University, London, "....departmental control of teaching is the root cause of all that is wrong with educational programmes in conventional universities". This refers perhaps to the framing of syllabi and courses of reading by the various Boards of Studies which have no nominees on these Boards of the Directorates of Correspondence Courses.

Sir Walter Perry does not mean that academic departments have a lesser role to play. He wants these departments to remain the nuclei for research (I personally see nothing wrong in correspondence education assuming that role also for itself, as pointed out earlier).

So long as the autonomy to frame their own courses of study and evolve their own syllabi is not given to Distance Education Centres, it should be ensured that Boards of Studies that at present function as framers of syllabi have on them a fair representation of correspondence shools which supply the major bulk of students to the university. Nor should there be frequent changes in the syllabi. We have to take into account the cost entailed in the preparation, printing and vetting of the course material. The publisher's and booksellers' gain should not be the loss of Centres of Distance Education.

Functional autonomy is needed. In some of the universities, the number of students enrolled with the Directorates of Correspondence Courses far exceeds the total enrolment with all the academic departments put together. The total budget of the university divided over the number of students, enrolled—

especially for Master's courses—would present an alarming picture, if the number of drop-outs or the over-all poor grade obtained by the majority of students are taken into account.

Wastage of human potential at the faculty level makes the picture still more alarming. Research produced by the teachers in academic departments is not proportionate to the money being spent on each teacher in the academic departments by way of salary, establishment, library etc. (This is more true of Humanities).

This situation was flippantly put in the famous not very laudable remark: "a lecturer is he who lectures; the reader is he who reads and the Professor is he who neither lectures nor reads but professes."

Whereas the system is hierarchical in regular departments, it should be cellular in Centres of Distance Education, each cell representing one academic discipline and headed by the core staff consisting of one or two eminent members on the faculty and all work being done on secondments.

THE SYSTEM OF ADMINISTRATION

Administrative Wing of the Distance Education Centres, on the contrary, should be hierarchical with a Registrar at the apex and other functionaries heading various operational sections so that a responsibility is ultimately fixed for every operation, from getting the written or audio-visual material prepared and having it despatched, received back and re-despatched as a feedback to students till they get their certificates and degrees.

The cellular approach is advocated in Academic Section because the responsibility must rest squarely on the cell rather than on the individual. Course work, team teaching, evaluation work relating to response sheets, itinerant teacher moving by turn on a circuit, staying at the well equipped-Resource-cum-Study Centres to give audio/visual displays are tasks, all of a cellular nature rather than hierarchical.

In stating that the teachers in University should take a public stance on issues of vital socio-political importance, Sir Walter Perry has made a highly provocative statement and put to debate the role of learned persons teaching in seats of higher learning. Here is a suggestion which needs be taken seriously. Particularly by a country like ours where we are torn as under by narrow considerations of caste, creed, religion or language.

This stance may be counter-productive in a formal system of education or limited in its ends in a formal system of education where the number of students in a classroom seldom exceeds 30 at the postgraduate level. Such a potential programme can be of immense value in correspondence schools where thousands of our students can be provided a wide spectrum of responsible opinion on issues of vital socio-political importance.

This must, however, be said that this suggestion is fraught with grave dangers if handled by men of ordinary calibre. Socially oriented teachers of Walter Perry's specifications must be persons of high voltage working with a missionary zeal not only to teach the prescribed subjects but also to evolve a newer man with a broad mind and generous propensities. This obviates a greater degree of personal contact between the teacher and the taught.

For a couple of years New Zealand Correspondence Schools had five teachers, each based in a particular area of New Zealand and responsible for correspondence students in that area. These teachers in New Zealand visit students' homes, study their familial environs, supervise students' day-to-day progress and report to the central units. Some such experiments can be tried in India.

We can have itinerant teachers moving on a circuit and staying at various places depending upon the concentration of students at that place or at places contiguous to it. But it needs be repeated that this is a task not be assigned to low graders, or persons with irresponsible nature. Itinerant teachers must be like monks, thoroughly disciplined so that they could address themselves to their students in a more effectual and dynamic relationship.

RESTRUCTURING THE SYSTEM

While deliberating over the management of distance education, we should work out the possibility of Open Universities on Zonal basis rather than on State or provincial basis. There are so many uneasy trends visible in the socio-cultural life of our country that we can no longer sit back in a state of inaction: If politically we could not bring about cohesion or unification, at least academically we can. Our educational planners can give thought to setting up five Open Universities under the overall control of Indira Gandhi National University.

Each Zonal University should have a common syllabus and common courses of reading with flexibility enough to keep provision in it for providing effective instruction in and ensuring growth of what is evocative of the peculiar ethos of each culture living for ages in that zone. Whereas History, Geography, Economics, Political Science and allied subjects together with Physical Sciences may be common to all States, dialect, legends, mythology, religion and rituals which constitute culture may be different. In our desire to evolve unity, we should not kill diversity. Unity in diversity is our motto.

The idea behind the suggestion can be concretised by restructuring our distance education along these lines. Our field being far more vast and the numbers larger and maturer, the aim can be achieved with greater precision.

Our Personal Contact Programmes held round the year and at different places can provide interaction of minds which will enfeeble and eventually annihilate chauvinistic, linguistic and other separatist ideas.

7

Distance Teaching Technique: The Concept of Tutor Comments

INTRODUCTION

In distance education there is no classroom situation and no close academic contact or interaction between teacher and the taught, therefore, the teacher counsellor as discussed earlier must guide the students to develop study-skills and his comments on the assignments evaluated by him must be very educational and effective to serve and guide the student which we will discuss in this chapter, but before we do so let us know some vital points about the distance teacher.

THE GENESIS OF DISTANCE TEACHER

A typical institute of distance education collects information relevant to a particular course of studies and shapes it into lessons, prepares the reading lists essential for it, and designs the learning tasks (assignments) or other types of worksheets suitable for its aims. All these put together take the form of a course-unit. The distance learner is expected to study the course-units and write answers to various questions or perform the learning tasks, which, when performed, are assessed and graded by the tutor, and subsequently sent back to the learners.

The average of grades obtained at the final examination together with internal assessment decides the final grades, and a certificate/diploma is awarded accordingly. It should not, however, be construed that every course given through the distance mode follows the same system of grading.

There can be numerous variations, but the basic principle that the final grades should be computed on the basis of a learner's performance at the final examination together with the quality of his work throughout the period of studies is not lost sight of.

This brief outline of a part of the learning-teaching process in distance education does not seem to account for the role of the teacher or the tutor, except as an examiner. Granting that the course-units, answer-scripts and examinations have their respective counterparts in the form of the chapters of prescribed texts, exercises written by students and corrected by teachers, and examinations held in the conventional system of classroom teaching.

The basic fact in modern formal as well as in distance education is the role of learner is most vital, therefore education now is a learner centred activity. Some other facts are as follows:

(*a*) a learner should be able to learn in non-classroom situations too,
(*b*) the so-called 'holy guide' should, in most cases, be more of a facilitator than anything else, and
(*c*) 'word of mouth' need not be the only means of help.

These truisms enunciate some of the fundamental notions the system of distance education is based on, and it is in them that we trace the genesis of a distance-teacher, who can and should do as much and as well as a classroom teacher.

The latter helps his students to communicate with the written learning materials presented as bits of information, delivered orally or referred to as materials to be looked up in libraries, and the former does much the same not through the 'word of mouth' but through the 'word of hand'—the comments on the answer-scripts.

This obvious theoretical resemblance between the classroom teacher and the distance tutor might get obliterated at the performance level because of the differing operational modes they follow. And this makes all the difference—a teacher who comes to the classroom must willy-nilly talk, and therefore, by implication, inform, guide, inspire or at least help the learner.

By not writing any comments on the answer-scripts, in spite of his having graded them, he ceases to be a teacher/tutor. As in such a case he is a mere examiner who evaluates an answer-script and is not called upon to explain his stand.

There is no lack of evidence to establish the fact that not every teacher/tutor handles answer-scripts with the attention and devotion expected of him. What could be the possible reasons for such indifference? May be any one or more than one of the following:

(*a*) he does not like his work, as he is working under some kind of compulsion,

(*b*) he does not really read the answer-scripts, but grades them to record an overt evidence of having done his duty,

(*c*) he reads the answer-script but does not have enough time to write his comments,

(*d*) he does not realize how significant his comments are from the pedagogic point of view.

(*e*) he does not know what comments to write and how to write them.

The problems outlined under (*a*), (*b*) and (*c*) have obvious solution but those presented under (*d*) and (*e*) deserve to be discussed in detail. As said above the cases listed under (*a*), (*b*) and (*c*) are not hypothetical cases. In many cases it so happens that academic staff are seconded from the parent departments of universities to the directorates of correspondence or distance education. If a particular teacher is not happy about the secondment, for whatever reasons, he does not take any interest in his work at the directorate [case (*a*)].

But then he must, in certain cases, show that he is working; for this he has to manipulate some kind of a semblance of work being done by him [case (*b*)]. Neither of these problems have pedagogic solutions, as in essence they are administrative problems. The obvious solution is that unwilling teachers should not be seconded for distance teaching, nor should we appoint such people as are not willing to undertake the tasks peculiar to distance teaching, for example, evaluating and writing comments on an answer script.

Turning to the case listed under item (*c*), we feel inclined to be sympathetic with him. His situation, obviously, demands more staff, which should be provided without any hesitation. It is obvious that this third case too is an administrative problem that can be resolved administratively. But, the last two cases, listed under items (*d*) and (*e*) are of a different nature; they belong to the domain of pedagogics. That is why we intend to study them elaborately as follows:

TECHNIQUES OF DISTANCE TEACHING

Most distance students are new to the distance mode of education. It is, therefore, the duty of a teacher to initiate communication straightway and he can initiate it best through his comments. As such teacher/tutor-comments are of undoubted significance to distance education, as they are both the content and vehicle of communication which effects learning. So as to effect gradual initiation of students to the ways of distance education, the teacher/ tutor has to be aware of the following three levels of communication:

(*a*) communication at the academic level,
(*b*) communication at the personal level, and
(*c*) supplemental communication.

(*a*) Academic Communication

At the academic level the function of a teacher/tutor is to (*i*) read the answer-scripts, (*ii*) write his comments on the answers and (*iii*) evaluate the answers to grade them. His comments are born of his attempt at correlating and comparing his own interpretation of a particular course-unit with the corresponding learner response in terms of both content and presentation.

The content of the course-unit, the tutor's own expertise in the field, the corresponding expertise of his colleagues, and his notion of the ideal response (for a particular assignment)—a variable that is affected as much by the teacher's/tutor's own views as by the range and variety of the answer-scripts he receives—form the bases of his comments and the grades he awards.

To stretch his reach fully he must understand each and every student, and unlike a classroom teacher who addresses the abstract average student of his class, the distance teacher-tutor has to address every student individually. And the only way of addressing his students is to write comments on the answer-scripts. This makes his task much more difficult and challenging than that of the classroom teacher.

The teacher/tutor must correct his student, elaborate what he may have attempted summarily, guide him where he may have gone wrong, confirm the acceptable aspects of his responses, assess the level of his achievement and explain the basis of that assessment so as to ensure better student-performance in future. And all this has to be repeated over and over again with every student—a task that demands great patience.

Approaching the problem of communication from the student's point of view, the tutor has to be conscious of the fact that his student is isolated from other students and his teacher/ tutor; that he is, in most cases, an adult with several social commitments and domestic responsibilities. Consequently, he is more susceptible to anxiety, slackness and frustration, and, therefore, may suffer from one or more of the following handicaps:

(*a*) Isolation from other learners seems to hang heavy on a distance student. The feeling that other students think, work and achieve differently may have a dampening effect on his enthusiasm and work.

(*b*) Isolation from the tutor breeds discontent and invariably accompanies the feeling that one can impress one's teachers/tutors better in a face-to-face learning situation.

(*c*) A long gap between the points raised by the students/ tutors and the corresponding clarifications received is discouraging.

(*d*) Since no two students can compare their assessed answer-scripts there is no scope for healthy competition, or peer group interaction.

(*e*) The distance learner has to depend entirely on the written word, he must be able to exploit it maximally for comprehension as well as utilisation.

Since such factors cannot be taken care of in course-units, it is the teacher/tutor who should help the learner to overcome the difficulties caused by 'isolation' and make their communication academically useful.

TUTOR'S COMMENTS

An answer-script is as much a product of the learner's reaction to the course-unit as his personality. It is, therefore, a manifestation of his personality which the teacher/tutor is expected to recognize. Very often distance learners are inclined to hide their weaknesses, they do not like to look small. Then, there are others who would like to look big.

Such attitudes might be genuine, but they can prove to be real hurdles in distance education, and their roots may be traced back to the learner's social status, family background, occupation, previous academic achievements, etc. No distance learner can avoid being influenced by such factors, as in preparing an answer-script he interprets the course-unit in terms of his own experience, and his answers carry a stamp of his personality.

One of the most obvious ways of modifying his approach to 'distance studies' is to influence his attitudes towards the teacher/

tutor, the course-units, the distance institution—and his learning strategy.

Therefore, there has to be a non-academic level of teacher/ tutor-comments, which will dispel the learner's misgivings and mould his attitudes to reform his concept of the role of the teacher/ tutor, the course-unit, the distance institution and his own learning strategies. The tutor will have to find occasions when he can show himself as the most sincere 'confidant' of the student, the most dependable exponent of the course-units, and the one who has a comparatively superior understanding of the academic issue at hand. He will have to present himself as one whose prime aim is to assist the learner in his studies.

His written comments must compensate for the peculiar gestures, smiles and tilts of the brows, which accompany and take away the sting from the teacher's remarks in a classroom situation. So that the teacher/tutor-comments may not hamper the motivation of the distance learner, they have to be well thought out, deliberate, palatable, precise and pedagogically purposeful.

Having analysed the two dimensional significance of teacher/ tutor-comments we shall now discuss the most crucial of the problems—which comments to write and how to write them.

In the previous section our focus was the "why" of teacher/ tutor comments. In other words we tried to suggest why such comments need to be written, and what they are all about. In this section we shall try to show that it is not always possible to write what we call well 'thought out comments' even more difficult is to make them precise and pedagogically purposeful.

The fact that most of the home-study programmes conducted the world over use written course-units as the major channel of transmission, and that it is the only channel in most distance education given in our country, warrants a certain degree of sophistication in formalizing the 'comment-types' which, as already discussed, are the basis of distance teaching.

Let us consider the following extracts which have been selected from comments actually written by 'distance teachers' working on learners' responses.

1. Horrible language! Pay some more attention to your language.
2. You have beaten about the bush.

3. Try to avoid the jargon if it is not clear to you.
4. What do you mean by this? Where is the illustration?
5. Is that all there is to say? Do you think you have put in all the relevant information? Read the topic of the assignment again and go back to the teaching unit.
6. Please go through the lesson once again and also the question in the assignment.
7. Since you almost fulfilled the criteria of effective Language Teaching Materials you have been awarded an "A" grade.
8. You can improve the organisation of your answer.
9. You could improve your answer by spending some more time on it.
10. Please read the question again. It seems you have not fully understood it.
11. A lot of unnecessary material has crept in.
12. Read the answer again and strike out all the unnecessary details.
13. Go trough the lesson once again.
14. You have some problems with the language about which you need not worry much.
15. Your answer is a faithful summary of the lesson.
16. You have not followed the question at all.
17. Is this necessary here?
18. Please read the lesson once again and redo the assignment.
19. Examples and illustrations are OK, but one example could have served the purpose.
20. Beginning of the essay is quite good, try to keep up the same speed.
21. Not clear, not to the point.
22. The treatment of the topic is not adequate.
23. You have failed to give a single illustration of how...
24. You need a bit more clarity in your understanding of the task given.
25. Your answer is too brief and incomplete.
26. Your argument about situations/themes determining vocabulary is acceptable and the illustration given about cricket is good.
27. Instead of giving negative illustration (i.e. of what is not wanted) you could have given positive illustrations.
28. You could have discussed the issues further with the aid

of your illustrations. Besides, you should have talked about the following points also.

i,.... ii,.... iii,.... and iv....

29. Please try to test the suggested reforms in your own classroom teaching situation. Prepare illustrations, based on your experience and send them to us for evaluation.
30. You would notice that you have overlooked the role of experimentation in the teaching of sciences. You should have touched upon this point to make your answer more convincing.

We have chosen these comments to identify a few comment types. As we did not want to be subject specific in our discussions, while selecting these comments care was taken not to include content/discipline based comments. We may classify these comments as follows:

(1) *Harmful (HL) Comments*

Consider the comments 1 to 5 above. Comments like 'Horrible language....', "You have beaten about the bush...." are harmful in so far as they put off the distance learner. Such comments are 'rude' by themselves; they not only fail to build any purposeful rapport between the distance learner and the distance teacher, but also build barriers between them and all possibilities of communication get blocked.

At times, some distance learners who are sensitive to words feel hurt by such remarks/comments. They not only start hating the tutor concerned, but also become indifferent to the subject he deals with.

Consequently, they drop out of the course. Others may write back objecting to the 'rude' remarks of the tutor concerned. In most of the cases, the tutor will justify his remarks. As a result, they fail to communicate purposefully, and the interests of the learner are damaged, in certain cases irrevocably.

(2) *Hollow (HW) Comments*

Take a careful look at comments 6 to 15. They are words and words and nothing beyond. They read like sentences which have meanings, but those meanings are 'hollow', for one cannot make out what they mean. For example, "Please go through the lesson once again and also the question in the assignment", appears to be an instruction, but it is not clear 'what' is going to happen, 'how' and 'with what effect', if the instruction is followed. Or, consider comment 12.

If the student knew what 'the unnecessary details' were, he would not have written them. Nor is 'reading the answer again' going to help in removing those 'unnecessary details'. In effect the comment is a 'hollow' one if it is a set of words, even a sentence, that does not convey anything purposeful or otherwise.

Comments 16 and 17 display the characteristics of both the *harmful* and the *hollow* comments. On the one hand they are 'rude', on the other without any purpose to serve.

(3) *Misleading (MG) Comments*

At times tutors write comments which put the learner on the wrong track—the learner is asked or made to do something which does not serve any purpose, or he is made to build untenable perceptions about himself, his activities and the environment in which he acts. For example, let us consider comment 18. The learner is asked to read the lesson once again; in all probability he may follow the direction honestly and read the lesson once again. And then he will redo the assignment.

Without having been told what the weaknesses in his first attempt were, he is likely to repeat the mistakes he may have made in his first attempt. Just reading the lesson once again or redoing the assignment in itself is not going to make any contribution to the learner's learning; instead he will be under the wrong impression that by having done what the tutor asked him to do he has gained something quite substantial academically.

So far we have talked about three types of comments—Harmful, Hollow and Misleading comments. For obvious reasons, the tutor should take all the care not to write such comments. Experiments and experience show that to avoid writing Harmful comments is not a difficult task, but it is rather difficult to do away with 'Hollow' and 'Misleading' comments. It needs deliberate effort and caution to avoid writing such comments. Our straightforward suggestion in this connection is that in no circumstances whatsoever should a tutor write any of these three types of comments.

(4) *Null (NL) Comments*

Such comments as don't confirm or question, illustrate or explain, refute or approve of anything may be called 'null comments'. These comments include all types of zero-meaning non-verbal remarks: question marks, double question marks, double check marks, underlining, side brackets, etc. Seemingly these symbols indicate that the answer has been read by the tutor, but they are not helpful to the students. He does not decode them, in fact he cannot.

Such comments could be made useful by giving every non-verbal symbol a predetermined verbal value known to both the student and the tutor.

In a different situation, the tutor could use these symbols to tone down the adverse effects of writing discouraging comments repeatedly. Consider a situation in which the tutor feels like making the same adverse remark, or more or less similar adverse remarks at half a dozen places in the same answer-script or on the same page.

Instead of wasting his time in writing such annoying remarks, he may use the same symbol at all six places. This method may have significant psychopedagogical advantages. In such a situation one could use numbers, Greek letters or any other set of symbols.

(5) *Negative (NE) Comments*

Such comments as negate facts, concepts, explanations, illustrations, analyses, elaborations and relevance of the content of an answer, and the very approach to a particular problem presented by the distance student in his answer-scripts may be termed 'negative comments'. These are perhaps the most important of all the comments a tutor has to make, because these are the correctives most needed by the students, who, when deprived of such guidance get exposed to the danger of 'mislearning'.

These comments may be written in the margin beside the particular wrong fact, explanation, etc. Whenever possible, reference should be made to the lesson number, page number and section number where the correct answer might be available. In certain cases the tutor will have to explain why a particular answer is incorrect; may be he has to supply written or prepared answers, illustrations or examples to support his stand.

A few illustrations of negative comments have been listed above—see items 21 to 25.

(6) *Positive (PE) Comments*

Consider comment 26 above. It approves of what the learner has written. Positive comments approve of the stand taken by the distance student. They indicate that his answer is upto the mark or excellent, or that in spite of some flaws in the answer, it is remarkably original and brilliant.

It is surprising that most tutors don't even think of such comments. Such comments encourage the distance learner to repeat his performance, because he realizes that he has already reached his tutor's 'wave length' and he would do his best to match it as many times as he can. It is these comments that actually result in and then further the mutually advantageous communication between the tutor and the student. Such comments may be written in the margin beside the answer they are applicable to.

(7) *Constructive (CE) Comments*

Comments 27 to 30 do not negate what the student may have written, nor do they approve of what the learner may have written. Instead, they offer constructive suggestions as to how the answer could have been improved. We may call them constructive comments. They are immensely helpful in effecting purposeful didactic communication.

It should be noted that a 'constructive' comment added to a 'negative' or a 'positive' comment, enhances the pedagogic utility of the latter. These comments like 'negative' and the 'positive' may be written on the margin beside the relevant portions of the answer-scripts.

(8) *Global (GL) Comments*

Having written the comments at relevant places in the main body of an answer-script the tutor must prepare a global comment to cover the entire answer-script with reference to various aspects of the answer. Such comments will have to be on a separate sheet of paper, or better still on a specially designed table of instructions. They may also refer to such drawbacks as are not necessarily related to the course-unit; spellings, syntax, legibility, etc.

Perhaps the most important function of this class of comments will be 'explanation of the grades'. Every student is keen on knowing his grades. The first thing he looks for in his corrected answer-script is the 'grade', and having known it, he would like to know why he gets an A or C. If every answer-script is returned with a comment on the grades it bears, there is every possibility of improved student performance.

What a global comment may look and read like is illustrated with the help of an illustration as follows:

Assessment

Student's Name: . . . .
Student's Number: . . . .
Unit: . . . .

Course: Nursery
Grade: A 80

Tutor's Comments

This is a very thoughtful and perceptive essay. You have very lucidly and systematically set out the essential points, and you have conveyed the spirit and the practice of the Montessori approach very effectively.

You are, of course, correct to refer to the cost of apparatus. I think one needs to think in terms of gradual acquisition, perhaps with a rota system of work. The basic principles can to some extent be applied with an imaginative approach even if the school is not fully equipped.

Content		*Presentation*	
Accurate Information	☑	Well Planned	☑
Inaccurate Information	☐	Inadequately Planned	☐
Comprehensive	☑	Concise	☑
Lacking Content	☐	Clearly Expressed	☑
Logical/Good Conceptual Analysis	☑	Not Clearly Expressed	☐
Illogical/Poor Conceptual Analysis	☐	Weak Grasp of English Structures	☐

	Grade		%		Grade	
Excellent	A	☑	80	Borderline (to be moderated)	D	☐
	A–	☐		Fail (Re-submit)	E	☐
Very Good	B+	☐		Tutor's Signature		
Good	B	☐		Received 17/3/86		
	B–	☐		Date Assessed 18/3/86		
Good Average	C+	☐		Moderation		
Average	C	☐				
Below Average	C–	☐		Date		

(*b*) Personal Communication

Personal level communication is most vital in distance education because apart other advantages it breaks learners isolation.

A distance teacher who intends to build personal level communication with the learners needs to have the following extra-academic attributes:

(*i*) a very high degree of patience,
(*ii*) a feel for the appropriate placement of personal-level comments, and
(*iii*) a certain degree of linguistic sophistication required to successfully blend academic comments, instructions and information into an 'intimate' whole.

A distance teacher may write as many personal-level comments as possibly he can, but we believe that even a *single* well-placed and appropriately worded comment of this kind per answer script will go a long way in breaking the isolation of distance-learners. Given below are a few examples of personal level comments.

'Yes, that is what most other students have been writing about the conventional methods of teaching a language'. 'Your answer is quite upto the mark. In fact I couldn't have thought of a better answer myself....'

'Your answer seems to have an edge over most answers I have received so far. It is so because your approach to the course-units has been flexible and you have tried to think in an unconventional way'.

(*c*) Supplemental Communication

Communication at the academic and personal levels gives rise to a third level of communication which may be called the 'supplemental-level' of communication. Such communication may emanate either from the learners, or from the teachers. In the former case a learner may like to question a particular comment written by a teacher, or ask for an explanation regarding a grade awarded or a remark recorded on the answer-script. In the latter case, a tutor may discover that a particular assignment is difficult, and most students need help in handling that assignment.

In such a situation model answers or such hints as would help students must be prepared and made available to them. It is not within the scope of this paper to discuss the 'supplemental-level' of communication; however, we need to add a word of caution here.

SUGGESTION

The system of tutor-comments that has been suggested here is not foolproof in itself. The most striking weakness in the system, one may point out, is that it depends on the sincerity of the tutor. Therefore, in order to make the system work more efficaciously, it is advisable to monitor the work of tutors from time to time, and remind them, at least 3 times a year, of the standards they are expected to maintain.

Such an approach should provide ways and means for students to comment on the course-units and the work of their tutors. Maybe the tutors themselves will come up with constructive suggestions regarding course-units or the system as a whole. These are healthy steps towards a really effective distance education.

8

Development of Course and Course Materials

INTRODUCTION

In the earlier chapter we have discussed the forms of instructional material for the use of adult learners in distance education. This material has to be classified for different stages of learning, hence, there is a need for the development of courses and according the course material, which we will discuss, in brief, hereunder.

MEANING OF THE COURSE

Course development in distance education takes a different procedure from that in the conventional system, for courses tend to be different in nature in the two systems. In the conventional system a course is teacher-centred and is instructed through a single medium, that is, the teacher. In distance education it is student-centred and the instruction is carried through multiple media. Several media are so integrated into the system that the course can never be complete without their joint operation or application.

Course development therefore becomes a process of coordinating the roles of various media to convey information to the students. Broadly, three approaches have been observed; single-member approach; course team approach; and hierarchical approach.

At the outset it is essential to clarify that we mean by a course. From a broad perspective, a course can be considered a process of intellectual interaction of students, tutors and course teams based on the course materials produced at the university. Mary Thorpe says: "I believe we should begin from the assumption that course materials are not the course; rather than the course is an annual process of interaction between students, the materials and the tutors and that, in this sense, tutors and students 'produce' courses as well as course teams."

Taking a narrower viewpoint, a course consists of the study materials such as printed texts, audio-video tapes and other materials which enable the student to equip himself for the final evaluation.

In India we often use the term course for the overall programme of study consisting of several 'papers' taught or studied during the fixed number of years. A 'course' in the British or American sense is equivalent to a 'paper' in Indian universities, and one has to take several courses to qualify oneself for the final award. A course in the Indian context is a 'programme' in the Western sense. Here the term course is used in the Western sense, i.e. equivalent to a paper in the Indian universities, as it is more convenient for analysis.

Course development implies four stages:

1. Course design and strategy,
2. Materials development,
3. Course presentation, and
4. Developmental testing.

A course writer entrusted with the writing of a full course or a part of a course is responsible for the development of the course through all the above stages. The course writer may be a single person or a group of persons. In the case of a team, the team is collectively responsible for the work.

COURSE DEVELOPMENT APPROACHES

Mainly there are three approaches for course development, which are being discussed hereunder:

1. Single-Member Approach

In the Indian universities course outlines are designed by Boards of Studies and Faculties, and finally approved by Academic Councils. Course design therefore is a collective work. Distance teaching departments of Indian universities, which generally teach the same courses as the conventional departments do, have to develop course materials within the framework prescribed for the latter. Distance teaching departments have no freedom to move out of the limits set by the tradition-bound Boards of Studies. They prepare a break-down of the outlines into several units before starting the work of course preparation.

This break-down is done by the institutes, teachers in consultation with other experts who are generally teachers in the conventional system. Each institute is supposed to have subject committees for each subject or discipline and these committees advise the institute with regard to course development. After making the break-down, units are assigned to several individual course writers.

Course writers are either full-time teachers of the institute or teachers working in other institutions and serving the institute on a part-time basis. They are generally given some guidelines regarding the scope of the unit, the number of pages or lines, the deadline for submitting the work to the institute, etc. Within these parameters the course writer is free to write the materials.

The unit thus completed is edited by an expert, either a full-time senior staff of the institute or an outsider employed on part-time basis. So in this case materials development and course presentation are the functions of the course writer and course editor. There are in some institutes a provision for further scrutiny or review of the materials at a later stage, and the comments made may be incorporated when the units are revised.

In the picture given above, course materials are the responsibility of the course writer, although editing is also done. But in many cases owing to exigencies of time or money the editing work may be dispensed with, and the course materials go to print straight from the writer.

Some enthusiastic teachers try to get the feedback from students in an informal way and make improvements in their courses at the revision stage. However, this cannot be done in the case of part-time course writers who are not attached to the institute by permanent ties.

These course writers have no collective role in the design and production of audio-visual software which may be made part of the course. Course writers are again assigned individual role in writing a radio talk or talk for audio taping.

There is no occasion for group discussion, mutual criticism or comment. This leads to a sort of isolation of the course writers. As a result a single course prepared by several members in their individual capacity is not collective product. Parts of a course may bear difference in emphasis, style or even content. A course may thus be good in parts.

It is possible for a single person to be held responsible for a course from design to production. In such cases there is no editor in addition to the course writer who is solely responsible for the course. Jon Stafford writes about his experience in the making of a course exclusively by himself. He was responsible for running the course fully, including the tutorial services.

He asserts that "one academic can present an entire course and can prepare, present and administer one distance education course although the number of students involved is relatively small."

One advantage of the system is that it places the responsibility and accountability of the course on a clear person. He can take the feedback from the students and make modifications to improve of the course. Students also find a specific person to approach rather than a group in which responsibility is diffused.

This fosters the client relationship between the teacher and the student, emphasising the fundamental professional responsibility of teachers. As regards the academic, the course is entirely the product of his labour and he need not share its prestige with anybody else. But when the same teacher is responsible for administering the course completely, he can do it only for small group effectively.

Here the sense of isolation that the course writer feels is worse, for he is responsible for the whole course. However, it must be noted that a substantial part of academic work is isolated as one has to think and write effectively in quiet solitude.

Practically the differences between the person who is responsible for the whole course and the person responsible for part of the course are limed. In the latter case there may or may not be an editor to edit the materials. Apart from this they work in similar circumstances.

2. The Group or Team Approach

Instead of a single person doing all work regarding the development of course materials, it is possible to have them done by a group or team. A course team is a group of persons (both academics and non-academics) engaged in the task of initiating, producing and maintaining a course. It cannot be an exclusively academic body, because a course which involves radio, TV cassettes, etc. has to be guided by expertise drawn from the fields.

There is no statutory provision regarding the constitution of a course team. A course team of the British Open University (OU) consists of a few academics, an editor, an expert from the BBC and many others as required. The team has a chairman who is generally the person who has initiated the course.

In the British Open University any academic can initiate a course whether or not he is a lecturer, reader or professor, and be the chairman. Someone may think there can be a course on Democracy, or on Politics and Technology. Some of those who are interested in the idea may join together to form the academic part of the course team.

As a course team is a heterogeneous body it may be interesting to analyse what each team member or category of members has to do. The chairman is responsible for pushing the plan through the concerned bodies and has to be in liaison with the administration. He runs course team meeting and allocates tasks. He is responsible for completing the work in time and keeping the expenditure within prescribed limits, although there are administrative sections that keep watch of the progress and keep themselves in touch with him. The academic members take the most active role in the course team work by writing texts, discussing them, rewriting them, generating new ideas and approaches, editing and proof reading as well, to some extent.

There are sometimes non OU academics who are associated as consultants; they also may write parts of the texts. In every course team there is an educational technologist whose main function is to advise the team on assessment, testing, feedback, etc. He is supposed to represent the student community and so keep the authors' feet on the ground. They are generally members of the Institute of Educational Technology (IET) which is a major department of the OU.

But there are instances of the faculty of the IET becoming text writers for course teams. The Graphic Design Department has to be represented where there is need for graphs, charts, pictures etc. The OU has a cadre of course team managers who help the chairmen in their routine administrative functions, and so managers are also present when course teams meet.

Although the chairman or team members do some sort of editing while scrutinising the drafts, there is a professional cadre of editors in the OU who are associated with course team work. An editor is invariably present at the meetings. The editor is responsible for getting the final product to and from the prints. It is said that he is often the only person who gets a grasp of the whole course.

The audio-visual ingredient of the course is the responsibility of the BBC. As all the courses have a small or big part of the audio-visuals, a BBC representative participates in course design and production. These days staff tutors also are associated with course teams as they can represent students' interests, they being close to the students. Sometimes there are critical readers—both OU and non-OU—specially for the purpose of checking drafts, accuracy of facts, timing etc.

Perhaps the most notable advantage of the course team method is the facility for constructive criticism of the drafts. This is strengthened by the willingness on the part of the team members to take the criticism in right spirit and modify the draft in accordance with consensus.

John H. Mason, a member of the Mathematics Faculty of the British Open University says: "The heart of any co-operative venture of course production is the giving and receiving of specific comments." Making comments in a superficial way may be an easy job, but constructive suggestions are products of in-depth study.

When a course is first conceived it is in a state of flux. There is a lot of confused thinking and prolonged discussion possible until ideas are concretised. Responsibilities are shared in a course team and there is great potential for cooperative effort. But the constraints of time, finance and human indolence are likely to distort the process of collaboration and bring forth a not-so perfect output. With a view to keeping the production schedule, the work is sometimes rushed through. As a result drafts are read hastily, comments insufficient, redrafting or editing poorly done.

People are not all hardworking and not all are born to serve the course team cause. Course production in the British OU takes three to four years, and sometimes even more. The course production schedule of the OU envisages that work should start four years ahead of the year of implementation. The average output per individual member of the Social Science Faculty of the OU in recent times has been one unit and a half per year.

The average cost of producing a Social Science course is much more than 6,000 pounds. If salary and other establishment charges are added it comes to 30,000 pounds. Expenditure on audio-visuals in the British OU are cut down today and course team size reduced owing to shortage of funds.

3. The Hierarchical Approach

It is possible to develop a course by a group organised on a different pattern as is done in the Fernuniversitat of West Germany. In Fernuniversitat the head of the discipline concerned has the power and responsibility to initiate the course and choose the partners. He allots course writing to his colleagues in the team, supervises the work and ensures quality.

Whereas in the British course team the members are equals (the chairman being the first among equals) in the West German system the organisation is hierarchical. The members are the sheep and the head of the discipline the shepherd. Some of the faculty with whom I had had discussion at the Fernuniversitat affirmed that it was in the German tradition to give the final say to the head of the discipline.

This approach in a way combines certain aspects of the first and the second approaches. Here is a course team led by the head of the discipline; and the team members prepare the materials individually under his supervision. However the German procedure does not assure freedom of thought and discussion as in the OU team.

DEVELOPMENT AND DISTRIBUTION OF COURSE MATERIALS

Print based course materials occupy key positions in instructions of distance education which is distributed to the students either directly or through study centres.

Generally the lesson scripts for each paper are available in book forms and are divided into 20 to 30 units. There may be two sets of lesson scripts for a paper containing these units. Each unit's size varies from 4 to 25 demi size printed pages with an average number of 8 pages. There is no standard format of lesson units followed in the case of all the papers and subjects of UG and PG levels. In the case of most of the lesson scripts the units are found in the text book format including the subject content of the courses and are followed by a list of further readings or reference materials.

Much emphasis has not been given to the self-instructional style of presentation. However, in the case of few papers, especially in Education and Commerce fields, good attempts have been made to take care of self instructional nature of presentation of units. In these cases one can come across a unit being divided into different sections like overview, objectives, division of contents into small paragraphs supplied by diagrams and examples, conclusions and objective test type learning exercises.

In certain cases the units have been presented in Skinnerian Programmed Learning Material (PLM) or semi PLM. The booklet, including 10 to 15 units learning material, contains additional information like courses of studies, list of suggested references, assignments, and examination questions of previous year. The materials are written in English for PG courses (except Sanskrit & Hindi), whereas they are available in Hindi and English for most of the UG courses.

Usually the course materials are revised by the group of experts in every third year. New lessons are written only in the case of alteration of existing course units or addition of new units of course papers.

The course outline of each course of the DCC remains same with that of regular courses. Therefore, the syllabi are approved by different academic bodies of the university meant for the purpose. The DCC takes liberty in development of instructional materials following its own formats. Of course, the heads of the post graduate teaching departments of the parent university are consulted for development of materials.

In the initial stage of the creation of the DCC, almost all the lesson scripts of the DCC were developed by the teachers of the PG teaching departments of the HP University, teachers of the affiliated colleges of the university, and academicians of other institutions and colleges within the country. In due course with the growth of the DCC, its faculty staff co-operated with the activities of writing lesson scripts, editing the units, reviewing the units and translation of needed units.

A glance at the career of the teachers involved in development of course materials revealed that besides the present faculty members of the DCC experienced teachers from other universities, colleges and other higher education institutions.

Indira Gandhi National Open University is the largest university imparting distance education and it helps other universities and institutions in many ways with regard to development of courses and various other aspects and hence the development of distance education courses in most universities and institutions is as good as those of formal universities, yet following suggestions would be useful for better results.

SUGGESTIONS FOR IMPROVEMENTS IN COURSE MATERIALS

With regard to improvement in style of presentation, the teachers suggested that the lessons be clear, systematic and illustrative suiting the needs of the students. Most of the students suggested that the lessons should include more examples, charts, maps and tables. Suggestions given by the students reveal that the lessons be self-instructional in nature with charts, maps, diagrams, etc. and perhaps be linked with TV and radio programmes.

From the point of view of content coverage of lessons, the teachers and students suggested that the materials must be comprehensive, contemporary and include essential aspects of topics, and be relevant to the Indian context. Similar suggestions have been rendered by large number of the students products of the system and the dropouts in this context.

The language aspect of the lessons need careful consideration since students studying in different courses belong to a multilingual background. The lessons should therefore be simple, should be written in English as well as in regional languages.

AN EVALUATION

From a theoretical perspective, the course team approach ensures most academic quality. It provides for deliberation, redrafting and comments, and focuses the co-operative effort of various interests and sections into the making of the course. It seeks to integrate the various media into the course under the overall supervision of the course team.

However, this is expensive owing to the large number of persons and stages of deliberation involved. The Athabasca experiment is an attempt to cut down expenditure but the academic in the team becomes a lone voice. He has nobody to consult and share the responsibility with, as regards academic quality.

It appears that where there is a strong contingent of permanent staff many of them can be involved in the work and external elements reduced. If the permanent staff are small, it is less expensive to associate externals than to increase the staff.

In the method followed by Indian universities the course design is a collective effort; but in the course design is meant for the conventional system. Distance teaching departments are compelled to prepare study materials within this framework. So they lack the freedom to mould materials in a fashion that suits them. This is particularly felt when audio-visuals are to be incorporated into the materials.

In the British OU designing of courses and formulation of strategy go together. In the Indian practice they are separated and so problems arise when strategy is to be fit into the prefabricated design. The open universities emerging in India may be able to overcome the problems of bifurcation as they are responsible for both designing and administration of their courses.

However it is possible to introduce an element of cooperation into the Indian system without introducing the course team. If the individual course writers submit their drafts for scrutiny by their colleagues writing for the same course and accept the suggestions for improvement, much of the benefits of the course team methods can be fruitfully absorbed. It is possible that personal spite and envy may divert the operations and cause a lot of waste. Much depends on the goodwill and cooperation on the part of the course writers.

No system is above criticism particularly as regards the duration taken for writing course materials. The human factor operates everywhere. Whether a single-member team or multi-member team, course writers need occasional goading as well as patting. It is always advisable to do a major part of course production before students are admitted to the course.

In the Indian situation there are cases wherein course production starts after admissions are notified. In such cases course materials will have to be rushed through, and sometimes not even completed.

9

Forms of Instructional Material in Distance Education

INTRODUCTION

By and large distance education differs from formal education, therefore, the instructional material in distance education must suit the adult learner, hence, before we undertake to discuss various forms of instructional material in distance education let us understand the concepts of 'self learning' and 'interaction' of the learner with man and material, as most vital ingredients of distance education.

Self-learning as an Essential Ingredient of Distance Education

Students enrolled in distance education institutions are mature and have better language competence and improved mental abilities. Such students are capable of learning on their own, if suitable instructional techniques are employed.

Modern instructional techniques like programmed materials, advance organizers, modules, organised seminars and discussions, guided practical and field work, suitably designed assignments and planned library work emphasise self-learning as it maximises learning. Learning through these techniques would largely depend upon the motivation on the part of learners.

Motivation for learning can be created and enhanced by properly organising the whole instructional process. In an organised system of instruction, clear guidelines are provided as to what the learner has to learn on his own and what would be learnt through other means.

If all the instructional components are properly related to the goals of instruction and evaluation procedures, reasonably high motivation on the part of students could be expected.

Interaction as an Essential Ingredient of Distance Education

Self-learning as referred to above, takes place only if there is purposeful interaction between the learner, teacher and materials. If the instructional material possesses certain built-in-mechanisms to promote active interaction, it would ensure learner's active participation, which will in turn make the whole teaching-learning process effective.

Intermittent slabs of human interaction in any instructional situation are likely to maximise its effectiveness. These slabs of human interaction are specially needed to develop, in learners, certain higher cognitive abilities, like critical thinking, techniques of analysis, synthesis and evaluation. Although these abilities can be developed through specific content situations, their learning effects do not remain confined to these content situations only.

They develop, in learners certain basic peculiarities in their ways of thinking and dealing with situations at later stages. It is this aspect of the contributions made by human interaction that are significant educationally. This aspect of interaction in instructional situations has definite implications for the development of instructional materials. The instructional materials should, therefore, be designed in such a way that they allow sufficient scope for active human interaction.

FORMS OF INSTRUCTIONAL MATERIAL

The various forms in which instructional materials have been developed and their efficacy studied are: programmed materials, advance organizers, modules and instructional materials having questions in the beginning and at the end. These are discussed below in some detail.

1. Programmed Learning

Instructional materials have been developed by following the principles of programmed learning which are based on the concept of Operant Conditioning. In programmed learning, the learning process is programmed in a particular sequence and the learning material is presented in written form to the learner in logically arranged small steps. The Programmed Learning Material (PLM) helps a student to learn at his own without the help of a teacher.

The other built-in mechanisms of PLM are active respondents, positive reinforcement and self-paced learning. In PLM, the learner is provided with small pieces of information, each of which is followed by a question, the answer to which is also given, generally, in the margin. (This piece of information, the question based on it and the answer thereof put together is called a frame).

The learner reads the subject-matter and the question. He answers the question in writing and checks his answer with the model answer which reinforces learning. Besides providing such reinforcement, various forms of cues are also used to facilitate self-learning.

The effectiveness of PLM has been studied by comparing it with traditional methods in terms of the achievement of students. The programmed material was found superior to the traditional methods in terms of the achievement of school students (Hughes and McNamar, 1961; Goldback *et al.*, 1962; Shah, 1968; Sharma, 1968; Desai, 1968; Sharma, 1968; Kulkarni, 1974; Shah 1969; Aven *et al.*, 1970; Nallaiah and Adinarayana, 1977; Mohanty, 1979; Shitole, 1979; Gupta and Gupta, 1979; Dean, 1980; Gupta, 1983; and Kumar, 1983).

It was also found superior to the traditional methods used at the college level (Kaushik, 1968, Bhushan, 1973; Govinda, 1975; Emery, 1981 and Buddhisagar, 1986). On the other hand, Feldhusen, Ramparter and Birt (1962), Hatchand Flint (1962), Spangoli (1965), Gupta (1968), Sharma (1968), Patel (1970), Cockwood (1980), Beauchamp (1980), Decarbo (1981), Fairbrother (1981) and Kumar (1982) reported that programmed learning as well as conventional methods were equally effective.

All studies were conducted in formal education settings. Simich (1965), Sjogren (1965), Sort (1968), Basu (1968, 1969) and Mullick (1968) found that PLM was quite effective in correspondence education also. Since PLM has worked in formal settings both at the school and the college levels and correspondence courses, so it can also work in distance education. It may, therefore, be said that the instructional material to be used in distance education should be prepared on the principles of programmed learning.

PLM can be used in various ways. It can be used independently to present the learning material as well as in combination with other media. In situations where the content to be covered is more of informative nature, the PLM as a medium can be very effective. PLM can be presented to individual learners in the form of booklets. It can also be presented with the help of a filmstrip projector or a slide projector to a homogeneous group of learners.

But in order to achieve different objectives use of only PLM may be inadequate. For example, in order to develop the ability for critical thinking and evaluation it may be necessary to combine PLM with discussions. While PLM will provide the necessary basic knowledge needed for a discussion session, the discussion itself will provide the opportunity for interaction among students and with teachers.

It will provide means to express various views, seek clarifications, react to other's views and also evaluate various points of view in the context of differing situations. In this way PLM can be combined with field work, laboratory work, seminars, library work etc.

From the above presentation, it may be said that PLM may be used effectively in distance education either alone or in combination with other techniques. It will make distance education more effective.

2. Advance Organizers

Efforts have been made to write instructional material based on the Advance Organizer Model (AOM). The AOM is based on the Theory of Meaningful Verbal Learning propounded by David P. Ausubel.

The Theory of Meaningful Verbal Learning deals with three questions, namely (*i*) How the knowledge (curriculum content) is organsied? (*ii*) How the mind works to process new information (learning)? (*iii*) How these ideas about curriculum and learning can be applied by teachers when they present new material to students (instruction)?

The major purpose of the theory of meaningful verbal learning is to help students acquire subject-matter. Further, Ausubel advocates the use of Advance Organisers to facilitate the learning of written materials. The Advance Organizer Model is designed to strengthen student's cognitive structure, which refers to a person's knowledge of a particular subject matter at any given time and how well organized, clear, and stable it is.

The main characteristics of an Advance Organizer: (*a*) It has to be constructed in such a way that the learner can perceive it as an idea distinct from the material in the learning task itself. It is an idea that is at a much higher level of abstraction, generality, and is more inclusive than the learning material itself. (*b*) The essential features of the concept or proposition must be pointed out and carefully explained. (Definitional statements do not always point to the essential features of the term being defined).

The teacher and students must explore the Advance Organizer as well as the learning task. The presentation of an Advance Organizer need not be lengthy, but it must be perceived (the learner must be aware of it), clearly understood and continuously related to the material it is organizing. The Advance Organizer may be written in a sentence or a paragraph. In the instructional material, it must be presented before the detailed presentation of the idea.

Advance Organizer Materials have been developed for college students in various subjects by Ausubel (1960), Ausubel and Fitzgerald (1961, 1962), Ausubel and Yousef (1963), Scandura and Wells (1967), Groteluescher and Sjogren (1968), Bauman, Glass, and Harrington (1969), Richards and McCormick (1977), Derr (1978), Schwartz (1980), Wilson (1980), Lalli (1980), Meena (1980), Haghighi (1981), Korezenowski (1981), Martin (1981), Change (1982), Mahajan (1983) and Buddisagar (1986). On the other hand Stenbrink (1970), Smith (1976), Alexander (1977), Thompson (1978), Giles (1981), Alvermann (1981) and Chitriv (1983) developed Advance Organiser Material for the school level.

All the above mentioned studies conducted both at the college and the school levels compared Advance Organizer Material with traditional methods and reported that Advance Organiser Material significantly facilitated the learning and retention of new information.

On the other hand, there are studies which have reported that Advance Organizer Material and traditional methods equally facilitated learning (Schulz, 1966; Woodword, 1966; Jerrolds, 1967; Neisworth; 1967; Neisworth, 1968; Weisberg, 1970; Livingston, 1970; Barron, 1971; Barnes, 1972; Clawson, 1972; Graber *et. al.*, 1972; Lucas, 1972; Caponecchi, 1973; Feller, 1973; Sowder, 1973; Shmurak, 1974; Moore *et. al.*, 1975; Callihan, 1976; Goodman, 1977; Zakkour, 1977; Parisi, 1977; Phelps, 1978; Frost, 1978; Solmon, 1978; Morganett, 1980; Singleton, 1980; Lance, 1980; McAdarag, 1981 & Siddaramaiah, 1982).

But, in general the researches point out that Advance Organizer Material scientifically developed can facilitate learning. Further, Buddhisagar (1986) compared Advance Organizer Material with programmed learning material in terms of learner-achievement and reported that both were equally effective, when groups were matched for intelligence through statistical method.

On the other hand, without matching the groups for intelligence, Advance Organizer Material was found superior to programmed learning material. This finding may be taken as a hypothesis for further investigations.

3. Instructional Material Having Questions in the Beginning and at the End

There have been instructional materials where questions are put in the beginning of the chapter and sometime at the end of the chapter. The purpose in each case is quite different. The main purpose of writing questions in the beginning of the chapter is to help the reader to have a gestalt view of the contents presented in the chapter.

Such questions will help the reader to be mentally prepared for learning the contents of the chapter. In other words, readers will know in advance the important points around which the discussion has been presented in the chapter.

On the other hand, the main purpose of having questions at the end of the chapter is to help the reader to know the extent to which he has understood the contents of the chapter. Such questions are meant for self-evaluation mainly and pertain to the cognitive domain.

Questions are helpful to maintain attention and to facilitate learning and remembering of important points. According to Dale (1969) a quest starts with a question, preferably our own. Instructional materials if wisely used can develop the inquiring mind as they answer the questions of the student. It is the spirit of inquiry that builds momentum for sustained and permanent learning, and the reward is the joy of discovery as the answers are found.

Witbourne and Weinstock (1979) wrote a book entitled "Adult Development: The Differentiation of Experience" wherein questions were given in the beginning of each chapter, and Johnson (1977) wrote a book entitled "A Review of Research Methods in Education" wherein questions were given at the end of each chapter. Both the books are good illustrations of this approach.

4. Module

Module represents one of the specific forms of instructional materials. In a workshop on the application of educational technology for the preparation of instructional material held at Tagaytaj city, the Philippines in 1976, it was agreed upon that "a module is a learning opportunity organised around a well defined topic which contains the element of instruction, specific objectives, teaching-learning activities and evaluation".

Gabriel (1981) said that "Module is a teaching-learning strategy of a system with a set of definite objectives to meet the divergent learning styles and individual differences by personalised instruction using multi-sensory approach and built-in evaluation schemes."

Similarly, Mukhopadhyay (1980) defined that "an instructional module is a small 'booklet' on any subject which arranged the instructional activities in a particular sequence with adequate instruction for the individual learner to progress with respect to the pre-determined objectives. It is individualized as well as group-paced".

Comprehensive Access to Primary Education (CAPE) programme of NCERT (1979) stated that "Module is a self contained unit with a definite set of expected behavioural outcomes, providing an experience or series of experiences resulting into learning or problem solving".

Above mentioned definitions highlight some of the specific characteristics, such as a specific and small self-instructional unit, self-paced, employing different types of media, having specific steps ranging from objectives to evaluation, etc. Modules can be a part of more comprehensive strategy of instruction. They can be used by different types of target groups.

Different researchers have followed different steps in developing modules. NCERT (1979) developed modules for teachers involved in the task of universalization of elementary education.

The steps followed for developing modules are: (*a*) statement (title), (*b*) general instructions, (*c*) expected behavioural outcomes, (*d*) learning experiences, (*e*) feedback questions, (*f*) answer key, and (*g*) evaluation. In the presentation of learning experiences, these modules have not adopted any set pattern. Subject-matter is given in different styles, such as the episode form, the tabular form, the debate form, the deductive form, etc.

Singh, Sansanwal and Gujral (1979) developed a "Module on writing a Thesis". The steps followed are: (*a*) rationale, (*b*) expected behavioural outcomes, (*c*) learning experiences, (*d*) testing questions, and (*e*) model answers. Later on Mukhopadhyay (1980) explained the use of different steps while writing "a module on module".

These steps are: (*a*) module statement, (*b*) prospectus, (*c*) pretest, (*d*) prerequisites, (*e*) resources, (*f*) objectives, (*g*) learning experience or activities, (*h*) self-checks, and assignments, (*i*) post-test; and (*j*) model answers to self-checks.

In presentation of activities, such as reading a book, viewing a film, discussing in a group, working in a laboratory, writing certain assignments, etc. corresponding to the enabling objectives, three sets of activities are designed—(*a*) essential, (*b*) alternative, and (*c*) optional. Essential activities are minimum and necessary, alternative activities are according to the interests and tastes of learners, whereas, optional activities are for the purpose of further learning.

The style of presentation in a module takes care of individual difference in interests, potentiality, tastes and attitudes of learners. Therefore, a variety of opportunities is provided to the learner to understand the expected subject-matter.

Not much research has been done in this area. Mukhopadhyay and Balguruswamy (1981) and Sharma (1982) developed modules for college students and compared them with traditional methods. It was revealed that modules for instruction were significantly superior to traditional methods.

10

Application of Conventional and Modern Media in Distance Education: Need for an Integrated Approach

INTRODUCTION

A brief account of the concept related to the application of conventional and modern media in distance education has been given in the chapter captioned "Application of Information and Educational Technologies in Distance Education". This chapter is devoted to discuss the concept of conventional and modern media as applicable in distance education as well as the need for an integrated approach for their application in distance education.

ROLE OF MEDIA IN DISTANCE EDUCATION

To be relevant, acceptable and long lasting, alternative system of the formal education, it has to be well designed, effective and affordable. Moreover, its speed has to be accelerated to provide education to the students all over the country through an effective communication network. A variety of subjects of high utility value covered both for vocational training and higher education make effective media involvement a must for distance education.

Media can be effectively involved in both curricular and enrichment areas. Coverage of students of wide range of educational and social backgrounds and ages, aspirations, learning styles, environments and convenience under distance education make the use of media very crucial. It can help adapt education to complex individual needs, wishes and conditions. The verbal explanations cater to the groups of learners having homogeneity. The teacher, the pillar of the present educational system is missing in distance education making the use of audiovisual aids very relevant.

In fact, distance education can be called essentially an audio-visual programme. The audio-visual aids can play a major role in making distance education, to begin with, a possible reality, for a large number of both illiterate and literate masses in the far flung interior villages as well as in the urban areas in the country. It can improve the quality of education at a comparative or a lower cost than that of the formal system.

Media also helps create a more dynamic learning environment in distance education. The diversification of objectives, content and form is possible through the communication media. The greater individualised and independent instruction in distance education to overcome the barriers of space and time, in a decentralised learning environment makes use of audio-visual aids imperative. In distance education, there is a shift from spoken word to an instructional methodology dependent on communication media.

The major objective of any media can be to help maximum learners to learn effectively: in other words to comprehend and retain knowledge. This hints at mass communication approach. The greatest constraint of the distance education can be its alarmingly high rate of drop-outs compared to the conventional education. At times it is accorded second class status.

The demand for distance education can be increased in future and its status raised through the effective use of communication media which allow far greater variety and flexibility of learning and teaching techniques. Distance education can employ both small media and advanced technologies. In a developing country like ours anything and everything must be seized to promote education.

MEDIA FOR DISTANCE EDUCATION

A. Conventional

Print materials—structured lectures, pamphlets, handbooks, manuals and books.

B. Modern (Involving use of new communication technologies)

(*i*) *Teacher made and self-operated*

- Slides, synchronized slides and tapes, slide commentary workbooks;
- Transparencies;
- Audio cassettes; and
- Telephone teaching.

(*ii*) *Academic and Technical Expert made*

- Radio broadcasts, motion pictures, televised broadcastes;
- Video cassettes;
- Electronic books; and
- Self-structured programmed materials aided by computers, if possible.

All media are educationally sound. Only their selection for distance education should be made on the basis of their effectiveness to serve at a reasonable price in a specific socio-economic and cultural situation. Some would be excellent for the individualised approach while others will provide mass communication approach. Print materials, slides, transparencies, and audio cassettes have the advantage of being tailor-made for the specific groups with no or little outside help from experts (photographer and artist).

Expensive and elaborate studio settings, editing facilities, sound proofing and air conditioning, imported equipment, technical expertise at almost all the stages and lengthy preparation are eliminated. Television clientele of distance education of middle SES can use them with the help of regional study centre as they involve the use of recorders and projectors which can be operated easily.

The printed book is still the most innovative storage and retrieval information system. It will continue to be the dominant component in distance education services in the developing countries. When print materials are easy to produce, duplicate, transport and use, and involve the use of literacy and no matter how judiciously supplemented with graphics—tables, graphs, diagrams, maps, line drawings, illustrations and photographs are still abstract.

So they will have to adopt styles, which besides motivating the distant learners, will also fit into the knowledge structure of many heterogeneous students. A sound national book policy will encourage authorship, making good literature available at moderate prices. This in turn will promote development of print media, fostering reading habits and contribute to the success of distance education.

Our efforts to take education to all the people requires use of new communication technologies. Motion pictures, video films and TV broadcasts can provide enormous range and type of visual resources to the teacher for the descriptive materials.

They can also help overcome the problem of abstractness and barriers of time. They can also be utilized at the convenience of the clientele of distance education. Educational technology and modern development in information communication networks can play a vital role in distance education.

Radio, telephone and television networks and computers have provided excellent distance education opportunities for increasing the number of educated persons and raising the quality of education by breaking the space barriers and coping up with the explosion of knowledge in other countries. Through them, the availability and quality of human resources are raised considerably.

The computers have created wonders, specially by storing information in unbelievably small volume, processing it and giving it out in record time. Santhanam (1985) writes that paperless electronic books, which promise to be common in West before the end of this decade, have less volume, lower cost, freedom from storage maintenance problems and additional voice output facility for the use of blind. They are already becoming popular as teaching-learning tools for distance education in the West.

The committee headed by Prof. G. Ram Reddy, Vice Chancellor, Osmania University (1982) which had recommended the establishment of an open university in Andhra Pradesh, believes that there is a growing awareness of updating and supplementing correspondence materials with new educational technologies.

However the role of the new communication media based on both the technical hardware and software need to be evaluated against Indian conditions as major constraints related to their management and financing are likely to impede the progress of distance education.

THE CONCEPTS OF MULTI-MEDIA AND INTEGRATED APPROACH

Distance education is a new-born baby in India. Much awe and wonder goes with the mode of communication we use for it. 'Multi-media approach' has brought with it a set of gross over-simplifications. 'Interaction' has become an easily usable catchword. It is time to understand that interaction in distance education does not happen simply because of the presence of a satellite or a TV. Facilitation of interaction is one thing and bringing in new media of communication does not guarantee it.

Another common misbelief is that the greater number of media we use, the more effective will be the interaction. Experiences of educators all over the world show that a new medium brings with it new philosophic problems. Let us not misconceive that a satellite-based course will be always more effective that a course that uses just printed material and face-to-face sessions.

No medium of communication has an absolute value to it and it is wrong to suppose that a TV is always more effective than a radio or a video more convenient than TV. Next, the value of medium depends on what you want to communicate. Teaching surgery through distance mode will require one medium and teaching writing skills, another. Lastly, we should also think of the combinations of media when we talk about 'multi-media approach'.

Should radio talk support the printed matter? Can slides go with satellite communication? Are radio and TV interchangeable? True, questions like these cannot be answered objectively and many of the answers will emerge from the situational context. Yet, there is always a need to place a medium appropriately in an 'Integrated-media' approach according to the following criteria:

(*i*) Value associated to the medium.
(*ii*) Its suitability with the subject-matter.
(*iii*) Its possible combinations with other media.

Let us see, in detail, the uses of and the problems associated with each of the media.

MULTI-MEDIA APPROACH

(*a*) Print Media

The printed word is no longer regarded by the educators as 'non-communicative' or ineffective. In the words of Holmberg, "By far the most important medium in distance education courses is the printed word. This applies to conventional correspondence study, as well as to highly sophisticated multi-media, presentations like courses of the open university" (Holmberg, 1985:62). Though we said earlier that the choice of media depends on the subject matter to be conveyed, the value associated with the print medium seems largely objective and independent of the nature of subject matter. Print medium has proved largely effective in each of the cognitive, affective and psychomotor domain, and there will hardly be any educator who wants to be little or ignore the place of this medium.

As Charles Zuber of the University of South Pacific said: "Any medium....can generally be regarded to a greater or lesser degree as support for course material in form of print. Care must always be taken that this existing and fundamental medium should not be over-looked". In my opinion, the words of Zuber are representative. Yet there are occasions when experiments show that printed word is more effective in certain domains than the other. In Nashif's opinion ".... if the objective is cognitive, involving analysis as in philosophy, the printed word will probably be more effective".

Secondly, accepting the indispensable value the printed word carries, one cannot ignore two evident shortcomings of the print media. Print media lack the personal touch and secondly are not flexible or open enough to allow for dialogue. This makes us state the need for supporting the printed word with the non-print media.

(*b*) Radio

Radio seems to be a very practicable instrument for adult education. Even in countries like India, it is easily accessible for the learner. It can add a personal touch by bringing in the voice of the tutor. However, radio raises the serious question of learner autonomy. It forces the learner to listen to the programme at a particular time and does not allow the learner to work at this leisure. This is applicable even to TV and the manner of using radio should be decided keeping this handicap in mnd. One way which is usually suggested is "... any audio-visual electronic programme used must be complemented by other media to ensure dialogue, such as telephone conversation or written answers or direct confrontation....."

A project for studying the effective use of radio in correspondence courses began in Japan in 1976. The results tell us how cautiously we should use radio programmes. The results showed that "....only 2 to 2.5 per cent of the respondents viewed the programmes successively from the first to the last. In terms of comprehension, 11.8 per cent reported that the lecture was 'very well understood', 29.4 per cent mostly understood and 35.8 per cent 'understood a little'."

(*c*) Audio Cassettes

An obvious advantage of the audio cassettes over the radio programmes is that they are under the control of the user, students can stop the player to take rest, make notes or can replay a difficult section. One more use of the cassettes, in the words of a student, is: "I find the tapes very useful, particularly the discussion ones. It is definitely a 'contact' with the staff even though it is remote.

A study of the Distance Teaching at Thailand's Sukhothai Thammathirat Open University (STOU) gives us an idea of the different purposes the audio cassette can be used for. STOU used the tapes to:

- — provide orientation of the course
- — clarify certain complex ideas
- — give feedback to the student's activities and assignments
- — summarize major ideas of each unit
- — present the views of external experts

Massey University (New Zealand) tried using cassette tapes for tutorials in History. Groups of learners listened to a lecture on the tape. Then they would discuss the given questions and record the conclusion on the tape. They sent this tape to the university which sent its comments either again on tape or through mail.

Dr. Robert Gwynn has analyzed the results and they would be applicable to all the subjects where tutorial forms an essential part and where no single answer is possible for a given question.

However one of Gwynn's observations can prove to be more significant. A number of groups failed to heed the directive that their responses be taped on the evenings the tutorials were held. According to Gwynn, this may indicate a sense of insecurity in handling a new mode of communication. This leads us to think of the necessity of including the media-study skills component in any Distance Education System. This component should enable the user to make an effective use of the media.

(*d*) Televised Teaching

The use of television requires a great care; especially in the matter of combining it with other media. Television generally cannot convey all or exhaustive information and so it needs to go with print and other non-print media. When televised teaching was tried out at Akita University in Japan, the results showed that students could attend the televised lecture class at ease with little physical fatigue, but because they attended with the attitude of an onlooker, they became gradually dissatisfied to participate in communicative activities.

This shortcoming of the television makes it wholly unusable in the case of some subjects. Another difficulty may occur at the production stage itself. Kelvin Grove College (Queensland) experimented teaching philosophy at a distance video. They tried to use vidęo to project philosophic discussion. The aim was to share with external students the philosophical experience of "talking things through" or philosophising. A paper on this experiment says:

> "We were cautioned by media services about the quality production. According to them, end prodction quality relies heavily upon camera work (obvious). When a production is scripted the cameraman knows who and what to look for. In an unscripted setting the cameraman does not have the same "lead time"... The cameraman found difficulty in locating the speaker until they recognised the non-verbals associated with a speaker's desire to speak...."

Moreover, it is quite impossible to write a "script" before the discussion. As Haines and others statue, their own approach to teaching philosophy made it impossible for them to write a script for events to follow.

Again, a training to use TV and video becomes a must for the learner. The introduction of television into the educational process has created the need for visual literacy.

Successful attempts have been made to increase the capacity of the television set. This had led to two new media: Video-disc and videotex. Video-disc is like a long playing record carrying both audio and video and working through the conventional television set. Videotex has the potential to make the home television function like a computer terminal. The owner of the TV can have access to vast computer data and can receive text information and graphics from a remote data base.

(*e*) Satellite

In 1980, satellite delivered TV was made accessible to everyone in Canada. Summing up its impact on Distance Education, Geoff Potter wrote:

> "In some cases, Hermes (the satellite) brought people together in a way that was every bit as emotionally moving as it was intellectually stimulation. In other cases, students became

bored, technical problems made effective interaction impossible, information seemed colourless and static."

Using satellite, on one hand, is a rewarding and rich educational experience. On the other hand it creates a whole multitude of problems of planning. Potter points out how satellite-based communication can be extremely impersonal. In the classroom the instructor is giving some "treatment" to the information. But the instructor and the information become inseparable in satellite communication.

The difference between the instructor and the information is very crucial and it is this difference that produces the spark in the heart and the mind of the student, which we call "comprehension", "recognition" or "understanding".

Secondly, because of the pressure on time, the organisation of a programme is always tight. If you believe in the theory of learning by doing or learning by personal exploration, satellite has much less to offer to you. Learning through satellite is basically 'learning by guidance'.

In his paper, 'Moral Ties and Satellite Networks', Griffin points out some basic faults in 'mouth to mouth' communication. They refer to the problems of duration, speed, absence of visual clues, uni-dimension, absence of phatic communication and disembodiment. According to Griffin, the role of the coordinator is very crucial and very difficult in a satellite programme.

(*f*) Face to Face Sessions

Residential study sessions are usually considered necessary only for a few subjects. True, they are indispensable for a subject like Philosophy (where a comparison of different attitudes is necessary) or Pronunciation of English (where some practice and remediation from the tutor is necessary), they will also help students for other subjects. The more important question is how to use these sessions.

Some universities use these contact hours mainly to summarise or reinforce whatever goes through print and other media. In fact, study sessions can be organised to serve altogether different purposes. An example is STOU which arranges its 4 sessions in the following manner:

— one for orientation
— two for tutorials
— one for review.

If telephone is being used as a medium, its use can run supplementary to the use of study sessions. Telephone can also be used to encourage, orient, counsel etc., the consolidation of which will take place in the final sessions.

TELIDON, VIDEOTEX AND SATELLITE

With the use of Telidon, Videotex and satellite, media has no longer remained just a matter of supplementing Distance Education. The problem has always been to integrate the new media with the course structure and in this process of integration, a number of changes are taking place in the fundamental nature of Distance Education. As said earlier satellite communication has raised a question about the theory of learning we believe in. Whatever model of learning our basic course structure proposes, once we accept this new media, it puts forward and begins to implement its own model: learning by guidance.

The position of the tutor is largely changed because of the use of media. The media could remove them from an interactive role. "It could redefine their role from that of a 'teacher' to that of a 'course designer', 'programmer' or manager of student-selected information services."

As we said at the beginning, interaction in education does not happen simply because of the presence of media. The educators have to learn that facilitation of interaction is a skill. And to acquire this skill, we must have an understanding of the process of communication and a clear understanding of the media technology. The introduction of media has changed the earlier simplistic design of a distance course. We now need coordinators, local managers, demonstrators and this has made the design of a distance course a unique process.

INTEGRATED APPROACH

An Integrated Approach takes into account the possible value and suitability of each medium and links each new medium with the existing media. The following diagrams illustrate the difference between these two approaches.

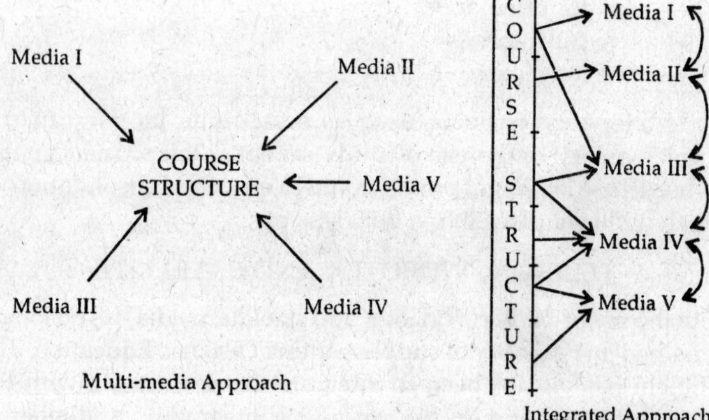

As an illustration of the Integrated Approach, I have given below a possible model for a distance education set-up. The model is meant for three different domains in a single-course: affective cognitive and psychomotor. Obviously, the given model is just an illustration and guideline. A model quite different from the one given can be worked out and may prove effective.

The diagram given below stands for the conclusion of this paper as it illustrates the need for an Integrated Media Approach and suggests a possible way of moving towards the Approach.

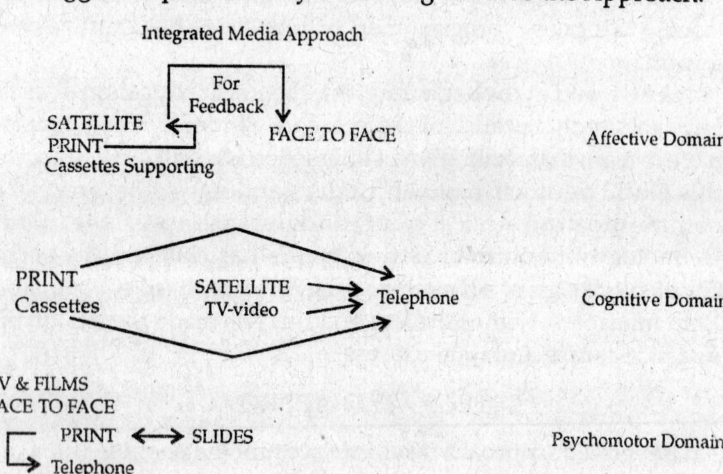

Size of the typeface suggests importance given to the particular medium. Arrows indicate the relationships and absence of arrows indicates that the media are used for mutually exclusive purposes.

CONSTRAINTS IN THE USE OF COMMUNICATION MEDIA

1. Language-wise complexity, of the audience, especially in the absence of multi-channel facility; example: The students of 800 colleges with subsidised TV sets cannot understand either, English or Hindi adequately. Inadequate and difficult production of language-free TV programmes.
2. Inadequate acquaintance with TV or even radio as educational communication technologists on part of the persons in charge of distance education; inadequate institutional facilities to acquaint them. In India, only 6 institutes, out of 30 relay radio talks for the distance education and TV support is almost nil.
3. Less coverage of the contents of education covered by the radio and TV media. The programmes specially on TV are of very general nature and not student based. In an effort, to make them applicable to masses, they are reduced to the most elementary levels.
4. Impoverished resources for the development and expansion of TV and computer based communication technologies. India at present buys high technology from the developed world in the fields of communication technologies and micro-electronics. The maintenance and repair facilities are simply non-existent in small cities, towns and villages.

   This is so much in contrast to the situation in open universities in developed countries like UK. Hodges writes, "The Computer Board for universities and Research Councils predicts that the British University students of 1992 will have powerful personal computers that can be plugged into a network in the study, bedroom or in the library and will use computers for sending and receiving electronic letters, for writing essays and answering tests and for choosing a library book."
5. Low socio-economic levels of the Indian students of distance education to afford audio and video cassettes.
6. Small number of students having a regular access to the radio and TV broadcasts.
7. Inability of the educational institutions to meet the financial liabilities for use of the new technologies, specially video production and computer technology.

8. Technical and expensive process of preparing excellent quality video films. This is observed through my personal experience as a team member of TV Teaching project funded by ISRO, engaged at present in production of video films for urban and rural adolescent girls and women. The video production centres in India are too few. The small audio and video production units in each university may burden already overstrained economy of our country.
9. SITE experiment has shown that while it was possible to reach a large number of people in the remote areas, it also indicated that this advanced communication system demanded advanced software facilities, trained personnel and competent utility and monitoring services hinting at a huge sum of expenditure.
10. Large size complexity of the background of the clientele to be covered under distance education. The masses include decentralized, tribal, rural and illiterate adult persons with apathy towards education and any new communication technology.
11. Inability of the learners and teachers to take to new methods of communication as Swaminathan says, "Beaming educational broadcasts is one thing, creating an impact of these broadcasts on education is another."

HOW TO OVERCOME THE CONSTRAINTS

Like many innovative approaches, distance education also may not register much success with raising quality of education or coverage of learners unless steps as suggested below are taken to overcome these constraints in the use of new communication technologies for distance education.

1. A survey to ascertain the abilities and experience of the students of distance education for suitable preparation of audio-visual aids. Without the development of appropriate learning and materials based on the theories of learning and perception, the hardware alone cannot help distance education to reach its goal. Learning materials of country-wide value need not to be developed.
2. Teams of first rate media persons and academic experts for technology based communication media to locate and evaluate suitable materials and give scholarly treatment

for depth and breadth of knowledge and to produce a harmonious picture.

3. Encouragement to low cost production techniques; example: Slides of expensive field processes first and later transferring them to video cassettes compared to straight video production will be cost effective. The new audio-visuals can play a highly significant role in distance education only if the country becomes self reliant and self supporting regarding the indigenous technologies.
4. Academic staff's access to training facility such as script writing, production and screening of video cassettes of developed countries.
5. If possible, gradual decentralised autonomous radio and TV transmissions by the open universities like the open university in Nigeria.
6. Encouragement to community TV viewing and both community and individual radio listening for larger coverage of clientele.
7. Encouragement to both the student and the teachers who are used to conventional media and methods to master some new skills involved in the use of new communication technologies.

It is hoped that India will soon overcome these problems, related to the electronic media to be able to take full advantage to their great audience appeal, capacity to record maximum information in a given space and facilities of easy transport, storage and long life. Basically, learning in distance education as in other approaches, takes place through various senses and stmuli. No one aid can be recommended, for all types of learning and all types of learners. A variety of both conventional and technology based audio-visual aids will help distance education. The audio-visual aid which cost less, are easily available, are easy to prepare, carry, use and store and which bring about the greatest clarity in learning will have to be given priority. One has to be realistic to which is immediately achievable and which can be achieved in many years to come. The despairing situation, arising out of the reduced use of conventional low cost media and nonavailability of modern electronic communication technology need be averted for the genuine growth of distance education. India still being a developing country, a mixture of traditional and sophisticated media can serve the instructional purpose of distance education.

11

Application of Information and Educational Technologies in Distance Education

INTRODUCTION

It has been stated earlier that growth and development of distance education is the result of growth and development in communication technology which is responsible for the growth and development of information and educational technologies. In the development of these technologies and in their educational application space research technology—the satellites play a vital role, therefore, first we would like to discuss the role of satellites in the promotion of distance education.

SPACE RESEARCH TECHNOLOGY (THE SATELLITES)

It all started in a big way after USSR. put space satellite 'SPUTNIK' into the earth orbit in 1957. During 1960s USA. embarked on a space programme that covered various activities which resulted in Apollo Eleven—Man's first Moon landing in 1969. During 1970s efforts were made to make use of space research and its benefits for the problems on Earth to protect the quality of environment and improvement of life in general for all mankind. One of the first uses of space technology for mankind was to improve weather forecasting and international communications.

Further, remote sensing satellites have added a new dimension to identification, evaluation and exploitation of natural resources. A new era has started with satellites and their application in various human activities. National and International Television networks have revolutionised in recent years which enable to telecast live programmes all over the world.

Space organisations in India deserve all praise for their launching of satellite INSAT 1B in geostationary orbit which has enabled the country to be integrated by national TV network. India has made much progress in satellites for educational application.

EDUCATIONAL PROGRAMMES THROUGH SPACE

Man has continuously engaged throughout human history to educate and train his fellow beings in the pursuit of happiness and excellence. But constraints were always faced because of limitations. In the wake of radio communication during 1930s, and availability of wireless sets to the common man in 1940s, concept of distance education began to take shape. Lectures and special lessons were being broadcasted regularly for the benefit of schools and colleges.

With the advent of Television and satellite communication, it has become possible to telecast live programmes all over the country through satellites such as INSAT 1B. Of course University Grants Commission (UGC) has started telecasting special programmes of lectures for the benefit of viewers during the day. Some of the programmes have made good impression on the viewers.

However, the whole problem needs to be given top priority regarding programmes, their impact on the audience, feedback and audience selection, wide publicity, experts, participation and facility for televising in regional languages. Special channel utilisation and interaction with various universities will have to be looked into. Special courses to be given through the mass media so that educational curricula would emerge and would lead to a programmed university degree or diploma.

DISTANCE EDUCATION

With the progress made in the area of communication satellites both at the national and international levels, it has been possible to operationalise the concept of distance education. Indian satellite which is already in orbit is enabling to make a beginning in the new venture. Next satellite to be in the orbit in near future would facilitate further to boost this new venture. A special channel earmarked for distance education, is very useful.

ORGANISATION AND IMPLEMENTATION

Once, the objectives of distance education have been accepted and satellite communication has been made available, it becomes mandatory for the organisers to implement the programme as a mission oriented project. For this purpose proper organisational set up is required at the national, state and district levels. It is an interdisciplinary activity.

PROGRAMME PREPARATION

As the task involved is a gigantic one, it needs careful thought for suitable programme formulation and coherent sequential televising of the programmes. Wide publicity and feedback monitoring and essential facets of the programme preparation and updating the information.

Programme preparation will have the following activities to be taken care of:

1. Identification of subject experts,
2. Suitable studies,
3. Infrastructural development for suitable programme preparation,
4. Language editing, and
5. Language experts.

All these activities need huge finances and the activity is of national importance and fundamental nature. Suitable allotment of funds can be made during the plan period and the programme can be executed. Considering the national literacy percentage, it may be worthwhile to support at least at the rate of one rupee per head/year for the programme which will revolutionalise the national image both with respect to education and general awareness. To mobilise funds for this may not pose a serious problem if all concerned departments could pool the resources including sponsored programmes. Working plan evolved with suitable consultations is progressing well but much has yet to be done.

APPLICATION OF INFORMATION TECHNOLOGY AND DISTANCE EDUCATION

The recent information technology revolution has transformed a communication-conscious human society into, metaphorically speaking, an information-obsessed global village in the sort span of just two decades. The course of development for the developing and the underdeveloped countries is no longer linear-sequential; it is increasingly characterised by 'leap-frogging' wherein one or more stages are bypassed in order to arrive at the state-of-art stage of information technology.

Today, our traditional concepts of 'knowledge' and 'information' call for re-examination. "Knowledge is power" is the slogan of this decade. Distance has been washed away, thanks largely to information technology.

Tele-conferencing no longer belongs to the world of science fiction; it is a reality on our national TV network. At present, our children face an incessant "information blitzkreig". India never had such a generation of knowledgeable youngsters who quite often know a lot more than their parents. Information technology has come to stay whether we want it or not and its implication in terms of accelerated socialization and learning are quite fascinating, sometimes even ominous.

The only option available to us is to ride this tigress of information technology and our skill lies in riding it to our advantage. "Knowledge and information" constitute the meeting-point between education and information technology. If we understand the range of possibilities available to us through information technology, we may be able to understand better some of the constraints that have characterised educational endeavour throughout human history and which have circumscribed its range as well as effectiveness.

Like its mother 'science' 'information technology' may prove 'a faithful servant or a fiendish master' depending on how judiciously and to what purpose we successfully master it. Consequently, there is a need greater than ever before to perceive the entire gamut of possible relationships between information technology and education so that the former is made subservient to our needs.

INFORMATION, EDUCATION AND INFORMATION TECHNOLOGY

Information experts now make a distinction between information and knowledge. Knowledge, consequently, is no longer the same as information. Information comprises data transformed into a meaningful guide for specific action. Knowledge, on the other hand, is an organised body of information that facilitates insights and judgements.

To quote Stonier, "what is information at one level may be data at the next". Thus facts, data, information and knowledge constitute a hierarchical order. One of the imperceptible shifts in our social order relates to the fact that political power has increasingly become information-based; till the recent past, it was capital-based. Hence, information and knowledge are the grist common to the mills of education as well as to information technology.

Information Technology (IT) has meant different things to different persons. However, the consensus of opinion is more inclined to define IT as the technology that deals with "the collection, storage, processing, dissemination and use of information" or "new ways of storing, processing, and transmitting information brought about by rapid developments in electronics, computing and telecommunications."

UNESCO has defined IT as comprising "the scientific, technological and engineering disciplines and the management of techniques used in information handling and processing, their applications; computers and their interaction with men and machines; and associated social, economic and cultural matters."

Thus IT is not entirely concerned with information processing hardware and software; it has to be equally concerned with the fall-out that it generates in man's social, economic and cultural life.

Distinguishing among terms like technology (i.e. total body of knowledge pertinent to the generation and innovation of tools, machines and systems), artifacts (i.e. the vital interface between human beings and their environment enabling them to bridge the gap between their native insufficiencies and a demanding and complex millieu), coping (i.e. the manipulation of three essential resources—matter, energy and information) and manipulation (i.e. various processes encompassing, producing, processing storing, transmitting and consulting) as various aspects of IT.

Hamelink defines IT as "the aggregate of scientific/technical disciplines basic to the production of devices (tools/machines) and systems for the capture, transportation, storage, processing and retrieval of voice, text, numerical and pictorial information." The following survey of operations related to IT as illustrated in Figure 11.1 would help us to understand its range.

Contrary to popular belief, IT has three forms, viz. primitive, intermediate and super; also called low IT, mid IT and Hi-IT. IT provides the essential infrastructure for an unprecedented variety of human activities due to increased significance of resource information in various fields. Its effects are not limited to a section of society; it influences all people at all times.

Operations	*IT Devices/Systems*
Capture	(*a*) remote resource sensing satellites (*b*) radar systems (*c*) electronic camera (*d*) VCR systems (*e*) video discs (*f*) optical character recognition
Transportation	(*a*) coaxial cable (*b*) optical fibre cable (*c*) microwave link (*d*) communication satellite (*e*) cellular mobile radio (*f*) laser beams (*g*) facsimile transceivers (*h*) videophone (*i*) electronic teleprinters (*j*) modems (*k*) multiplexors
Storage	(*a*) memory chips (*b*) magnetic film/tape/drum (*c*) holography (*d*) laser emulsion (*e*) microfilm
Processing	(*a*) integrated circuits (*b*) computer software (*c*) peripheral equipment
Retrieval	(*a*) high definition television (*b*) teletext (*c*) videotex (*d*) pay television systems (*e*) on-line databases/databanks

Fig. 11.1: Operation X Devices Spectrum of IT

It has been hypothesized that "the most advanced stage of information society will be high mass knowledge creation society...... The spirit of the information society will be the spirit of globalism, a symbiosis in which man and nature can live together in harmony, consisting ethically of strict self-discipline and social contribution.

Education has all along been an activity related to a very sensitive area of human relationship—the development of children. Transmission of knowledge and information have been central to educational endeavour throughout its history. Expert and lay opinion might have differed about other purposes of education but so far as transmission of knowledge and information is concerned, they have been almost unanimous.

Educational systems have always been expected to enable its consumer-learners to acquire maximum knowledge and information in minimum time to promote the simultaneous progress of the individual and society. Education has occasionally been described as 'the knowledge industry'.

Thus we find that both education and information technology work upon and process the same substance, albeit with different purposes: IT has been working for faster and more comprehensive presentation of information to human beings while education has been exerting itself to bring about more intense interaction between information and the individual for better comprehension and assimilation and generating greater possibilities of its use in making men and their life better in quality.

Education and information technology should, therefore, be perceived as natural synergists—made-for-each other partners to play a possibly predestined role to bring the dream of a better life within our reach, to help realize what has so far appeared to belong to the realm of utopia.

OPEN LEARNING SYSTEMS/DISTANCE EDUCATION SYSTEMS AND INFORMATION TECHNOLOGY

Distance education is in a way a new name to open learning but still some experts and in some nations it is known as open learning system therefore hereunder we will use open learning for DE.

If we examine the nature of Open Learning Systems (OLS) and Formal Learning Systems (FLS), we find that by their very nature, OLS are better suited to use IT for making themselves more effective. An OLS is by its definition less teacher-intensive. It has to make up for the disadvantages resulting from the absence of the teacher who otherwise would have mediated between the instructional material and the learner and in doing so facilitated a more fruitful interaction between the two in the desired direction.

The OLS has also to cater to variety in its presentation in order to ensure a minimum level of motivation for expected interaction to take place. An effective OLS can neglect the role of an occasional human mediator between its programme and materials on the one hand and its consumer-learners on the other at its own peril only. The role of tutor-counsellor made available to the consumer-learners of OLS is of crucial significance. It is he who can make the OLS a viable alternative to its counterpart FLS which is highly interaction-based through regular face-to-face instruction sessions.

The range of programmes and various modalities evolved for making OLS more responsive to its learner's needs and their cognitive, affective and psychomotor differences need to be developed beyond their present level. Unlike the Indian OLS, which is limited only to Distance Learning and the three programmes, viz. Open University, Open School and Correspondence Institutes, the OLS programmes in the UK, the USA, Japan and Australia, to cite a few examples, range through Distance Learning to Flexi Study to Directed Private Learning to Outreach.

These countries have an OLS characterized by easy 'accessibility' and 'flexibility' to accommodate the needs of their learners and to bring education to their door-step. It is through the use of IT that these countries have been able to achieve high accessibility and easy flexibility in their OLS programmes. The Indian OLS can also use the experience of other countries and the recent advances in IT to evolve a better functioning of OLS that is more need-based in terms of individualized curricula and that simultaneously responds in more satisfying ways to local, regional and national expectations and development goals.

APPLICATION OF INFORMATION TECHNOLOGY TO INDIAN OPEN LEARNING/DISTANCE EDUCATION SYSTEM

The role of the new IT in evolving a fuller OLS in India and strengthening it should lie in making available newer techniques for printing, storage and retrieval of information and knowledge and for promoting, faster, more comprehensive and more meaningful interaction between learners and information.

A comprehensive treatment of all IT-related operations (viz. capture, transportation, storage, processing and retrieval) and various IT devices/systems is obvious beyond the scope of the present paper. It would be more fruitful to delimit the treatment to areas of more directly evolving and strengthening the Indian OLS. The possible role of IT could, therefore, be examined in terms of printing, telecommunications, computing devices, microelectronics and software.

(*i*) Printing

As far as printing, dispatch and availability of instructional material is concerned, the Indian OLS is limited largely, if not exclusively, to paper-intensive modes. To come of age, it shall have to switch over to electronics-intensive modes. Unlike paper-intensive modes, electronics-intensive modes do not lead to ecological imbalances, nor are they susceptible to limited life-span or vulnerable to attacks by insects; they require less storage space and allow for re-use to an almost unlimited extent. IT-based electronic publishing offers cheaper, faster and longer lasting devices for processing-transmission and retrieval of information. It holds tremendous potential for mass production and distribution of information.

Word-processors and text-processors have made text-editing much less cumbersome and they now provide easy availability of simpler versions of text to suit the competence of individual learners. Electronic publishing could be videotex-based or teletext-based. Videotex system comprises a telephone, a television set for monitoring, a computer-fed database, a key board controller and a modem unit.

'Modem' is an acronym for a modulating-demodulating device because it converts a digital square-wave signal that cannot be processed by a telephone into an analogue signal that can be easily processed by it. It also provides for reverse function, i.e. conversion from the analogue into the digital form. Figure 11.2 represents a schematic diagram of a videotex systems.

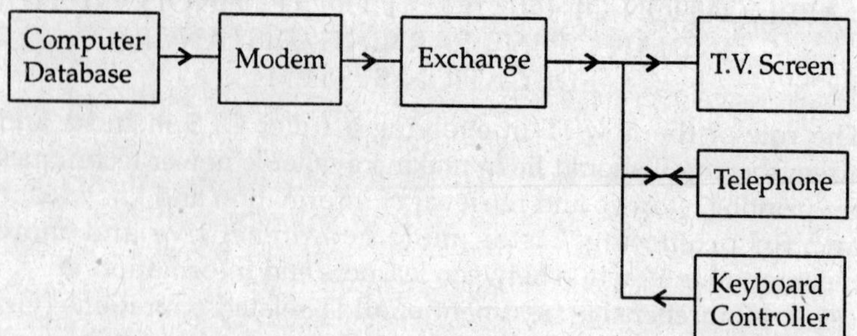

Fig. 11.2: Components of a Cablecast Videotex System

The listener/viewer operates the key controller and the aural information is available through modem over telephone and its visual counterpart is flashed on the TV screen. The telephone and modem allow for a two-way interactive system wherein the listener/viewer can ask questions, seek clarifications or get supplementary information. Prestel (Great Britain), Antiope (France), Captain (Japan) and Telidon (Canada) are good examples of successful videotex systems.

Among these, Prestal was the first to become a world videotex service in 1979. Teletext, on the other hand, provides for one-way facility. The listener/viewer cannot seek additional information. Vieotext is relatively faster and provides easier access to and more fruitful use of computer database. Videotex thus holds greater promise for Indian OLS.

Information can be stored in large quantities in databases. The Council for Educational Technology of Great Britain provides a good example of a fast developing educational database. Large databases stored on mainframe computers with multiple access points can put learners in contact with an almost inexhaustible store-house of information.

The American Centre at New Delhi through its instant access to various databanks in the US now makes available the latest information on almost any topic to any scholar who is sure of the nature of information that he seeks. Data vendors like DIALOG, MEDILINE, MUXUS can be hooked on to the telecommunication network in the USA and made available to information seekers almost all over the globe.

Microforms, videotapes and videodiscs are other powerful alternatives to conventional printing. Microforms store, display and retrieve optical image. Computerized microform retrieval systems can now process as many 3,000 documents a day. Books, magazines and dissertations can be easily transferred to micro-form and preserved in much smaller space for future use. Video-tapes have literally taken over the entertainment world from Indian cinema.

These tapes store magnetic signals for simultaneous subsequent retrieval of the visual and the audial information components. Lectures by experts, demonstration of process/techniques and field trips to inaccessible/remote regions could be recorded on videotapes for subsequent use. TV series like 'Secrets of the Sea' and 'The Living Planet' illustrate the numerous possibilities of its use in OLS as well as FLS. Videodiscs have not been as popular as videotape in spite of their obvious advantages. Compared to videotape, videodisc "....represents the densest storage medium in existence.

It is very durable and because of the nature of the system, free from wear.... its radial format provides almost instant access to anyone of 55,000 clear, sharp and rock-steady images, instead of having to wind foot after foot of video tape". Compared to videotape, videodisc recording is less cumbersome and though its front-end cost is much higher, it is almost thrice as cheap as videotape in the long run."

(*ii*) Telecommunications

This term refers to transmission of signals through electric or electromagnetic media. All India Radio, Doordarshan and INSTAT-10 are good examples of telecommunications-based transmissions/ dissemination-of-information. Telecommunications convert audio and/or visual information into electromagnetic signals which further modulate radio or microwave carrier signals. These signals are bounced back by the ionized layers in space or space satellites and are picked up by radio or television receivers.

These receivers demodulate the received signals and separate the audio and visual components for providing sound messages and optical images respectively. The recent decision to provide a separate channel for educational telecast in view of the excellent technical infrastructure provided by Doordarshan which has established more than 100 low and medium power TV transmitters is a welcome step and it offers tremendous possibilities for strengthening and broad-basing Indian OLS.

The sky should be the limit for our ambition and effort in strengthening our OLS through telecom network. When linked to a computer databank, telecommunications become a still more powerful delivery medium. Functioning at the speed of light, it provides optimal acceleration in carrying information to its consumers.

(*iii*) Computers

Computers are going to be the "whizz-kids" of our future educational system. Computation, information storage, communication and control are the four major functions of most computers. Super-computers are endowed with artificial intelligence and they are capable of intermediate level reasoning as well. Intricate calculations or multivariate data analysis become almost "kid-stuff" with their help.

Huge amounts of information can be very systematically stored in its memory (depending upon its memory size) for subsequent retrieval and use. Computers can provide flexible interaction with learners within the limits of the programme that defines their functional range. Computers can help us exercise extrafine control over various processes like satellite manoeuvring, satellite tracking and rocket launching.

A computer memory may be of ROM (read only memory) or RAM (random access memory) variety. The ROM variety is more widely used and its four sub-types, viz. mask-programmed ROMs used for storing programmes during its manufacture, PROMS (programmable only once at manufacture stage), EPROMs (erasable programmable read only memories that can be programmed many times) and EAROMs (electrically alterable read only memories) have been described in detail by Hankridge and Bradbeer *et al.*

Use of computers in education has resulted in CAL/CAI (Computer assisted learning/instruction). Arrival of computers in American classrooms has been compared to an avalanche. A variety of computer languages both low-level and high-level (algebraic) enables users to work with various computers, e.g. ADA, APL, BASIC, C, COBOL, FORTRAN, LISP, PASCAL, PL/I, RPG-II, SNOBOL, SPITBOL, WATFOR, WATFIV, LOGO, etc.

Computers can be immensely useful in providing individualized repetitive of analogous practice to learners, problem-solving exercises as well as activities for developing a variety of skills in a training programme. Project CLASS should prove a catalyst for increasing the use of computers in Indian education.

(*iv*) Microelectronics

Microelectronics is the science of producing technologies related to miniaturisation of various components of electronic circuits replacing loose wire circuits, integrated circuits pushing out printed circuits, and finally, the discovery of the magical silicon chip has all the elements of a fairy tale. ENIAC, the first electronic digital computer in the USA weighed 30 tons, filled the space of a two-car garage and contained 18,000 vacuum tubes which failed at the mean rate of one every seven minutes.

Thanks to the microelectronics miracle, an equivalent amount of computing power can now be placed on a pea-sized silicon chip. Microelectronics has resulted in the convergence of electronics, computing and tele-communications and brought about a tidal wave of technological revolution.

Miniaturization has brought about 'user-friendliness' (ease of use) and acceleration in computer processing. 'Touch' has increasingly replaced 'type' operations and now 'speech' is increasingly replacing 'touch' operation as well as synthetic speech at input as well as output stage. The lessons of microelectronics for Indian OLS lie in adopting leap-frogging approach in using IT. OMR (optical mark reading) or OCR (optical character recognition) provide for automatic reading of course assignments from learners and evaluation of scripts.

"Reading of assignments is the most unenjoyable activity in any distance learning programme" is what most teachers in OLS would confess in their unguarded moments. OMR/OCR could take a great deal of this drudgery out of the teachers' chores.

(*v*) Software

Software describes programmes that control computers as well as the instructional material the learners are exposed to. The importance of providing training of OLS faculty for developing their programming skills can hardly be over-emphasized, more so in view of awaiting countrywide introduction of CAL/CAI.

One of the desirable features of administration and leadership relates to forestalling an emergency and providing for preemptive measures before the situation explodes in its face. The importance of software is far more for the OLS faculty than for its consumer-learners unless of course they happen to have opted for computer programming courses as and when made available to them.

APPLICATION OF EDUCATIONAL TECHNOLOGY IN OPEN LEARNING/DISTANCE EDUCATION

In earlier chapters a reference has been made about the distance education/open learning systems, therefore, hereunder we will discuss some vital aspects of educational technology as being used in distance education/open learning in India.

Considering the fact that India has its own communication satellite in space and a large network for and television broadcasts with enough manpower having potential to produce educational programmes, the distance mode of education is ideally suited for mass education. Making optimum use of the existing facilities a large number of people hitherto untouched by education can be brought into the fold of education and teaching-learning process therein can be revolutionized.

The British Open University which has greatly influenced the Indian distance education systems, brought in certain radical innovations when established in 1969. Its teaching system in particular was based on a combination of broadcasting and especially written printed texts. As Bates (1984) puts it, 'from its inception the Open University was technologically based.'

In this quest to reach education to the masses, distance education had to think of an appropriate delivery system other than the traditional face-to-face teaching. Mass media footed the bill quite admirably. Mass media gain relevance for distance education from their capacity to disseminate educational information to a great number of people.

In a well designed instructional strategy, mass media can either be an indispensable component of learning environment or it can play a role which is to supplement learning.

Stressing the importance of mass media and their relevance in educational system a UNESCO commissioned International Committee on Education envisages in its report that 'one of the merits inherent in mass media is that they relieve teacher of exclusive concern with transmission of knowledge and thereby enable him to pay greater attention to his mission as educator.'

Developments in technology have greatly influenced the distance education systems. A wider range of media such as radio, television, audio and video cassettes is now becoming more and more accessible to a distant learner. Choice regarding the use of media for distance education has become more difficult to make. The modality of using texts as the core material and radio/television as support systems needs to be given serious rethinking.

Questions such as whether some media are more effective than others? Whether it is socially justifiable for distance teaching institutions to use media that are not universally accessible? Whether it is better to deliver learning material through alternative media? Are cropping up in the minds of planners and designers of distance learning courses.

Educational technology, viewed as systems approach to education, provides a perspective to tackle these and many related questions concerning distance education. With increasing availability of diverse educational resources the teacher becomes not only the designer and planner of instructional system but also someone who can integrate these resources into total learning environment.

Given the speed of technological development and the emphasis laid on its use in education in the national policy on education there seems to be an increase in the interest shown by educationists in this area. Nevertheless, technology has not been sufficiently used in distance teaching.

According to a survey, printed material and contact seminars occupy a major role in distance teaching schemes. Radio and television support is almost negligible, audio and video technology is yet to be introduced and more recent developments in computer, video-disc, word-processor and teletext technology are still distance education. It may not be difficult to think of the reasons behind their neglect.

Generally, the academics and administrators are unaware of the potential of educational technology in distance education, are inexperienced in their use, and probably even frightened off by their imagined costs. Though it is very much desired, it is extremely difficult if not impossible to make a detailed presentation on the types of technology available for distance teaching in a write-up such as this. However, in the following paragraphs an attempt has been made to list some of these technologies with very brief statements on the advantages attributed to them.

Radio

Radio can be considered as a medium as it consists of transmission through broadcasting of audio signals to listeners. The number of listeners of a radio broadcast may range from those within the radius of a few kilometres in the case of FM transmission to several millions in the case of national broadcasting. Educational broadcasts is a part of the programmes of several AIR stations. Largely, the radio broadcasts are for listening at the time it is broadcast.

However, with the availability of storing devices the message can also be stored by concerned persons/institutions. These two possibilities make it necessary that a decision is taken before broadcasting whether the material is for direct hearing or to be recorded for later use. Another related question is whether the message is to be broadcast once or more than once and with what interval.

Radio and television broadcast are of particular importance in distance teaching as alternatives to face-to-face contact which is almost missing in it. Researchers have found that the use of radio in correspondence education is accompanied by increases in the percentage of written assignments submitted by the students of the Delhi University correspondence courses as compared to their counterparts without radio lesson facilities. There could be various programme formats for education broadcasts. It could be a lecture or radio talk by experts, interview/discussion involving a team, sound recording of complete text or excerpts of historic interest, or radio-vision consisting of talk to be accompanied by diagrams/pictures/ slides.

The use of radio broadcasts in the open universities abroad, however, has been decreasing with a dramatic increase in the use of audio-cassettes which are mailed to the students alongwith the printed course material. This is largely due to the inconvenience in listening to a programme as and when it is broadcast.

Television

TV broadcasting is an important component in the open universities in other countries. With the acquisition of its production technology and falling prices, home receiving sets of TV broadcast are available in large number of Indian households and the number is increasing day by day. The specific value of TV broadcast will vary according to the context in which it is used. But there is no doubt that it can provide distance learners with unique resource material.

Demonstration of complex or expensive experiments, field visits, microscopic observations, advanced technical equipments, industrial processes, social and interpersonal interaction and interviews with outstanding persons in a field are just some of the experiences that can be offered to students in their own homes through broadcast television. Generally, the broadcast television programmes have their strength in encouraging interpretations by individual learner, stimulating thinking, providing an overview or synthesis, demonstrating continuos processes, raising awareness and developing skills of evaluation.

At the same time they have their weakness in achieving mastery learning, giving feedback, presentation of complex ideas and probably even development of abstract thinking. The TV programmes are short-lived, they cannot be reviewed, are presented at the same pace for all learners and do not provide scope for reflecting on an idea or thought during a programme unless one looses the thread of the programme itself. However, it would be too early to talk of its effectivity in certain terms since much needs to be explored in terms of its use in distance teaching.

Audio-Cassette/CD

This and the video cassettes/CD are the media which would probably be crucial for the success of distance education. For students, study material presented on cassette offers considerable freedom. It can be used when it appears most relevant to the individual needs of students and at a time and place convenient to them.

This is precisely the reason why it might be more appropriate for distance teaching. Moreover, the hardware viz., cassette-player provides the learner with a scope to stop, pause and replay the text according to the personal preferences of students. It has been argued in the past that cassettes provide students with a learning medium which shares many of the advantages inherent in a written text such as skimming, reviewing and control of pace while restoring the advantages of voice modulation.

Video-Cassette/CD

Video cassette/CD is more recent and an evolving educational medium. Video-cassettes are like broadcast television in the sense that they combine moving pictures with sound. At the same time they are different in the sense that they can be viewed in ways which are independent of predetermined transmission time. Video-cassettes have the advantage over broadcasting of increased student control of the medium.

Their more flexible control characteristics allow students to adjust the pace of the material to an individually appropriate level by replaying sections that move too quickly or by skimming forward over sections that are too slow. Even though at present a majority of the distance learners do not have any access to video cassette players, considering the fact that it is a high growth industry it is expected that in about a decade or two its accessibility figures would be far more satisfactory.

Video-Disc

The video-disc technology is at present not available in India. A video-disc is a brilliant silver coloured disc about 30 centimeters in diameter. Use of a laser-based photochemical process makes it possible to produce a reflective surface master which faithfully reproduces the audio-visual properties of the original programme material. From this master disc plastic copies can be relatively inexpensively produced by moulding or stamping processes similar to those used for producing gramophone records. One can think of a video-disc as a high fidelity gramophone disc with pictures to accompany the sound.

With the existing technology a video-disc can contain upto 55,500 individually numbered pictures or can play continuously for more than one hour. A beam of laser light is used to play the disc. It can be viewed on a standard TV set and hence has all the advantages of a video-cassette.

However, there are two features of the video-disc player which makes it unique. One, since only a beam of light is striking the surface of a video-disc, the disc will last indefinitely. Two, the location on the disc from which the laser beam is receiving information can be changed rapidly and precisely. The precise rapid single picture access makes it possible to step through the whole video disc one picture at a time. In addition it provides slow motion forward and reverse and rapid scan forward and reverse.

Most video disc players are equipped with an input port to accept digital signals directly from a computer. This combination of computer/video-disc player is the basic interactive video-disc system. This system makes it possible to develop computer assisted learning materials that combine the logical control and flexibility of computer software with the audio-visual characteristics of a video disc.

Considering the fact that the physical capabilities of the computer/video-disc system are much more than any of the educational lessons now available, its educational uses can only be speculated.

Word-Processor

If the technologies mentioned so far were mainly for the delivery of the educational programmes a word-processor is more for planning, designing and production of programmes. Considering the fact that the printed text has been and will continue to be for some time the basic medium for providing learning experiences in distance teaching, one can imagine the manpower, materials and energy being spent in production of texts.

Word-Processors are like electronic typewriters with additional abilities for electronic as well as permanent external storage, computerised house keeping and visual display of at least 20-30 lines of text. Since the material is first stored in memory instead of direct typing on paper, a lot of amendments in the text in terms of spacing, sequencing, deleting, right/left justification etc. can be done before arriving at the final script to produce any number of copies through a printer unit.

These facilities are extremely helpful in preparing a distance teaching text which routinely undergoes several processes such as drafting, typing, redrafting, retyping, editing, illustrating, and printing. Having these facilities in one single machine helps in keeping the production of a course on schedule.

12

Application of Audio-Visual Aids in Distance Education

INTRODUCTION

Audio-visual educational aids, in modern concept, are part of educational technology, hence, we made a reference of these aids in the earlier chapter captioned 'Application of Information Technology and Educational Technology', but this chapter specifically deals with the application of these aids in distance education.

THE CONCEPT

In educational planning today, a move towards an 'open' educational system is simultaneous with a proposal to induct the 'new media' into the teaching programme. Newly-initiated distance education programmes thus tend to begin with a series of consultations between educationists and professional media personnel; and as an educationist who has been using the new media for some years.

Two divergent themes recur on these occasions. There are those who stress the years of careful planning that must go into the production of educational software; into the selection and sequencing of subject-matter, into the choice of mode of presentation ('format'), and into the identification or evolution of cohesive teams of subject experts, script writers and producers. And there are those for whom these are non-issues.

Intriguingly, the same two divergent themes may be detected in reports of projects around the world, which have used the new media for distance education. (Since these are reports *after* the event, the differences will be seen to occur *between* projects rather than within projects). Intriguingly (again), there is a familiar failure of articulation of the premises about media and education which must underlie the opposing themes:

(*i*) The media provide a technological tool for substituting for, or extending the 'reach' of the traditional educational system (chalk-and-talk, book-and-exam.).

(*ii*) The media provide the opportunity and the occasion for the induction of educational reform (education as experience, learning as opposed to teaching, and so on).

Obviously, the choice of premise will affect the planning, the software and the outcome of the educational project. We shall illustrate this by describing a few such projects, placing them in two major categories, which we may conveniently label as the 'instrumental' and the 'reformist' [according to whether they choose premise (*i*) or (*ii*)].

The purpose is not to make a value judgement, and suggest that the choice of premise may be guided by its (perceived) 'intrinsic' worth. This choice will be guided, rather, by factors inherent in the distance education programme as we shall see below. What is imperative is to determine, at the outset of a distance education programme, which of the two premises about media is best suited to that particular programme.

A number of decisions which must be made fairly early will hinge on this choice—crucial decisions about hardware, about studio facilities, and about hiring. We can show how some education programmes 'drift' between the premises with a consequent reallocation of budgets and priorities; such 'drift' is a luxury that a developing country can ill afford.

Finally, it may be argued that the 'instrumental' and 'reformist' categories set-up here serve to provide a useful perspective on some fairly recently launched distance education programmes in the county, e.g. the UGC's *Countrywide Classroom*, the Andhra Pradesh *Open University*, and the A.P. Board of Intermediate Education's *Open Education Programme.*

There are differences of aim, audiences, content and method which dictate the classification of these distance education programmes into different categories; unhappily, a failure to recognize these differences has led to a scramble by the concerned agencies for identical (or at least comparable) facilities and resources.

Distance education programmes which make an instrumental use of the new media have some distinguishing properties.

Principally, they are distance education rather than truly *'open'* education programmes: that is, they have a clearly defined target audience, who enrol (pay fees) for specified courses and work towards specific degrees. Not only is there no incentive to make the software of more general interest, or of broader relevance, quite often the technology chosen limits the audience allowing access only to the target.

The postcards of Sir Isaac Pitman could obviously benefit few others than the registered shorthand student (and perhaps the odd inquisitive postman). In the Australian case, the University of New South Wales did not (perhaps could not) use the existing broadcasting facilities, setting up instead the first University-owned and controlled broadcasting, setting station in Australia (quite a few others are reported to have followed suit).

The interesting fact is that the bandwidth allotted to this station placed it outside the tuning range of an ordinary receiver a modification needed to be made to the set to receive the broadcasts. (The University initially provided modified sets on hire; later these sets became available in the market).

From these features of a targeted, enrolled audience and a formal teaching package, must inevitably follow other features' characteristic of distance education programmes based on premise (*i*), e.g. the establishment of a network of extension centres or study centres, and the availability of teaching materials on cassette (a tape-correspondence service) to groups of interested students.

USE OF TELEVISION

Two other features of the Australian enterprise are of interest. The first is their special use of the television studio. The major closed circuit TV studio is equipped with two colour cameras, a telecine chain incorporating a camera control unit, facilities for audio and vision mixing, two-inch transverse scan videotape recorders and several helical scan videotape and cassette recorders.

Audio-visual aids include graphic of various kinds, chalk-boards, magnetic boards, 8 mm filmloops and photographic enlargements. The telecine equipment is used for the presentation of 35 mm slides and 16 mm film. Other aids include a caption roller, microscope projector, near projection equipment, models, mock-ups, etc. Facilities are also available for 16 mm animation. Broadbent sets down with great clarity the mode of operation of an instrument oriented video studio.

In this special studio there are no cameramen, and in the early days there was no producer either; from a console the lecturer himself punched up the picture he wanted to show and about which he was talking from one of the outputs of two cameras, a slide projector or a cine-projector. The layout of the console and associated equipment enables the instructor to select video and audio from five sources, and to record his selection on videotape.

The console includes three miniature monitors, which show the video from each of the two cameras and from the telecine chain, a text generator or a computer. One camera is normally fixed focussed on to a blackboard or perhaps the lectures face; the other camera, which is fitted with a motorized zoom lens controlled by the lecturer, focuses on to a part of the console top on which demonstrations may be shown or diagrams drawn.

The lecturer makes up his programme as if he were before a normal class, using a wide selection of visual aids. With this arrangement it has been found that production costs are low, and flexibility of operation is considerable, when compared with normal television production methods.

The system works well but usually it is so organised that a staff producer, who is familiar with the material of the lecture, assists in positioning the displays, in operating the zoom lens of the overhead camera, and in generally organizing the production.

A further development of the lecturer-controlled console was introduced in 1979 for the many computer programming courses offered. The display was restricted to the video output of a computer, with an audio accompaniment in the form of the lecturer's voice.

This, however, raises an important issue. The lecturer-controlled mode of television programme production implicitly relegates TV to the role of a teaching aid—a glorified, many-in-one aid, bit a teaching aid nevertheless. Is this a legitimate use of the medium, or is it an under- (or mis-) utilization of it? Can the new media be content with delivering the old substance, or do they intrinsically demand a different style of education? In other words—do educationists have a choice at all between the premises (*i*) and (*ii*) set out at the beginning of this chapter.

We need to raise this issue, more so because it appears to have been raised—in some measure and in a preliminary sort of way—by the Australians themselves. Thus Broadbent writes:

"It quickly became evident that the new medium had its own special advantages and special limitations, and a new technique was required for successful transfer of ideas from lecturer to listeners. Many of the speakers were helped by the fact that they had taken part in radio and television broadcasts, but all had to adapt themselves, and their material, to the new medium. While most of the lectures consist of material presented by a single speaker, some take the form of a discussion between two speakers, with one interviewing the other, or both jointly developing a theme. A number of panel discussions have also been used, groups of three to five experts in some field discussing a topic."

COST EFFECTIVENESS

The next case of a distance education programme manifests a similarly late recognition of the demands of a new medium. In this case, the solution was to redesign the teaching package, to make a more cost-effective use of television.

The Institute of Chartered Accountants in England and Wales has, since 1975, been developing a range of package training materials, to be used by qualified accountants and their staff for trainees required to pass the Institute's examination. As in the Australian case, education-at-a-distance was necessitated by the failure of the learners to go to the teacher: the Institute found that only ten per cent of its members attended any of its conventional courses. As in the Australian case (again), the Institute initially decided on a purely instrumental use of video:

"......the use of video enabled a good lecturer to be seen and heard all over the country without having to repeat his performance..." (M. Tyrell and R. Davies, 1980).

NEW MEDIA IN EDUCATION

The 'instrumental' approach to the use of the new media in education is perhaps the original approach (and therefore, a widespread one). Richard Hooper, formerly senior Producer, BBC Open University Productions, writes about what he calls the 'media justification' problem.

"......the 1950s justification of the use of the new media has in later years been the very cause of their decline. The closed-circuit systems at universities like Pennsylvania State were set up specifically to distribute lectures to more students at less cost. Existing methods of teaching and learning were taken as given. These methods were stretched by use of new technologies—stretched but not changed."

Hooper lists two other contributory factors for the still peripheral role of the media in higher education, viz. 'media fragmentation' and 'media status'.

"There has been a continuing war between the various new media... In individual universities the television service, audio-visual centre and language labs are all busy practising media apartheid.

"Another problem.... has been the status of the media people. The television producer, for example has tended to be regarded by the academic staff as a technician. He is consulted, if at all, after the course content and objectives have been selected by the academic staff."

With these preliminaries, we may turn to distance education programmes adopting premise (*ii*). The obvious choice is the Open University of Britain. But we may first profitably acquaint ourselves with a course at the Pennsylvania State University, USA—a course whose interest for us lies not merely in its 'reformist' approach, but also in the milieu of its origin, when we recall that this University has a history of using closed circuit television in a purely instrumental manner.

This basic Interdisciplinary Arts Course is described by M.C. Mills (1980), as ordinarily encompassing film, theatre, painting, print-making photography, sculpture, music, opera, dance and architecture. Students are expected to understand the elements in a work of art that create its effect, to evaluate unknown works of art by learning to relate them to previous experience, and to relate elements across various arts that have similar cognitive values and affects.

What is noteworthy here is that a course design has been evolved for the arts, which is predicated on the availability of the media. Normally, the advantages and the centrality of the media are better recognized by science courses, for which the benefits of video (for example) are more easily perceived—such as control of time (slow/fast motion) and viewpoint (micro-macro), and accessibility (everyone can have a ringside seat at the laboratory experiment, provided there are enough viewing sets to go round). Anthony Bates tells us that at the Open university in Britain,

> "Science alone had argued from the beginning that television was essential for its foundation course, and had advised students not to take the course if they did not have access to television. 'Science-based' courses (which included mathematics as well as technology) were awarded a greater allowance of television programmes....."

In the other Foundation Courses, Bates informs us:

> "......academics often had to write extensive and detailed drafts of correspondence texts before they were able to specify precisely what they wanted to teach. Only then was it possible to decide on the contents of the television or radio programme. This meant that the major conceptual ideas were contained in the correspondence text, and the television and radio programmes merely reinforced or discussed these concepts."

Bates argues convincingly that better results would be achieved if the programmes and the correspondence material were developed at the same time.

Nevertheless alone among the Distance Education Programmes considered here, the Open University takes as its point of departure a philosophy of media usage in distance education. Consequently it has ensured that its structures and facilities evolve out of this philosophy. Thus here too we find courses which could not exist without media involvement, e.g. war and society (based on archive film material), The History, Design of Architecture, Language and Learning. "In the Open University", we are told "the decision to use broadcasting preceded decisions regarding the content of most courses."

Perhaps the most reassuring aspect of the Open University's approach to media is that, along with the results (in terms, e.g. of course design and software) of a consciously 'reformist' policy, they seem to desire, as a bonus almost, the results one would expect from an 'instrumental' programme. More than one reference may thus be found to the role that broadcasting plays in building up 'the corporate feeling of a University'.

> "Broadcasting is also essential to break down the isolation of the student. Many students never attend tutorials (at the study

centres)....many of them value the opportunity to see and hear their professors, and...seeing them—often nervous and awkward—before the television camera makes more human and personal what would otherwise be a very remote and impersonal teaching situation.. For instance, there is a strong feeling in the mathematics faculty that without the support given by television the dropout rate would be much higher. The assumption is that the television programmes assist the students' understanding and lead to quicker assimilation of material, and, at the same time, give students the psychological boost of feeling that they belong to an organisation with real people, however, remote or distant these may be physically".
(A. Bates).

This is strong recommendation indeed, coming as it does from a premier user of the media with a 'reformist' orientation, for a frankly 'instrumental' utilization of audio-visual aids in distance education—in the preliminary stages, at least. I must conclude as I began, by stressing that the virtue is not in the choice of one orientation over the other, but in recognizing the choice and making a clear commitment to one of the alternatives. There is time yet for us to decide on an instrumentalist use of the media for distance education courses which have a prescribed syllabus and a set of enrolled students working towards a formal degree (etc.).

This use of the media in such courses will allow us to see its use in instances such as the *Countrywide Classroom* in better perspective. In the latter case, the audience is truly 'open'; there is no set syllabus; and none of the policy statements.

Here we have the opportunity—indeed, the responsibility—of setting education into its broader context of indicating more clearly and creatively the interdependence of many of the spheres of our knowledge, the excitement of discovery, the logic of science, the recycling of concepts.... The challenge of making the *Countrywide Classroom* live up to its name is a large one. The merest acquaintance with the experience of the Open University shows that even when the goals are clearly articulated and the academic/ administrative structures set up with the greatest care, the results may yet fall short of expectations.

13

Student Support Services for Distance Education

INTRODUCTION

Higher education provides people with an opportunity to reflect on the critical, social, economic, moral and spiritual issues facing humanity. It contributes to national development through dissemination of specialized knowledge and skills. It is, therefore, a crucial factor for survival. Being at the apex of the educational pyramid it has also a key role in producing competent personnel for the various important vocations. With this demand in focus higher education in India has grown speedily.

In spite of so much expansion of higher education many students are deprived of admission to the formal system of higher education. There could be several reasons like limited seats, geographical and social isolation of the students, students not able to fulfil the requirements for entry into the formal set up etc.

Though, these students are deprived of joining the university system due to above reasons, there are several other who are turned down even though they fulfil the criteria for entrance. Thus, higher education in Indian conditions is facing major issues like, lacking in quality, increase in quantity and not able to maintain equality.

In order to meet the demands in India a beginning was made by starting correspondence courses in the Universities. In March 1961, an expert committee recommended that correspondence courses leading to a degree or equivalent qualification should be administered by universities only.

Main emphasis should be given on development of good quality correspondence material and also personal contact between teacher and taught. This is to be supplemented by good radio broadcast, educational TV programmes, audio and video materials.

From these beginnings in correspondence education in India, we now find tremendous growth in this system of education.

The essential aspect of modern distance education are well thought out and well planned correspondence materials which are self-instructional, set books, charts, posters, reading materials, television and radio broadcasts, audio and video pre-recorded cassettes, which provide academic support to the learners. Also tutoring and counselling services play a vital role in the personality development of the learners.

Keegan (1980) comprehensively analyses a range of attempts by a large number or eminent authorities to define distance education. According to Holmberg (1977) distance education is any one of the various forms of study which are not under the continuous, immediate supervision of tutors present with their students in lecture rooms and it includes teaching through print and electronic devices.

Before discussing various aspects of student services for distance education, we must bear in mind the vast and varied clientele served by distance education as listed below:

Clientele Served by Distance Education

1. In-service persons who for economic or other reasons had to take up jobs at an early age but are on the look out for an opportunity to improve their educational qualifications.
2. Drop-outs who later become motivated to resume their education.
3. Persons in geographically remote rural areas where there are no institutions of higher education.
4. Socially and economically backward sections of society.
5. Overflow from colleges/university teaching departments where admissions are made on merit and for a fixed number of seat.
6. Retired personnel who want to take up studies to keep themselves occupied.
7. Persons who want to learn and earn simultaneously.
8. Persons who want to study a subject just for the love of it, or to satisfy their curiosity.
9. Handicapped persons.
10. Persons who need some additional training in their vocation for updating their knowledge.
11. Persons (in affluent societies) having plenty of leisure time

who want to pursue some hobbies and other spare time activities.

12. Those students who are not able to fulfil the criteria for entry in the formal stream of higher education.

ADVANTAGES OF DISTANCE EDUCATION

The added advantages of distance education system may be summarized as follows:

(*a*) It is very economical. After a critical stage more the students, the more economical it is.
(*b*) There is no fixed student teacher ratio.
(*c*) The achievement of limited number of excellent teachers can reach thousands of students.
(*d*) Very few full time academic staff are needed. Part-time teachers of the conventional institutions often fill the bill.
(*e*) There is no need of academic buildings, students' residence halls etc.
(*f*) Students are not concentrated in the campuses and there is little chance of student unrest.
(*g*) In-service personnel, housewives, disabled persons, underprivileged people residing in remote areas, school drop-outs etc., all can avail of the courses offered.

The inherent flexibility of distance education system is conducive to greater variety of subjects of study, introduction of interdisciplinary options in various courses and wider choice of subjects for the learner. The system is eminently suited for instruction at all levels of education.

There is, however, a strange fallacy among some academicians in some countries that technical and science subjects cannot be serviced through distance education system. They are probably not aware of the tremendous success with which some correspondence polytechnics in Russia have been imparting instruction for full-fledged engineering and technological course as well as refresher and updating course for topmost engineers and technologists throughout the country.

We also know of some technical universities and institutes of Australia, teaching technical courses through the distance education methods. In fact the potential of distance education of serving technical and vocational courses needs to be fully exploited by the developing countries, so as to make distance education more broad based, meaningful and relevant to the needs of society.

SIGNIFICANCE AND NEED OF STUDENT SUPPORT SERVICES

The modern distance education system is the product of a gradual process of evolution over a period of 100 years or so. The driving force in this long process of evolution has been the challenge to established credibility of a new system vis-à-vis the age old conventional system of classroom teaching. This challenge necessitated consistent efforts to develop a non-conventional and alternative channel for imparting education. Beginning with modest Home study/Independent study/Postal tuition, it developed into somewhat better organised Correspondence education.

With the integration of various teaching-learning activities and communication technology, correspondence education seemed to be a misnomer. Distance education was considered to be a more appropriate nomenclature and it came to be internationally accepted when the International Council for Correspondence Education was renamed as International Council for Distance Education at its Twelfth World Conference in Vancouver in 1983.

Being an innovative system, distance education has always been open to all teaching methods and media. It is a teaching-learning system which combines both teaching and learning activities. It imparts education to students at a distance. The earlier exponents of the system, correspondence educators laid greatest emphasis on instructional printed course material. But in due course of time the concept of two-way communications was inducted into the system to make it more effective.

The tremendous development of communication technology in recent years provided a wide choice to distance educators to integrate new media into the distance education teaching-learning processes. This led to a change of thinking among distance educators and it was realized that even though the printed course material would continue to be the mainstay of the distance education system, integration of (communication) technological devices could greatly help in strengthening the teaching-learning processes.

As distance education gained more and more popularity, varied target groups were drawn to the system and the institutes had to devise varied teaching-learning programmes to cater to the needs of ever increasing number of learners. In this developmental process, distance educators realised the need of well organised student support services. And communication technology came to be recognised as an effective support service both for the teacher and learner.

An improved form of DE insists on two-way communications, and facilities for occasional group interactions. Self studies through course materials and other specific exercises are supported by tutor-students interactions and occasional group interaction sessions to strengthen efficiency of learning processes guided by DE system. In other words, DE system encourages different kinds of students support activities with a view to give feed backs to students' progress, clearance of doubts of learners, evaluating regular progress of students and giving appropriate counselling to needy learners.

Such activities can be organised in different forms, such as (*i*) two-way communications between tutors and students through written response sheets, postal correspondence and telephone talks; (*ii*) personal contact programmes at regional levels; (*iii*) local, regional study centres; (*iv*) regional/local level libraries; (*v*) regional/local level workshops and laboratories, and (*vi*) computer assisted feed back. In the Indian context the traditional system of DE as well as open universities have made some such provisions for DE learners.

AVENUES OF STUDENT SUPPORT SERVICES

These avenues include the following:

(*a*) Use of Communication Technology

A number of distance education institutes, particularly the Open Universities in the developed countries took to the new communication technology in a big way. Besides the usual radio broadcasts and television programmes, they have evolved various innovations of these media to convert them into two-way communication devices. In New Zealand and Australia for example, they have developed Radio-tutorials and Radio Conferences.

Similarly, some of the developed countries have evolved useful combinations of Cable TV, Electronic blackboard, Fibre Optics and telephone. These combinations convert the simple television set into a powerful educational tool called the Telidon—a Canadian

Video System. The Video tape and Video disc are also very useful innovations which remove the constraint of viewing TV programmes at set times. Another good innovation of TV is the *Cyclops* developed by the Open University in England. It is an extremely versatile audio-visual teaching medium based on the conventional TV set, standard audio cassettes and microcomputer technology.

Audio cassettes and video tapes are also very effective teaching media. They have an advantage over the radio and TV in that they enable the learner to have control over the learning material: he can listen to or view the programmes at any time convenient to him, he can stop the cassette or video tape at any stage, go over any section of the cassette or tape as often as he needs and use it again and again for revision or recall.

Phonograph records and Flexi discs are also good devices which are cheaper and more easily accessible. Educational film strips and films too could be very useful and effective media in the teaching-learning processes.

Telephone has great potential for providing two-way interactor between the learner and the teacher, as also among the learners themselves. It is particularly useful when an institution has to deal with students scattered over vast areas and in countries where there is shortage of specialists. Some of the latest innovations of telephone are Tele-tutoring and Tele-conferencing.

Tele-tutoring can be developed into a very useful student support service in the distance education system. The institutions which have adopted these innovations allocate learners to telephone tutors and the learners can discuss their problems with the tutor on telephone. The learners and the tutors do not have to travel for interaction, seminars, etc.

Distance education institutes in the developing countries may not be in a position to make use of all the innovations of modern communication technology, but they should chalk out a phased programme of the integration of these devices into their teaching-learning system to make it more effective. In the first phase we should take immediate steps to adopt such devices as are easily available and within the reach of our learners, e.g. radio, television, telephone, audio cassettes and video tapes.

In the second phase we should try to develop the various adaptations of radio, television and telephone. In the third phase we should keep an eye on the future and try to develop the latest and sophisticated communication technologies in collaboration with the developed countries. It would be worthwhile exploring possibilities of assistance from and collaboration with UNESCO, various Education foundations and International organisations for this purpose.

Now that the government of India is laying special emphasis on new technology, the Open Universities and correspondence education institutes in our country should initiate special projects for harnessing communication technology for educational purposes. Of course we must be very pragmatic in our choice of communication media and choose a judicious mix of the media relevant to our needs and resources.

Unfortunately, correspondence institutes in our county hardly provide any properly organised media support to their students though some institutes do arrange radio talks. TV support is altogether absent. The Association of Indian Universities and the University Grants Commission should impress upon the government the urgent need for Radio and TV support for distance education programmes.

The establishment of Indira Gandhi National Open University would, in due course, help in developing systematic and properly organised media support for distance education programmes all over the country. Considering the special relevance of distance education system to the educational needs of our people and the society the government should give priority to the provision of Radio and TV support for distance education programmes, and explore the possibilities of building up effective telephone support as well.

However, apart from the media support, the distance education institutes need to build up various others support services for their students. Here again we lag behind the developed countries. Although as many as 32 universities in our country have set up full-fledged institutes/Directorates of Correspondence courses, very few institutes have developed study centre and library facilities.

It is time we paid special attention to plan and build up an effective infrastructure of student support services which are so essential to the distance education teaching-learning processes. Here again some advanced countries have tried a number of innovations. These support services, their functions and innovations may be classified as under:

(b) Study Centres

A network of study centres is of vital importance to a distance education institute for providing useful support to the students in their learning pursuits. Each study centre should have a counsellor who should be competent enough to give general counselling, advice, and guidance to the students on methodology of learning through the distance education system and general aspects of the various courses.

He should also be able to provide to the public in that area, detailed information and guidance regarding courses of study available in the institute which may be relevant to their needs. The centre should also have subject tutors who may be available to the students for consultation and guidance.

These tutors could also handle evaluation of students' assignments, and teach at the face-to-face contact programmes. Tutorial support is of crucial importance to the learners and serves as a great morale booster for them. It helps them to overcome the feeling of isolation.

The study centre should also have a good library, audio and video equipment, telephone and listening lab facilities. It should have suitable working hours according to the convenience of students and must remain open on Sundays and holidays too.

The study centres can also organise distribution of course material.

Some of the variations of study centres and face-to-face contact programmes tried by some distance education institutes in different countries are:

(i) Mobile Learning Centres

Mobile Learning Centres as devised by North Island College in Vancouver island, Canada, are smaller and more compact editions of the Static Conventional Study Centres. Each mobile unit has study carrels for about 4 students, a tutor's cabin, radio, telephone, storage for files, library books, audio visual viewing equipment for multiple viewing of different programmes by different students, a micro computer station and space for laboratory work. It is manned by a single tutor who performs multiple roles to guide varied learners studying varied courses, to advise them how to learn and to help them in making their learning as independent as possible.

However, he has the support of two other tutors—the subject tutor for evaluating students' assignments and the local telephone tutor for sorting out the learner's problems that cannot be resolved by him. Students can avail themselves of the services of mobile learning centre by prior appointment. They are free to spend any length of time talking to the tutor individually or as a group, using resource material, writing assignments, etc.

These mobile units serve the purpose of publicity vans also and enthuse a number of persons, in the areas visited, to enrol for various courses. The mobile learning centre could form a very useful support service for Distance Learners, and should be specially suitable for developing countries.

(ii) Local Study Cell/Circle

A Local Study Cell organised by the institute or by the students themselves, as in Teleuniversite Quedec comprises 2-5 students who meet to interact and share their learning experience, activities and difficulties. There is no animateur at these cells but each cell is assigned to a resource person, and in case of need the students can contact him on the telephone. This form of support has proved very useful in language courses. But in areas where students are widely dispersed it is not easy to organise such cells.

In Finland, Study Circles are a common feature. Each Study Circle comprises 3-10 learners and it is supervised by the Director. The circle meets regularly for lectures and seminars but the learners also work individually with the help of books specials audio-visual materials and occasional TV and Radio programmes. A University lecturer visits the Circle regularly to deliver lectures, lead seminars and provide consultation. The Study Circle is a flexible and well adopted form of study organization specially suitable for sparsely populated areas. Each Study Circle enjoys considerable autonomy regarding working hours, methods, etc.

(iii) Workshops

Regional workshops as organised by Teleunivesite Quebec, for groups of 15-20 students with the help of a local animateur has proved to be a popular support service. The workshop programmes include discussions on learner's difficulties, exercises, question-answer sessions, viewing of audio-visual material etc.

(*c*) Personal Contact Programmes

Personal Contact Programmes or face-to-face teaching sessions constitute a commonly accepted support service in most of the Open Universities and Distance Teaching Institutes in the developed as well as developing countries. These programmes help in giving to the learners some sort of orientation and guidance regarding the methodology of learning and provide condensed classroom teaching to cover the important and difficult topics of the student's courses of study.

There should be adequate provision for consultation periods so that students may discuss their individual difficulties with their teachers. It would be good to invite some eminent scholars as guest-speakers for delivering special lectures on a few selected topics. That would give wider academic exposure to the learners. The students should be encouraged to mix and interact with their fellow students at these programmes. Some cultural activities thrown in could lend colour and social value to these programmes.

The venue of these Personal Contact Programmes should be the campuses of study centres, universities, colleges, schools, etc. which may have adequate classroom, laboratory and residential facilities.

(*d*) Evaluation of Student's Assignment-Responses

Well prepared course material and student's assignments are two distinct aspects of the distance teaching-learning process that give the distance learners an edge over their counterparts in the formal education system. Special attention, therefore, needs to be given to these features. Submission of assignments, at least a reasonable percentage of them, must be obligatory for the distance learners.

And evaluation of these assignments should be carefully and promptly done so as to sustain the interest of the learners in their courses of study and to inculcate in them a regular study habit. It would be ideal if the assignments of a group of students are evaluated by the same tutor throughout the duration of the course of study. Apart from awarding marks, the tutor must also give his comments on the students' performance and suggest improvements, etc. The turn-round time of assignments must be the minimum. Where computers are easily available, some of the assignments could be computer-marked.

(*e*) Library Facilities

By virtue of the independent learning concept of the Distance Education System, library facilities should occupy a prominent place in the students' learning process and form an essential part of support services. The Distance Education Institutes must have a well-stocked Central Library which should provide extensive library facilities to the students.

The Central Library should also have a Book Bank so that students are able to borrow prescribed texts and suggested books for the entire duration of the course. The catalogues of all such books should be sent to the students when they enrol with the Institute. Mobile Library vans too could serve a useful purpose, specially in remote rural areas. The Institutes could also have arrangements with public libraries and libraries in the universities and colleges, etc. to extend library facilities to the distance learners.

(*f*) Home Experiment Kits

Home Experiment Kits as devised by the Open University in England should form an essential part of support services for students who take up science or technical courses. A brochure of instructions on the use of the kit would also be necessary. However, for complicated experiments, the Distance Education Institutes must organise facilities for practical work for their students in some good laboratories in universities, colleges or polytechnics, etc.

(*g*) Resource Packs

These could be very helpful in providing some additional information and reading to the distance learners for updating and supplementing the course material, and for circulating leaflets, posters, study guides, cardboard cut outs, information booklets, schedule of TV and Radio programmes, etc.

(*h*) Information and Enquiry Desk

Every Distance Education Institute should have a special Information and Enquiry Desk for providing information and guidance concerning the various courses available at the Institute. This would ensure prompt disposal of enquiries regarding admissions, eligibility conditions, etc.

THE CONTENT, METHODOLOGY AND DESIGN OF STUDENT SUPPORT SERVICES

A brief account of this aspect is as follows:

To organise student support services for distance education system at higher education level, following structure is suggested. Distance education system should establish national level centres. These centres should develop the necessary self-instructional materials. These main cetnres should appoint region wise centres for catering to the needs of regional students. This will take care of admission, instructions and guidance and counselling and evaluation of these students.

In certain remote areas also national level centres should be established taking into consideration a cluster of villages. These centres should be well equipped in terms of library facilities for books, journals, audio and video cassettes. Also specially trained tutors and counsellors should be appointed at these centres. These tutors should know the local language.

Secondly, a face to face contact sessions should be held at these centres. These could be planned according to the nature of learners—either in vacations or during academic sessions. But these tutors and counsellers should be available.

Thirdly, in order to provide good facilities, the students should be charged for these facilities by these national level centres and also some fixed remuneration per student should be paid to the tutors and counsellors, and all other administrative staff.

The student support services will concentrate on academic and personal problems of learners. The content, methodology and design of these services will be such that it will:

(*i*) solve the learning difficulties of the learners,
(*ii*) provide feedback to the learners regarding assignments, practicals etc.
(*iii*) establish cogitive support with the learners,
(*iv*) organize instruction which will correspond with student pacing,
(*v*) organise activities leading to enrichment of personality,
(*vi*) identify and foster desirable personality traits,
(*vii*) prepare and conduct tests and evaluate the same, and
(*viii*) organize remedial teaching.

There should be adequate provision in the courses to pay individual attention to the participants. The courses will include brain-storming, buzz sessions, discussions, group-work, demonstrations, practicals, and a few lectures and peer group discussions. Along-with academic activities these centres will cater to the personal problems of the students. The group being heterogeneous, the problems of learning will be varied in nature. Especially, here the entry being open, many will not be exposed to the formal university system. In the present set up of 10+2, those students who could not pass +2 stage, will like to join distance education system.

These learners will have special characteristics and their needs will be different. They may need counselling. Here, the national level centres will have to appoint qualified counsellors, who can understand the problems of these learners.

To sum up, it could be said that the best student support services are quality materials which are not totally dependent on other aids, institutions feedback etc. This will depend on the main centre producing master materials which will be sent to the regional centres for reproduction, distribution and support.

As the learners of distance education would be heterogenous in nature, there is need for academic and personal contact. This is the best necessary support that the student support services should provide for the effective distance education programmes.

AN EVALUATION

In order to make the support services really effective and efficient, it would be necessary to give a good deal of thought to planning and organisation of these services. One way to ensure this would be to set up a Support Services Cell in the Institute which should keep itself fully informed about the latest departments in communication media, distance education methodology and research; obtain regular feedback and suggestions from the learners regarding adequacy and efficiency of various support services; and exercise proper supervision on the functioning and effectiveness of these services.

Policy makers and educationists are supposed to keep an eye on the future while framing policies and plans. With increasing awareness among people, the demand for education at all levels, particularly in the developing countries, is bound to swell, and no democratic or socialist government can deny the people their right to education. But with limited financial resources and shortages of qualified teachers, the developing countries will not be able to cope with this ever-increasing demand through the formal system of education.

Distance education system alone will be able to meet this challenge. It would, therefore, be in our national interest to give serious thought to the proper development and strengthening of this innovative teaching-learning system. We should give top priority to the strengthening and streaming of the Institutes of Distance Education in our country and give maximum autonomy, adequate finance and all possible help to enable them to develop a proper infrastructure of student support services.

Possibilities of collaboration with Open Universities and among Distance Education Institutes need to be explored. I am sure these measures can go a long way in reinforcing and strengthening the distance education system which has a big future in extending and equalising opportunities of higher education and brining about qualitative improvement in education at all levels.

14

Counselling in Distance Education

INTRODUCTION

Counselling is a way of human life since early days. Elders guide the youngsters and younger in need seek advice from elders and wise man, but as a concept in education and other fields of human life it is hardly seventy five year old and includes information-giving, advice giving, psychotherapy etc. It can be formal or informal in nature focussed on personal development and social adjustment. It is a vital concept in distance education. Hereunder, we will discuss various aspects of counselling for its useful application in distance education.

MEANING OF COUNSELLING

Rogers defines counselling as "A series of direct contacts with the individual which aims to offer him assistance in changing his attitudes and behaviour." Shostrom and Brammer define it as "A self adjustive process, which helps the client become more self directive and self responsible."

Counselling in its modern connotation means more than advice giving. The counsellor helps the counsellee to think through his own solutions, he does not provide him with ready-made solutions. Counselling does not confine itself to the solution of immediate problems only. The function of counselling is to help the individual develop skills so that he may take wiser decisions in future as well as steer out of immediate difficulty.

Counselling relationship according to Pepinsky and Pepinsky refers to the interaction which (*a*) occurs between two individuals called "Counsellor" and "Client", (*b*) takes place within a professional setting, and (*c*) is initiated and maintained as a means of facilitating changes in the behaviour of the client.

Counselling has long been regarded as an important, indispensable component of traditional institutionalised graduate/undergraduate programmes in other countries.

Maslow says "Counselling is a systematic exploration of self and/or environment by a client with the aid of a counsellor to clarify self understanding and/or environmental alternatives so that behaviour modification or decisions are made on the basis of greater cognitive and affective understanding."

Recently, a number of interesting unorthodox developments have made us realize that counselling and its "information giving" function is a vital and integral component of a distance education system.

Education is no more a privilege of the elite. When education was restricted to the elite the school and college populations were homogenous in nature and providing suitable education was a comparatively easy job. With education thrown open to everyone, the student population is more heterogeneous and so requires a more diversified curriculum and facilities.

Distance Education system is open to all who may satisfy the minimum standards set for admissions. Under these circumstances the students are coming from a varied social background. A significantly large number of students are the first generation learners. In their families they have no one with experience of college education to guide them in the choice of a career. Counselling help can be meaningful in this development.

Counselling involves problem solving and learning, it can be considered as special teaching which involves both intellectual and emotional aspects of individual's personality. Counselling thus becomes a legitimate and integral part of education.

However it aims at attitude change and does not concern itself with action. Counselling functions at the emotional level and does not confine itself to the intellectual learning. It generally deals with the problems related to (*i*) Vocational goals and educational aspirations, (*ii*) Administrative and procedural complexities and ambiguities, (*iii*) Academic motivation or progress, and (*iv*) Emotional adjustment and personal development.

A counsellor helps the students to cope with problems. So counselling must promote purposeful rapport between the student and the counsellor. A counsellor should be able to identify and respond positively to the individual student's problems and his requests for advice. Thus the counsellor needs to demonstrate empathy in dealing with students' enquiries, provide assistance and encouragement, wherever necessary.

The counselling process, should help the student to reach a decision, but it must place the ultimate responsibility for decision-making with the student. Tyler says "Counselling is mainly neither a matter of solving problems nor of making decisions; rather it is a developmental experience in which attempts to solve problems and arrive at decisions are the events out of which through reflection and the process of 'working through' personal growth takes place."

In other 4words, the counsellor in his relations with the student should try to work himself out of, rather than into a job, by promoting and encouraging the student self-help. The student will become increasingly more confident about seeking and finding his own answers and solutions to problems and less dependent on the counsellor.

SIGNIFICANCE AND METHODS OF COUNSELLING

In seeking to establish a meaningful counselling relationship with distant students it is first necessary to find a suitable means of communication. The means employed will be determined by such variables as the location of students and density of numbers, the distribution and accessibility of counselling points, the number of counsellors and range of counselling skills available and the level of educational technology which the university or college invokes to support its off-campus counselling programme.

But correlation of the range of counselling levels and types of media used in counselling may be effected through: (*i*) Correspondence counselling; (*ii*) Audio-cassettee counselling; (*iii*) Telephone counselling; (*iv*) Face-to-face counselling.

Counselling through correspondence is the only popular made in India. In fact we don't have other options to do the same. Of course, recently the Government has acknowledged the importance of counselling for correspondence learners and attention is being paid to develop other media like TV and Radio broadcasting. But yet we have a long way to go.

Correspondence counselling has got its own limitations. It is strictly a "one-way" process. Moreover, the postal delays cause a great deal of anxiety in the minds of the students who are badly in need of counselling at the time of answering their assignments.

Secondly, it is observed that external learners derive greater satisfaction from personal conversation and face-to-face counselling. This is largely psychological. Innovations in audio tape and telecommunications have been integrated into external delivery systems, making it possible for more personalised counselling to be accessible to all students.

Needless to deny the fact that India is a poor country with all its limited resources. But the scientific and technological development of India is quite respectable. Therefore, we would expect that though this medium, 'Audio-cassettee', is now not fully possible in the Indian context, soon we will be able to make use of it.

Audio tape cassette replay system is an inexpensive medium for conveying information and advice to students. The advantages of this medium are: (*i*) It seems to be more personalized than written comments; (*ii*) Students regarded the information as being more informative and complete than that obtained via correspondence; and (*iii*) Students' level of academic achievement significantly improved as a result of the use of the audio tape system.

Unlike audio-cassette counselling, Telephone counselling is totally absent in India. It is said that "telephone counselling is the most effective tool for distance teaching and learning—Capable of individualizing, humanizing, personalizing and optimizing instruction." As a result it is capable of generating highly interactive counselling relationships.

Telephone conversations have the advantage over cassette tapes is that they provide spontaneous two-way communication and discussion. The additional advantage of telecounselling is its flexibility. Wherever there is a telephone, it is possible to obtain information without travelling, thereby saving time, effort and money.

There are basically three ways of providing face to face counselling for distant students.

(*i*) A professional counselling service can be established and located as a centralized function of the learning institution itself;

(*ii*) Another means by which face to face counselling can be implemented in distance education schemes is through an organisational structure which may have decentralised agencies and resource centres and regional or provincial locations; and

(*iii*) Another method of conducting face-to-face counselling in distance education programme is by means of itinerant counsellors or educational guidance officers who travel to different regions to help local students sort out their study problems and help them overcome their anxieties.

Besides the abovementioned three ways of providing face-to-face counselling, there is the personal contact programme. As per recommendation of the various committees and guidelines laid down by the UGC most of the correspondence courses institutes organize personal contact programmes for their students in order to supplement instruction imparted through the printed lessons. These programmes provide a good opportunity to the students to come in close personal contact with their teachers.

Apart from the intensive classroom teaching imparted at these programmes, the students get a chance to sort out their individual difficulties and problems.

The common reason due to which such a large percentage of students are unable to attend these programmes are (*i*) difficulty in getting rail/bus travel concessions, (*ii*) difficulty in getting leave from the employer, (*iii*) family commitments or hard circumstances, (*iv*) financial hardships, and (v) non-availability of board and lodging facilities.

However, it is learnt that the reaction of the students who attend the personal contact programmes are generally very favourable and they go back with added confidence and enthusiasm to pursue their studies.

(*i*) Counselling services are still an underrated activity where distant learners do not represent the major or sole interest of educational institutions.

(*ii*) Majority of distant students are poor and economically not well to do. Very few freeships and financial inducements are available to them.

(*iii*) Lack of proper mode/media of counselling.

(*iv*) India is a large country with its mutilingual population. Moreover, cultural background, social status and economic factors differ from person to person and from one region to another. Therefore, only one mode of counselling may not be useful for each and everyone.

COUNSELLING FOR DEVELOPMENT OF 'STUDY-SKILLS' IN DISTANT STUDENTS

Suggestively this aspect must include the following vital points and techniques:

1. Time and place for Study?
   A. When to study? B. Where to study?
2. How to read and write better?
   A. SQ3R B. How to make useful notes?
3. How to read faster?
4. How to learn from Television and Radio broadcasting?
5. How to deal with examination?
   A. For effective preparation
   B. 'Technique to be used in Examination Hall'.

1. Time and Place for Study

A. When to study

(*i*) Make out a study time table, (*ii*) Do some study nearly everyday, (*iii*) Tackle the toughest work at times when you are at your best, (*iv*) Leave enough free times for recreation, (*v*) Make a note of what you hope to achieve in each study session, (*vi*) Begin your work at the very start of each study session.

Firstly, review what you did in your last session on the topic. Secondly, force yourself to keep concentration. Thirdly, take a total of five to ten minutes break within each hour of study. Fourthly, ending up with reviewing what you have achieved.

B. Where to study

(*i*) Find a place as free from distraction as possible, (*ii*) Try to study always in the same place, (*iii*) The only equipment you need apart from your books and distance Education materials is a table, a chair and a good light, (*iv*) Let it be known that during study sessions you cannot be interrupted, (*v*) Let plenty of fresh air in.

2. How to Read and Write Better

A. One very useful approach to study an article is known as SQ3R (survey, question, Read, Recall, Review).

SURVEY the material first to get a general view of what you will then study in detail, scan the table of contents, the introduction, headings, emphasized sections, summarise exercises and final paragraph.

Think up QUESTIONS that will give purpose to your study and allow you to read with anticipation.

Read the material (preferably three times faster rather than once slow).

Stop after each section of material to RECALL what you have read (and make notes of the main ideas and important details).

REVIEW what you have (and test the accuracy of your notes) by running quickly through the four previous steps again.

During the READ stage of SQ3R:

(*i*) Look from the work for the author's idea—the plan upon which he constructed the material. (*ii*) Pick out the main idea in each paragraph often contained in the first or last sentence. (*iii*) Look for important details, e.g. proofs, examples, supports for main idea. (*iv*) Don't ignore the diagrammes and illustrations—they may make the things clear where the text does not. (*v*) Be sceptical. Don't take author's words as gospel truth. (*vi*) Think of your own examples—look for the application in our own experience. (*vii*) Skip paragraphs and whole sections if you find them irrelevant.

B. How to make useful notes

(*i*) It helps to make notes because it keeps you active and concentrating, and provide a written record for revision. (*ii*) Store your notes in a loose-leaf binder. This gives maximum flexibility to rewrite the sections of one's notes. (*iii*) Some suggestions for writing the notes:

(*a*) Contents should include author's/speaker's main ideas and important details.
(*b*) Logical structure of the author's argument.
(*c*) Any important references he maintains.

(*iv*) Make notes at the recall stage of SQ3R:

(*a*) Use your own wording
(*b*) Make use of such standard abbreviations like, these:
e.g.-for example;
i.e.- that is;
c.f.- compare, remember in the context;
N.B. Note, important;
= equals, is the same as;
does not equal;

$<$ less than;
$>$ greater than;
$\therefore$ therefore; and
$\because$ because.

3. How to Read Faster

(*i*) Make sure you don't mouth the words or say them aloud as you read.
(*ii*) Try to read in 'thought—units'.
(*iii*) Build up your vocabulary by;
  (*a*) Reading widely.
  (*b*) Using a dictionary whenever new words crop up in your reading.
  (*c*) Making glossaries of words commonly used in your subject.
(*iv*) Practice reading faster (force yourself).
(*v*) Calculate your speed of reading in words per minute as follows:

$$\frac{\text{Length in words}}{\text{Time in seconds}} \times 60 = \text{words per minute}$$

4. How to Learn from TV and Radio Broadcasting

(*i*) Pay close attention to what is said (or shown).
(*ii*) Pick up the main line of argument from the programme.
(*iii*) Make a few key notes.
(*iv*) Immediately after the broadcasting, with your notes in front of you, try to reconstruct the programme in your memory or in a "note" form.
(*v*) Discuss with other students (if possible) if you are not happy with the broadcast.

5. How to Deal with Examination

A. For effective preparation

(*i*) Study systematically from the time you begin your course.
(*ii*) Begin revising at the end of the first week.
(*iii*) Criticise and rewrite your old notes working for all possible memory links between subject and topic.
(*iv*) If possible get together with three or four other students and have a discussion.
(*v*) Check through previous examination papers, if available.

(*a*) Write outline plans for answers.
(*b*) Write complete 'model' answers.
(*c*) Give yourself 'model' examinations.

(*vi*) On the day before exams:
(*a*) Don't try to learn new things.
(*b*) Revise normally or relax completely.
(*c*) Gather examination equipment.
(*d*) Go to bed early.

B. Techniques in the examination Hall

(*i*) Take time to read right through the examination paper and decide exactly what, you have to do and which questions you prefer.
(*ii*) Budget your time by allowing so much per questions and ten minutes at the end for checking.
(*iii*) Plan your answers by jotting down the main ideas and important details in outline form.
(*iv*) Answer your best question first, stick to your time budget.
(*v*) Write simple, direct and to the point. Watch your grammar and spelling, write legibly.
(*vi*) When you have finished writing, check through all your answers for more necessary corrections.

15

Instructional System in Distance Education

INTRODUCTION

It has been repeatedly stressed that in a democratic set up, social justice demands provision of educational facilities to the maximum number of people. The establishment of the institutions for providing education through correspondence is a step towards this objective. The system has enabled thousands of young and even not so young people to see their dreams come true.

In a way the concept of social justice is inbuilt in the system of distance education. The basic concept behind distance education is to provide some effective means to equalise educational opportunities. Higher education is no longer the exclusive preserve of the elitist class. It has reached the doors of those who are its keen seekers. As is well known, since independence there has been a manifold expansion in the field of education—schools, colleges, universities have all multiplied with tremendous pace.

However, well-meaning efforts are afoot to eradicate illiteracy and the task is very complex one; for giving shape to the policies and programmes of enormous dimensions, sustained efforts are needed for long periods before satisfying results surface. As elsewhere, in India also education was provided at almost all levels through the formal system alone, with the exception that a certain section of people, like women and some categories of employees, etc. had the facility of preparing and taking some examinations from the school-leaving-stage to the postgraduate level, in the capacity of what is called 'private candidates'.

This facility did help quite a number of people in satisfying their urge for higher education mainly on the basis of self-help. However, distance education has come to fill the void in an organised, systematic and scientific way. The formal system of education shall continue to play a vital role in the field as nothing can supplant it; but the non-formal system has come to the aid of thousands of people is realising their aspirations. It is supplementing the formal institutions which in a way are inhibited by many constraints to take up the enormous task of providing education in various fields and professions to the ever increasing number of young persons.

The credit for blazing the new trail in the matter of education by correspondence in our country goes to the Delhi University which took the initiative sometime in early sixties. However, the University Grants Commission (UGC) undertook to provide substantial assistance to the universities which instituted correspondence courses, as the Kothari Commission Report (1964-66) strongly advocated the adoption of the system of non-formal education as a means of providing greater opportunities for higher education to those who had no means to get the benefit of college or university education as such.

The UGC laid down certain well-considered guidelines for the organisation and management of correspondence courses, preparation of written material and lessons, evaluation of assignments prepared by the students, number of teachers to be appointed for the purpose, and the like.

In the guidelines, it was, inter alia, suggested that correspondence courses should be started only by those universities which have well-established teaching department noted for their high standards. It was added that the academic responsibility for the contents of correspondence courses in any given subject, and its standards, must be taken by the corresponding subject department in the university.

Unfortunately this has not happened. In fact the hope of a cooperative venture has been belied and the correspondence course teachers and their counterparts in University Departments took up attitudes which could well be said to be the very anti-thesis of what the UGC had suggested or visualised.

Distance learning in higher education was initiated in India during the early sixties in the form of correspondence courses started by a few universities. The seventies saw a vast growth in the number of universities coming forward with their own correspondence programmes. By early eighties there were more than 30 universities and colleges providing correspondence courses of varied nature.

These programmes although provided the flexibility of learning through correspondence mostly had the rigidities such as entry qualifications and examinations comparable to the formal programmes of those universities. A breakthrough in these rigidities occurred when the Andhra Pradesh Open University was established in 1982 exclusively for distance education purpose. This university has adopted the autonomous and flexible structure similar to the Open University of UK.

INDIRA GANDHI NATIONAL OPEN UNIVERSITY

In the last twenty five years (1960-85) of the open university system of distance education through correspondence courses, many weaknesses of the system came to light, therefore, there was a vital need to make the system impactful through the establishment of a national open university, hence IGNOU was established and the system of higher education through distance learning entered a new stage in India with the launching of the Indira Gandhi National Open University (IGNOU) in September, 1985. The university has been assigned the responsibility to coordinate the distance learning system in the country and determine its standards.

A few features envisaged by the Government of India for the IGNOU are as follows:

(*i*) Programme will consist of undergraduate degree as distance education. Diplomas will be in areas such as distance education, management, rural development, computer service and creating writing.

(*ii*) Emphasis will be on the areas of relevance to the needs of women and teachers.

(*iii*) Structuring of courses will be on a modular pattern with the facility for accumulation of credits. Arrangement for transfer of credits from formal to non-formal system and vice-versa is to be provided.

(*iv*) Separate Radio and TV channels will be sought.

(*v*) An open university system is aimed at, IGNOU taking the lead in integrating and cooperating with State level open universities also. Academic guidelines and finance will be provided to the open universities.

The above features provided only a very superficial picture about the nature and structure of the new National Open

University. Probably a detailed formulation of aims of such a university, analysis of the needs and characteristics of the target population, studying the nature, potential and feasibility of variety of media which suit not only the instructional aims but also the characteristics of the target population, selecting the most suitable contributions of media, deciding the mode of utilizing and presenting the media and formulating the pattern of feedback mechanism may have to be worked out for effective organisation of the programmes.

The preset paper attempts to suggest a few concrete ways of integrating the various media and resources available for distance education in order to evolve an effective and feasible instructional system for the open university. The already proposed framework of the IGNOU is broadly accepted and the focus of this chapter is to suggest details concerning the instructional system within that framework.

Aims of Higher Education

It may be worthwhile to reiterate the main aims of higher education. Generally it aims at not only imparting and enchancing specialised knowledge and skills in different areas of learning, but also develop leadership qualities in its clientele in order to take up leadership roles in various fields. These qualities would include, both the cognitive abilities as well as certain affect attributes.

The cognitive abilities are of crucial significance when one considers that personnel trained in higher education would be called upon to examine critically different situations, analyse them to identify the problems in the context of the needs of the community and take decisions through a problem solving approach.

Since the leadership role shall have to be played in different walks of life in close association with members of the community, certain affect attributes such as social sensitivity, and social justice, objective and democratic outlook, sense of quality, and scientific attitude are of extreme importance.

The distance learning system in higher education also will generally aim at these objectives; however, the focur may vary to some extent from the formal system according to the varied needs of the target population.

Learner Characteristics of Distance Education

Learners at high education level are mature enough in case of language comprehension and mental development. They are also expected to be self-motivated; this is especially true in the case of clientele of distance education.

These qualities of the target population enables the clientele to carry out instruction through self-learning ways as well as through intersectional processes. The clientele of distance education, although may have such common attributes, would vary considerably in terms of their educational needs, and socio-economic conditions, and background qualifications.

The varied aims of higher education and the characteristics and needs of learners who enter the system would be the main consideration while organising instructional system in the Open University.

THE TEACHING-LEARNING CONCEPT

Teaching by correspondence has become an accepted mode of learning in the system of education and it has acquired for itself a position which is quite unique. A new system in a way generates a set of sceptics. But fortunately the 'doubting thomases' in this case has a short span of life because of the actual impact made by the system and the number of students enrolled in various countries for these courses. The Open University, London has been a pace-setter in the matter of providing quality education through correspondence.

This university had created a niche for itself in the world of higher education. It has set methods and standards of instruction which, to say the least, compare favourably with those of any other well established university in England or elsewhere. Apart from the multi-dimensional nature of its courses, including those of professional and technical faculties, the uniqueness of this University lies in the fact that its courses and learning programmes are based on inter-disciplinary approach and a multi-media technique.

The methods of instruction comprise correspondence courses, radio instructions, TV viewing, use of taped education material, discussions and teacher-student contacts. Most of the teaching is done over television and radio. The very fact that the Open University has large number of students on its rolls and who devote 10 to 12 hours of study per week, is an indication of the measure of the success of its programmes, the seriousness of the students and the impact of its highly talented faculty.

It is not only the provision of opportunity for higher education that is important, but the success or otherwise of the whole system depends upon the quality of the teaching programmes and the way in which these are carried out and the contact established with the students.

In countries like Sweden, France, USA, Australia, Canada to mention just a few, a large measure of success has been achieved in working the system because steps to ensure quality were thoughtfully initiated, evolved and carried through. In India our main concern has, so far, been in terms of number as such.

Rapid physical expansion of correspondence education, establishing of open universities in some States and finally of the Indira Gandhi National Open University in New Delhi, is a matter of great satisfaction for the reasons which have already been ascribed; above but the real success of these institutions would be judged by their clientele in particular, and by the society in general, on the basis of the quality of instructional material which their students receive, its time factor, proper and regular delivery of the lessons and the seriousness and sincerity with which the assignments given to the students are evaluated and returned to them with proper guidance and encouragement.

It has well been said: "correspondence department is more than a mill receiving and grinding out study guides because qualified teachers who are trained in the specialised kind of teaching conceive it their duty to set up and keep oiled the machinery which encourages and rewards excellence in teaching".

Two things need to be noted here. First, that people who are to teach through correspondence should have acquired specialised kind of teaching skill, and second that the ideal should be to attain excellence in teaching which in a general way is considered to be the objective of every institution of higher education like a university. But in our case the hiatus between what ought to be and what in actuality obtains is quite wide.

A scrutiny of any advertisement for recruitment of teachers in any correspondence course institution would provide ample testimony that no special skill or training course, etc. for the purpose are required; rather there are hardly any facilities provided by the universities for the acquisition of such specialised skills or training.

It has to be accepted that the back-bone or correspondence teaching is the quality of the material produced and its proper printing, etc., which alone can create an appreciative impact on the mind of the student.

Not only that; the regular instalments of lessons or unit of lessons, is the *sine qua non* of the proper working of the system. There should be no haphzard manner of splitting the prescribed course to be gone through in a year into some number of lessons. As a matter of fact it has well been suggested that adequate care needs to be taken to see that the split of units is logical, viable and sound.

The system of education through correspondence would remain incomplete if the students who enroll themselves for study through this system just have an attitude of accepting something which has been sent to them, indulging in rote learning as is done by other students, and then reproducing the information so stored at the time of the examination. The material received should inspire and impel the student to write back his genuine impressions; he should be required to do his home assignment to the maximum extent as part of the process and no laxity should be shown in this matter.

But just as in the case of colleges, the house-tests have lost their relevance or seriousness, so, in the same manner and for mostly the same reasons, the written assignments in correspondence institutions are not taken care of in very serious manner by the students, and whatever small percentage of these are received, is casually gone through by the teachers it has become more or less a routine thing, something like the ritual of marking the university examination answer-books. Perhaps we read less, we write far less and thereby hangs a tale.

The regular receipt of studiously prepared lessons and honestly done assignments by the students alone can ensure the success of education through correspondence. The UGC guidelines have very correctly stressed the need for compulsory submission of response sheets on assignments given to the students.

As a matter of fact the universities should insist that at least 50 per cent of the total number of assignments given to the students are responded to by them as has been done by the University of Mysore, even though the UGC has prescribed a lesser percentage. One sided flow of instructional material without any adequate response and feedback from the students is not in the larger interests of the students themselves.

The quality of education imparted through correspondence courses would greatly depend on the steady and continuous two-way flow. If there are fewer and irregular submissions of home assignments given to the correspondence students then the quality of education acquired by them would be poor.

Besides the home assignments given to the students, it may perhaps be appropriate to think in terms of giving them 2 to 3 tests per term. This would make them more serious in their studies and may result in improving the quality of the academic programmes undertaken by them. It is not being suggested in any manner to introduce an element of routine examination with which many an evil is associated.

The tests could be on the reliable basis formulated in open universities elsewhere. We can with advantage adopt many of the good processes in vogue in those institutions like tutorials, etc. but should be careful in avoiding those things which do not fit into the conditions obtaining in our country on account of poverty and certain other related factors.

In the system of distance education the effectiveness of its academic programmes would depend to a large extent on the efficient and smooth handling of the job by the administrative apparatus of the concerned institutions. The procedures and the rules, etc. formulated for administrative purposes should be flexible but the principle of accountability should not be overlooked.

The idea is to ensure that no bottlenecks are created to affect adversely the pursuit of the academic programmes by the faculty and the students. The timely despatch of lessons to every student, and the distribution without delay of the assignments received back from them to the members of the faculty, would enable the institutions to provide satisfactory services to the students some of whom may be actually belonging to far off places.

The work regarding despatch of lessons etc. should not be treated at par with the disposal of routine office dak. For this purpose, the administrative staff also should be provided adequate type of training so that they are able to realise the importance of instructional material reaching the students in time; similarly, equal importance needs to be bestowed on sending back assignments evaluated by the teachers without delay.

The usual hierarchical pattern of administrative units may not be of much relevance or use in the correspondence education. The whole structure of administration should be functionally so organsied as to facilitate smooth two-way flow of educational material. The success of distance education, at least to some extent, would depend upon the way and the manner in which the administrative set-up has been organised and functions.

There is nothing wrong in borrowing with advantage some of the good things and practices from those open universities which have achieved commendable success in their programmes. But any attempt to adopt in a wholesale way, the programmes, procedures and methods etc. which are relevant to the students in those countries, would perhaps not be of much use to the institutions here.

Again, one sometimes finds that we are caught in the web of some cliches and high-sounding phraseology used in the material coming from countries like America. This attempt to blindly import something not relevant to our circumstances and conditions should be discouraged. We should make attempts to evolve our own pattern, our own methods and procedures to deal with the task facing us. It would do us some good to be innovative ourselves.

CLASSIFICATION OF ALTERNATIVE MEDIA FOR DISTANCE LEARNING

Here we attempt to provide the educational potential advantages and limitations of various media specially in the context of higher education through distance learning in the Indian conditions. An understanding of these aspects of each medium is important in order to arrive at effective and feasible distance learning systems. A variety of media has been presented here mainly with the purpose of highlighting their place in distance learning.

This becomes necessary especially due to the over-emphasis being placed on hard technologies such as computer and television; while these media are to be utilized wherever necessary other media cannot be completely ignored. Table 15.1 presents a classification of various media available for distance learning system.

Table 15.1: Classification of Various Alternative Media Available for Distance Learning

Media Category	*Media Items*	*Further Specifications*	*Potential and Merits*	*Limitations/ Demerits*
A. Printed Material	1. Self-learning Material	Linear FLM, Branching PLM, Deviated PLM, Modules, etc.	Providing basic understanding, self-instructional	Mostly verbal, human interaction missing
	2. Assignment and workbook	Field work, Practical Work, Written Work, etc.	Development of skills, interest, application ability etc.	
	3. Supplementary reference material	Library books, Magazines, Enrichment material, News-papers, etc.	Additional information	
B. Audio Material	1. Radio	Educational telecast broad-casts and general programmes	Providing basic information, relatively cheap medium, great accessibility	Verbal and hence can not attract for long
	2. A.T.R.	Recorded lectures radio programmes, discussions, etc.	Providing basic information, repeatable	Limited accessibility
	3. Telephone	For interactions	Comes quite handy in clarifying things	Relatively expensive and inaccessible
C. Video Material	1. Telecast	Educational telecast and general programmes	Great accessibility, better impact due to visual attribute	Relatively costlier, lack human interaction
	2. C.C.T.V.	Recorded and live programmes	Manipulation possible	Limited accessibility
	3. V.T.R.	Stored lectures, interactive programmes, life situations, etc.	For later use	Limited accessibility
	4. Other visual gad-gets and materials	Projectors, graphic material, charts, pictures, etc.	More accessibility	

(Contd.)

(Contd.)

Media Category	*Media Items*	*Further Specifications*	*Potential and Merits*	*Limitations/ Demerits*
D. Computer	1. C.A.I.	Systems such as PLATO	Basic knowledge, understanding and applications to some extent, self-instructions, interaction to some extent	Relatively expensive higher cognitive abilities and affect attributes not taken care of
	2. C.M.I.	Managerial purposes through computer network	More effective and efficient management of instruction	Relatively expensive
E. Interaction Session	Discussion, Seminar, Lecture, etc.	Human interaction to varied extents	Development of higher cognitive abilities and affect attributes as well as basic understanding of subject matter	Has to be supported by media such as printed material audio and video presentations

PROPOSED DESIGN OF INSTRUCTION

Management of instruction under the open university system would mainly involve three agencies. The Central Open University Campus, the Regional Centres and the Study Centres. Apart from these the institutions under the formal system of higher education is also expected to provide its infrastructure and human resources, wherever needed.

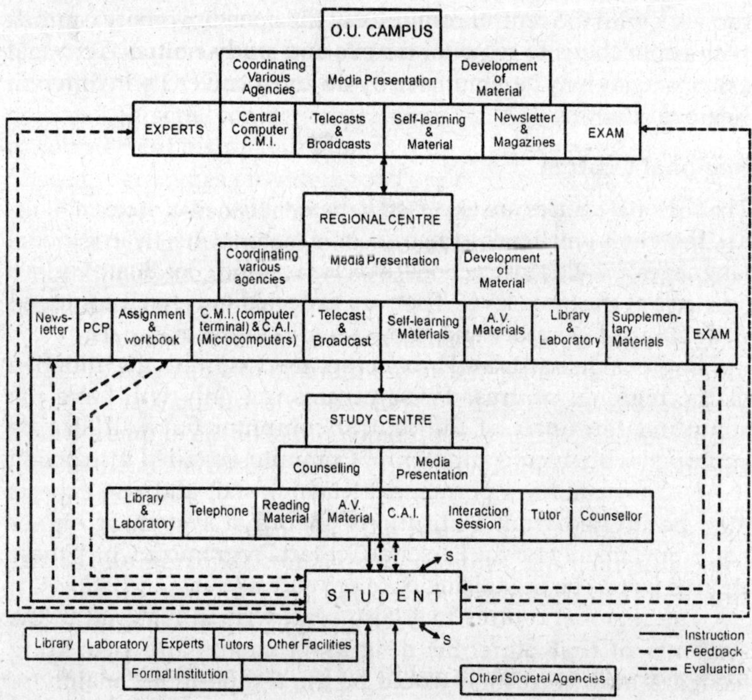

Fig. 15.1: Proposed Design of Instruction in the Open University

Facilities under other societal agencies such as museums, libraries etc., should also be utilised for distance learning. Figure 15.1 provides a diagrammatic representation of the proposed design of instruction in the Open University.

OPEN UNIVERSITY CAMPUS

There are three major functions expected of the open university campus. These are the production and development of instructional materials, instructional presentation through certain media and coordinating various agencies involved in the open university system. The campus is expected to telecast educational programmes through a separate channel for various courses for country-wide utilization. Self learning modular material for certain courses may be sent to the students by post from the campus.

The open university can publish a magazine or/and newsletter for the use of the clientele. There could be a nation-wide computer network with the central computer at the open university campus with connections to regional centres and study centres. Terminal examinations may be conducted by the open university in different Regional Centres.

Regional Centres

The regional centres are expected to be established at state capitals. These centres will develop instructional material mostly in regional languages, provide instructional experiences and coordinate various agencies at the State level. They are expected to be well equipped with library, laboratory and various audio-visual materials.

Regional telecasts and broadcasts are done with the initiative of the regional centres. These centres not only will have the computer terminals of the central computer but will also be equipped with microcomputer for Computer Assisted Instruction (CAI). They can have permanent teaching staff and also experts may be invited from institutions of formal system of higher education, mainly for the Personal Contact Programme which these centres would be organising once or twice a year.

The regional centres may also send written material to the students of that State. Sending assignments and providing feedback after correction would be the responsibility mainly of the regional centres.

Study Centres

The study centres are expected to be quite accessible to the students. They are expected to visit the nearest study centre for clarifying issues with the tutor, making use of the reading and audio-visual material, and also to learn through the computer assisted instruction.

The tutors attached to the study centres may be on honorary arrangement from the nearby colleges or universities. These centres would also provide opportunities for the students of a particular area to interact with each other. They may clarify certain issues through telephone too. There could be a person, always available at the study centre to deal with students' questions and doubts.

Institutions from Formal System

Institutions such as colleges and university centres from the formal system would provide their physical as well as human resources for the benefit of the students of the open university. They in turn may make use of instructional material developed by the open university. For this purpose an arrangement at the national level will have to be established with the help of the UGC.

Other Societal Agencies

Several educational and non-educational agencies of the society such as industries, research institutions, national and regional research laboratories, museums, libraries may be brought into the open university system. Coordination at central, regional as well as local levels may have to be established for this purpose.

Curriculum Development and Evaluation

In the context of the federal nature of India, and the present position of education being in the concurrent list, it may be required to have a definite stand regarding the roles of the IGNOU, the State open universities and the regional centres with regard to curriculum development. While it is desirable to have a central control regarding the nature, structure and content of the curriculum the regional centres and State open universities should be provided with the freedom to have various courses separately, for the concerned States, based on the local needs.

This would mean that the decision-making regarding the curriculum development and organisations would rest to a great extent at the regional levels. However, it is emphasized that the central open university campus has a significant role to play regarding curriculum development and maintenance of standards of instruction.

The central campus should have in the long run a full-fledged team with all necessary equipment for materials development which is quite a specialised job, especially when various new technologies are used. As a suitable and effective integration of these media is also a necessity for evolving an effective system, a team of specialists in different content areas and media working at preferably one place is desirable.

Getting material developed by different people on honorary basis, from various institutions may be initially required but this brings in its lot discontinuity and lack of sequencing among the various media used in the system. Material developed once should go through necessary modification and refinement through its use over a period of time.

As far the evaluation of students is concerned the regional centres and the study centres would take the main responsibility of formative evaluation and feed-back through tests, assignments, workbooks, etc.

The summative evaluation in the form of terminal examinations can be conducted by either the regional centres or the central open university campus depending on the geographical distribution of students offering a particular course.

16

Distance Learning—A Cost Effective System of Education

INTRODUCTION

Even today India in not a fully developed rich nation, but we need education for all, hence cost effectiveness has to be ensured from the point of view of an individual and nation both. Hereunder, we would like to discuss this aspect in respect of distance education.

ECONOMICS OF HIGHER EDUCATION

Even before independence, the Indian leaders and people had realised that in the transformation of the Indian economy in particular, and the society in general, higher education would have to play a determining role. With freedom, fresh vistas were opened for developing human potential and expertise which could be used in a progressive realisation of economic goals and social objectives.

The Government of India, in coordination with the State Governments, was anxious to initiate immediate steps not only for a radical reform of the entire higher educational system built during the British period, but also for large scale expansion that would bring higher educational facilities within the reach of majority of youth who had long been decided this opportunity.

Continuous expansion of higher education has wide-range financial implications. It requires large financial resources of both kinds—fixed as well as working capitals—in order to accommodate the rising student population and escalating costs. Expenditure on higher education (provided in the regular institutions) is bound to be high, particularly in the context of diversified courses; professional and technical courses, especially, are highly expenditure-oriented compared to general types.

Recent years have witnessed an escalation in expenditure for college/university education due to a rise in the salaries of teachers (constituting about 60 per cent of the maintenance expenditure) and outlay on buildings, hostels, laboratories, library books and journals, equipment and other research and teaching tools. Over the years, however, the proportion of expenditure borne directly by the students has declined steeply.

The contributions from other private sources, such as by way of donations, endowments, gifts and other charities for higher education too have constantly been on the decline, largely owing to the inertia of the institutions in tapping this source, the increasing expectation (or dependence) on the Exchequer of the Welfare State and/or due to high inflation; heavy taxation, extension of public regulation, control and ownership of all forms of assets, and so on.

The private sources of finance for higher education including fees have, in short, ceased to make any appreciable contribution to higher educational development.

With the decline in contribution of fees and drying up of private munificence, and the fast rate of rise in annual expenditure of universities and colleges, the major responsibility of financing higher education has fallen on the public source of finance, i.e. the Government. The policy of expansion has already meant the Public Exchequer sharing the expenditure upto 75-80 per cent, the rest being met by fees and other private sources.

The gap between the fees paid by students and the quantum of expenditure required to be incurred on them, has been getting more pronounced from year to year, particularly on the side of science, engineering, medical and other technical courses. As Gore has rightly pointed out, the more expensive the course of study one pursues, the greater is the Government subsidy.

The fees charged by colleges/universities are set much below any plausible estimate of what it costs to educate a student, and there is utter lack of rationale in the present arrangement. There is no provision, under the present pattern of financing, for occasional revision of the rates of fees, if and when there are notable changes in the overall price levels.

The same is the case in respect of hostel and other services of the higher educational institutions which are highly subsidised. The mixed fee-subsidization system is gradually changing into a near pure subsidy system, and the financial dependence on the Government is almost complete.

In recent years, much of the debate as to the future of higher education has revolved around mainly the financial resources needed to match the increase in enrolment and escalating expenditure. There are already sure signs that Government funds for colleges/universities would become more and more scarce in the years ahead.

Probably the likely growth of expenditure in colleges/universities had been underestimated by the policy makers—it has grown much more rapidly than on other educational levels. Also, measured in terms of per capita income, it is relatively more expensive to roll out a graduate in the low income countries like India than in any of the economically advanced countries.

In short, we have not been successful so far, to evolve a cohesive plan of action for the growth and financing of higher education. The inability of the Government now to meet the growing needs of the institutions and the financial squeeze that looms ahead make inevitable a reappraisal of the policy.

Expansion of higher educational institutions is not bad per se; it might generate economies of scale by way of a reduction in the average cost of provision of higher education in colleges, universities and other institutions. However, these economies of scale will be wiped out if there is over-expansion. There is also an inverse relationship between over-expansion and higher educational efficiency.

Over-expansion can be achieved only at the cost of watering down quality. This has been witnessed in the case of many higher educational institutions especially in urban centres where they are concentrated. The result is overstretched universities and colleges, oversized classes and sub-standard buildings and equipment which are aggravated on account of paucity of funds. In the process, the human inputs of teachers required for the system has also been overlooked.

The increase in the university/college population has not only meant worsening of the teacher-pupil ratio but also aggravation of the amenity gap. The present policy of higher education has in short led to lowering of standards, mismatch between expansion and availability of money, men and materials, and the 'haves' benefiting more than the 'have-nots' from the system.

EDUCATIONAL PLANNING—COSTS OF ALTERNATIVE METHODS

In educational planning, the determination of the costs of alternative methods of realising set objectives that are feasible is the first step towards working out the economics of a system. When the costs are compared with the benefits that are likely to accrue to the society after the given resources are invested, an idea about the alternative choices of development paths is obtained which, in turn, form the basis for taking an appropriate decision about a policy choice.

Such an exercise is essential because in every country, irrespective of its stage of development, financial constraints do exist since the budget is never unlimited. It is, therefore, imperative for the policy-makers to devise cost-effective methods for imparting relevant education to a cross section of students.

In India, the cost consideration is more important because educational efforts, as measured in terms of income elasticity of educational expenditure have declined over the successive plan periods in spite of the fact that a large segment of population is yet to be covered under the existing network of education programmes. This calls for devising an efficient and economical system of education which can cope with the emerging challenges.

There is a consensus among the educationists that the conventional system (CS) of education has proved to be inefficient in respect of (*a*) ensuring equality of educational opportunity to various groups of aspirants, (*b*) enhancing the quality of education, and (*c*) minimizing the cost of expansion of educational services.

Among the major causes of these-shortcomings in the Indian context are the pressure of enrolment of students on the university system and increasing demands of education on public finance especially when government funds under plan allocation are declining. The budgeted plan expenditure on education has come down from 7.2 per cent in the First Plan.

The approach of imparting knowledge at a distance by making use of various forms of educational media is considered an alternative to CS and is popularly known as distance learning system (DLS). On the consideration of the expected economies of scale and extensive coverage of both educational programmes and the target groups, this system has received wide recognition in developed and developing countries alike. While taking into account the cost aspects of teaching-learning process, we shall discuss below the economic viability of the DLS.

An exercise in cost analysis aims at relating costs to some measure of output and in educational systems, the students form the usual measure of output. In the CS, staff salaries, which are related to the predetermined structure of scales of pay for various categories of employees, constitute more than two-thirds of the total expenditure on higher education. The proportion of fixed costs of supplying teaching aids and equipment, library and other infrastructural facilities is, therefore, relatively small as compared to the variable costs which are related to the unit of output, i.e. students.

Since in the CS, the number of students in a classroom is fixed, the influence of student number in minimising the costs of educational services is limited. As against this, the share of fixed costs incurred on inputs (i.e. preparation of teaching material and related infrastructure facilities) is relatively more in the DLS than in CS and this is determined independently of the student numbers.

The economies of scale are therefore considerably high since under the DLS, teaching is not confined to a limited number of students as in the case of a classroom. The variable or marginal costs, therefore, decline as the number of students increase. There are, however, limits to which economies of scale can be realised even under the DLS.

In the following discussion, we shall isolate the factors which have significant bearing on the costs of DLS. An attempt shall also be made to indicate the methods and forms of teaching which would be cost-efficient and cost-effective.

In the generalisation of the thesis that DLS is less expensive than CS, a great deal of caution needs to be exercised while drawing conclusions in regard to the economic and social gains of investment on the development of DLS. In this respect, the following factors should be borne in mind. First, the choice of different educational media like printed materials, radio, TV, etc. for imparting education through various forms of distance education, such as correspondence and audio-visual methods, would have varying degree of impact on both economic costs as well as efficiency in teaching.

Second, the extent of coverage in terms of selection of the number of courses to be offered to different categories of students would influence the quantity and quality of inputs; thereby affecting the costs of education. Lastly, in each of the above cases, the costs of organisational set-up and training of distance educators would vary considerably.

Moreover, as India is a multilingual country, the teaching of various courses in different languages will accordingly multiply the costs. The extent of economies of scale therefore may not be reaped as expected. And if the duplication of courses by different institutions of distance education remains unchecked, the costs will escalate further.

It follows that while planning for education, a planner has to bear in mind the following two dominant considerations. First, the cost-efficiency and cost-effectiveness of the system; and second, the educational benefits which might accrue to an individual in terms of value added gains in social status and incremental gains in income.

These benefits should accrue to people in such a way that they stimulate economic and social development. In the field of education, the cost-benefit aspects are, by and large, not easily susceptible to measurement owing mainly to conceptual and statistical problems. The decision for promotion of educational activities therefore, cannot be strictly based on rigorous economic analysis.

However, since limited resources are required to be invested judiciously, a distance education institution has to consider different kinds of costs and devise methods to minimise them. Broadly speaking, there are fixed costs, which are not influenced by the number of students, and common costs (or overhead costs) related to the whole operation.

The latter types are also known as variable costs and are related to activities like course production and distribution of course materials, etc. Variable costs are influenced by two major factors: one is related to the number of students, while the other is associated with the number of courses offered. The courses on offer have two components: the new courses that are to be initiated and the courses which are continuing and need to be maintained.

The choice of educational media has significant bearing on both cost efficiency as well as cost-effectiveness of the DLS. We may reiterate that of the various media those which are used for imparting knowledge are books and journals, radio and television, films, video tapes, board and chalk and teaching machines like computers. The role of all these media in extending the benefits of lectures given to one group of students to the students in other regions is significant as these provide an opportunity to all those who otherwise would not benefit from the lecture.

Such tasks are easily performed through the use of video tapes, audio cassettes and printed materials which can be distributed at a low cost through correspondence method. The choice of educational media has, therefore, significant bearing on the following aspects.

(*i*) Widening of opportunity for learners of different educational backgrounds and the needs for improving standards;

(*ii*) Due to wider coverage of educational service, a considerable degree of the economies of scale may be realised which, in effect, may generate savings for further investments on such activities as expansion of the distance learning programmes as well as constant revision of course contents;

(*iii*) Effectiveness of an educational programme would improve considerably since the slow learners would be able to proceed at their own pace; and

(*iv*) Profession of teaching would become challenging since the teacher using educational media would find himself communicating with a far larger group of people than he previously interacted with.

The choice of media is thus crucially important for widening the reach of education, increasing its cost-effectiveness and enhancing its relevance through constant revision of course contents.

The forms of educational media through printed materials, audio-visual method and teaching machines can meet educational requirements of different categories of learners. But, the cost function for each medium of instruction would vary depending upon the package of courses that are offered and the number of students using them. The dimension and effectiveness of costs associated with different forms of media may be briefly outlined as under.

In the category of printed media of instruction are included books, programmed texts, journals, pamphlets, booklets, etc. The reading of printed materials is one of the oldest means of acquiring knowledge which is still very common at all levels of education. The production of printed materials has the tendency to become cheap as the number of students using such materials increases. The advantage of this form of media lies in making the learning process cost-effective.

A student can learn at his own pace and revise a lesson which is not so well comprehended. For teachers, it helps avoid duplication of lectures which are available from the best lecturers in the world. It, thus, provides them ample time and opportunity to concentrate on improving instructional techniques in order to facilitate the process of comprehension.

For learners, programmed texts are so designed as to make the lesson easily understood and a student himself can assess the extent to which he has learned the printed materials as he proceeds. Of all the forms of educational media, books, journals, etc. are therefore, heavily relied upon as an effective means of imparting knowledge.

The cost components of preparing reading materials are spread over two major items. One is salary of the staff (academic and secretarial) and the other is stationery (paper, ink, duplicating machine, etc.) used for production. The total costs including the costs of printing, design and editing of course materials will depend on the standard of material being produced.

The average cost per unit will, however, come down as economies of scale are achieved over long print runs. It follows that learning at a distance through correspondence system is more cost-efficient as the variable costs per student decline due to increase in the number of students. Also, the fixed costs of maintaining the organizational set up including material and service components remain reasonably low because of involvement of high labour intensity and low cost equipment in the process of production of study materials.

As against the method of learning through printed word, the audio-visual instructional techniques are capital intensive and therefore costlier. In this category of educational media are included radio, audio-visual tapes, gramophones, telephone, television, video tapes, films and overhead transparencies, etc.

The costs of material inputs like buildings, equipment and media personnel including course designers and producers are much higher than production of courses for distribution through correspondence method. Moreover, transmission and reception costs significantly add to the total costs.

The costs of transmission, which depend on the number of hours and the number of centres being used by the media, of course, magnifies the fixed costs, while the reception costs relating to (*a*) equipment like radio, television and their maintenance, (*b*) teachers' guides and training, and (*c*) students' cost on stationery contribute to variable costs. However, the increase in coverage of distance teaching programme encompassing a large beneficiary group of students generates economies of scale.

In the present era, the phenomenon of rise in prices of almost all the goods and services has become a major factor which influences the costs of inputs. The total cost of education is determined by the extent of increase in price index. Of the total education budget, the staff salaries account for more than two-thirds of the gross expenditure in the CS.

Even a marginal rise in price index leads to substantial increase in the total cost of education. As the proportion of staff salaries in the DLS is much less than in the CS, it can be expected that the former will be chapter than the latter. Within the DLS the extent of increase in cost of education through correspondence method (i.e. printed media) may be said to be higher than the corresponding rise in costs of audio-visual methods (i.e. through radio and TV), because the prices of stationery are observed to be increasing at a higher rate than the prices of video tapes and cassettes.

Moreover, with the advancement in technology, the costs of the latter methods may be expected to decline further. It can, thus, be reasoned that in inflationary conditions, the DLS will tend to be cheaper than the CS and the utilisation of information technology like radio and TV would be both cost-efficient and cost-effective.

However, a major shortcoming of teaching through radio and television transmission is that the student cannot control his learning situation. The programme is transmitted at a particular time and there is no way of playing back any material which has not been understood. Such a problem can be solved by using cassette or video-tape. This will, however, increase the individual costs of learning and therefore, the expected economies of scale may not be realised.

This is true particularly of such devices as teaching machines like computers which require appropriate development of software and hardware, the costs of which are enormous. Obviously, the magnitude of resources required for operationalising teaching machines in the prevailing Indian situation would be very high but it is not a vital concern because we have a high level of development in communication technology.

DISTANCE EDUCATION AND THE GOAL OF EQUALITY OF OPPORTUNITY

The other side of the coin is that after experience with the attempt to promote the goal of equality of higher educational opportunity, serious doubts are being raised now about its actual implementation. The so-called higher educational boom, instead of equalising opportunities, has in fact legitimatised, or even aggravated, inequality over the years. Most of the seats in the existing higher educational institutions have been appropriated by those belonging to middle and upper income strata of society, leaving the vast masses out of the ambit of benefit.

Nearly 80 per cent of our university/college entrants come from the top 30 per cent of the society. Those that really come from the 'poor' families, will not be more than 5 per cent of the total student population. The utopian hope of democratization through higher education has thus failed to happen although higher education remained the locus of the myth of equality. This has got further exacerbated as the benefit of subsidy really has gone to students belonging to the well-off section of society. Everyone is entitled to the same amount of the generous public subsidy regardless of his/her capacity to pay.

For the majority of the students it has meant money that their parents or they could well have afforded while for others, the minority, this is inadequate, and they are not therefore in a position to take advantage of university/college education. The main reason for keeping fees low in universities, colleges and other professional/technical institutions was to help the poor families and promote equality, but what has taken place is the monopolizing of seats available in colleges and universities by the well-to-do classes in the society.

The present arrangement under which nearly two-third of the expenditure on higher education is met by public funds is neither equitable nor efficient. The privileged groups forget the fact that a good majority of their age-group population is unable to go to higher educational institutions. If we opt for a system wherein the privileged group, which account for a majority in colleges, universities, IITs and other technical/professional institutions, meets a reasonable proportion of the expenditure instead of leaving the tax-payer to foot it almost fully, what is wrong with it?

Under the existing situation, to defend grants for higher education on the ground of social and economic equality is a monstrous perversion of the truth. Two-thirds portion of the grants go to "the haves". It is clear that the economic burden on the people may well require some adjustments. Perhaps a combined system of grants and loans, as is prevalent in many other countries, can be devised.

In order to alleviate infrastructural bottlenecks, a considerably high magnitude of resources would be required for strengthening the network of communication media. More importantly, for making full use of such facilities, the purchasing power of people has to be augmented through appropriate economic and media policies so that people can afford to buy equipment like TV/radio so as to take advantage of education services.

The management and administrative aspects of such services, including maintenance of equipment, should also be taken into account in planning for DLS because the costs are considerably high and, by any reckoning, the resource constraints have been a major impediment.

Till the time educational media are made accessible to a large population, the print media through correspondence courses would have to be heavily relied upon for dissemination of knowledge under the DLS.

It is, however, essential for a planner to make it sure that the demand for correspondence education is high enough to generate economies of scale and that the DLS serves the category of students for which it is principally designed and developed. Conventionally, the DLS is expected to cater the educational needs of housewives, employed persons and those who belong to weaker sections of the society and the therefore unable to meet the costs of formal education. The fact is that many institutions of correspondence education are termed as non-viable because of less than desirable level of enrolment, which indicates that expected economies of scale cannot be realised in these institutions.

The correspondence method has, however, limited impact on the equality of education, especially because prepared texts are by and large non-interactive since in most cases the reading materials are not developed under the 'course team system' or author/editors combined system. The practice has been that while preparing the text books, the author has hardly any knowledge of the standard of the students and, therefore, there is no way to know whether the material put in by the author is understood by the students or not.

In order to make the process of learning more interactive, programmed texts however need to be prepared and by indicating correct responses, the texts should enable the student to see whether he understands the material as he proceeds. This method however may not be as effective as audio-visual instruction or face-to-face teaching in class situation, because in the latter case students may seek clarifications, wherever required.

Another reason for the low quality of education under correspondence method may be attributed to the admission of largely such students whose academic performance has generally been poor. It has been observed that most of the students who are not able to secure admission in regular institutions for various socio-political and academic reasons, are studying through the method of correspondence. This is evident from the fact that more than two-thirds of them are non-working and educationally deprived persons.

Keeping in view the inherent limitations of printed materials (i.e. books, pamphlets, etc.) and the social and academic backgrounds of the students of correspondence courses, it can be said that the quality of education would be much lower than desired. Therefore, in the discussion on cost analysis which generally shows that the DLS is economical as compared to the traditional methods of teaching, we should duly take into account the quality factor in order to make an objective assessment of a programme on the basis of proper comparisons of both the cost of inputs of various methods of realising a set of objectives vis-à-vis the value of outputs as measured by the quality of teaching.

These is, however, no ingenious technique to quantify educational variables especially those related to quality aspects. This problem, therefore, poses formidable difficulties for carrying out cost-effectiveness analysis which should ideally form the basis for taking a proper decision in regard to investments for promotion of educational activities.

What follows is that while keeping in view the societal needs and requirements of the economy, a great deal of care has to be exercised in choosing courses that are to be offered through the DLS, because this system can be both costly as well as cheap depending upon the choice of an educational medium and its capacity to impart education effectively to a large group of knowledge seekers.

THE NEED, CHARACTERISTICS, ECONOMIC ADVANTAGES OF DISTANCE EDUCATION

(*a*) The Need

High education has to adapt itself to the increasing demands from various sections of the people. For this we ought to have alternative higher educational pathways; we need to have an efficient but at the same time flexible system which makes possible for young people to learn while they work, i.e. combining learning and work. It should not however be aimed at substituting or replacing the existing formal system of higher education. Many individuals who cannot complete school education could still make very useful contributions to the society and could have creative lives of their own if there are alternatives.

A properly motivated person, as Alvin Toffler observed, can learn anything he wants to learn without sitting in the classroom. The present higher educational system is based on certain assumptions which are no longer true, one of which is that there is a fixed body of knowledge to be learned, and that once you have learned this fixed information, you can then use it for the next 50 years because the world is going to be the same. This is no longer the case. There is a mismatch between what is taught in the conventional formal higher educational institutions and the needs of the people in the society.

These institutions continue to be strongly tradition-bound, have resisted transformation and are too rigid and too institutionalised. They are preoccupied with producing graduates to fit into a world that is not going to exist when those young men get there. So much emphasis is placed on how to get bigger, and not how to change. As Sir Eric Ashby says they display what a biologist calls 'phylogenetic inertia".

In order to bring about some semblance of social justice, it is imperative that this skewed distribution of educational facilities should be altered in favour of the traditionally deprived sections of the population. This can be done by utilising modern communication technologies, which "have the potential to by-pass several stages and sequences in the process of development encountered in earlier decades. In order to avoid structural dualism, modern educational technology must reach out to the most distant areas and the most deprived sections of the beneficiaries simultaneously with the areas of comparative affluence and ready availability". (National Policy on Education-22). Distance education is the only remedy to achieve these objectives.

(*b*) Characteristics of Distance Education

What does distance education mean? Holmberg (1977) defines it as the various forms of study at all levels "which are not under the continuous, immediate supervision of tutors present with their students in lecture rooms or on the same premises, but which, nevertheless, benefit from planning, guidance and tuition of a tutorial organisation.

Distance education includes all those teaching methods in which, because of the physical separateness of learners and teachers, the inter-active as well as the pre-active phase of teaching is conducted through print, mechanical and electrical devices. Elements of oral tuition and group work (contiguous teaching or face to face teaching) belong here as auxiliary components."

In its application, distance education has come to acquire certain intrinsic characteristics that make it attractive also to people and society, who do not need it as a second chance study opportunity. These characteristics, according to Holmberg (1977), are:

(*a*) The applicability of distance education to large group of students as a kind of mass communication, particularly attractive at times, when educational institutions are over-burdened.

(*b*) The possibility of improving the quality of instruction by assigning the best subject specialists and educationsts available to produce courses for large groups of students.

(*c*) The effectiveness of methods, proved by the students' acquisition of knowledge and skills.

(*d*) The economy of the large group approach and of the facts that the need for residential teaching is eliminated or diminished and that study can take place during leisure time.

(*e*) The possibilities of individualization of the study pace and—to some extent—of study content.

(*f*) The students habit forming experience of work on his/her own, which is felt to develop independence and lead to greater autonomy than other types of study.

(c) Economic and Financial Advantages

Distance higher education through open universities represents what is at present the most significant major innovation in many countries. It is a technique which is getting accepted the worldover as a viable alternative for reaching the deprived sections; it uses extensively a combination of correspondence teaching and new (educational) technology such as radio, television, computers, etc.

The Open University in the UK, for example, is the best known, and extends genuine equality of opportunity for many people. It is a significant departure from the present conventional system; it combines part-time study with full-time employment, and enables the students to spend their period of study in a different, more flexible way than in conventional regular types of institutions.

It will offer opportunities for taking appropriate higher educational courses to those who could not avail of them earlier due to lack of opportunities rather than lack of ability, and that too at any period of their lives when they are so motivated instead of one initial period of full-time higher education. It can thus meet the large backlog of demand from adults for a 'second chance'.

Many of the potential students, as if found in other countries, will be those who could have left school at an early stage. It will be genuinely 'open' in the sense that it will be without walls; formal educational qualifications will not be needed for entry. Besides, women are significantly under-represented in the conventional college/universities; distance education through open universities can recftify this long-countinuing imbalance in the higher education system.

In short, a diversified system of distance higher education can no doubt contribute to the enhancement of personal, social, economic and cultural standards generally. The talents of all classes of people can be developed through this new technique. There will not be any case of "wasteful negligence which allowed genius that happened to be born of lowly parentage to expand itself in lowly work." (Marshall).

There is no question of offering a make-shift project inferior in quality to other conventional institutions or treating it as a dumping ground for those who cannot get themselves admitted in regular colleges/universities. If planned and implemented well, as for example in the UK, West Germany, the USSR and Japan, the students will treat it as good as, or even better than, the higher education provided in regular institutions.

The open universities can also maintain close ties with industrial enterprises, public services and other institutions, vocational establishments etc., and relate some of their courses and training to the economic needs of the society—extending higher education where it is needed, and withholding it where it is not. There is also scope for inter-disciplinary studies and studies in non-traditional areas, which are socially relevant, to be built into the curriculum. It could be broadly based and of a multi-sandwich type.

According to the eminent political scientist H.S. Ferns "Broad education with untilitarian objectives need not be a soft option." "High specialisation," he states, "is often a soft option representing an escape from the need to face the world and society and to contend with the confusions of human experience." Open universities can besides provide courses of an updating or refresher nature to those who wish to make a significant change in their activities.

Teacher education programmes can also be arranged by the open university system especially at primary and secondary level. Distance education can contribute immensely to solving problems of mass illiteracy. This new form of extending higher education, besides, is less expensive. The average cost per student is found to be one-third of the cost in regular conventional institutions the worldover.

The following are some of the important identifiable *financial* advantages of distance education.

(*a*) The possibilities of economies of scale is larger here as it rests on imparting instructions extensively to large numbers. Also the modern media of communication will enable a small number of competent teachers to reach more students and stimulate more response. When enrolment increases, there will be a continuing reduction in cost per student.

(*b*) Expenditure on academic staff will form a smaller proportion of total maintenance expenditure than they do at conventional institutions. In the latter type of institutions, the need is for a much wider range of teaching method as they rely on the lectures. The proportion of total expenditure allotted to personal or external professional research in distance (higher) education will also be smaller relative to conventional institutions, as also the expenditure on building, equipment and technical and administrative resources used by research. The deduction for these purposes will be quite substantial especially at advanced levels, thus increasing the return on higher education.

As Charles Carter rightly observed, "Teaching and research in conventional universities, especially at postgraduate stages are like mutton and wool, joint products of the academic sheep; and the academic sheep in regular universities would not be willing to do without this wool." He thinks, perhaps rightly, that "a nude sheep would make bad mutton." There is also the question of general library facilities. The open university library is meant to be a teaching library rather than a research library, and the expenditure on library facilities will be much lesser as compared to conventional universities.

(*c*) Another crucial difference is that students at the open universities are not required to be present on the campus. This means that the open universities will not be incurring periodical expenditure on students' cultural, recreational and other miscellaneous facilities; besides, the need for providing hostel accommodation will not arise.

An almost similar situation exists with regard to providing staff quarters. As the number of open universities will be limited, there will not be the need for large campuses with all infrastructural facilities; considerable saving can be made as far as construction of buildings is concerned in the case of open universities.

REVIEW OF STUDIES—COST FACTOR IN DISTANCE EDUCATION

A number of studies have also been made to compare the cost of educating students trough the conventional and the open universities. Perry (1976-1) came to the conclusion that "however, one tries to make a comparison of the cost of educating a student in a conventional university and whatever basis one uses for making those comparisons, one is forced to the conclusion that education through open university is relatively very cheap."

According to a crude estimate reported by Perry, the cost students in the UK Open University in 1973 was £ 2749 (which can be an over estimate) against a figure of £ 5250 per student in the comparable faculties of the conventional universities.

In another study, Wagner, Laidlow and Layard, in their paper on the UK Open University assumed a consistency in the quality of graduates produced by the UK Open University and conventional UK universities and on the basis of data available concluded that the Open University was cost efficient relative to conventional UK universities.

In another study, Wagner (1973) calculated the average recurring cost per equivalent undergraduate for the two types of universities. He took the total recurring costs divided it by the number of equivalent undergraduates. One of the problems in estimating comparable costs was that the conventional universities have to bear increased costs on teaching postgraduates. For this purpose, he applied the weightages to postgraduate costs indicated by the British University Grants Committee.

In a similar study of costa at Costa Rican Universidad Estatal a Distancia, Rumble (1981-398) showed that the average cost per year of US $ 795 (at 1980 price and exchange levels), compared very favourably with those found in two of the conventional campus based universities, where they were $ 1,301 (Universidad) de Costa Rica) and $ 2,033 (Universidad Nacional).

Muta (1985-286) reported that the 'direct current expenditure (per student) of the University of Japan is 1/4, 1/3 and 2/3 of that the national universities, public universities and day programme of private universities'.....Otsuka (1984) reported that the direct current expenditure at the Radio and Television Universities in the Peoples' Republic of China is two thirds that of full time students and one third of part time students.

It may also be mentioned that comparatively speaking, the distance learning programmes are not only more cost-effective than the traditional teaching programmes, but they have shown a tendency to come down in the times to come. For example, according to Bates (1984-1).

> "AC-60 audio Cassette, containing one hour of material, can be delivered to an open university students for less than 50 pence. Similarly, a 25 minute television programme can be delivered on video cassette for 75 pence per student—or for

just over $ 2 for an hour's material—if the student returns the cassettes for re-use at the end of the course. 16K microcomputers are now retailing for less than £ 100, and a 48 K microcomputer at pound 125. A video disc player retails for under pound 400 and a video cassette player can be rented in Britain for less than pound 12 a month. All these prices will move lower relative to inflation—rather than higher in future. In comparison, print costs are rising faster than inflation and open university broadcast television productions were averaging over pound 35000 a programme in 1983".

ITEMS OF EXPENDITURE

The open universities will be required to incur expenditure mainly on the following items:

(*i*) Academic and non-academic staff who will be on the regular pay-roll—under the former category open universities will have Professors, Readers, Lecturers, Research officers, etc., and the latter category will consist of administrative staff, editors, proof readers, cartographers, designers, lesson-keepers etc. Besides the regular full time academic staff, if needed, the services of outside component teachers may have to be availed of on payment.

(*ii*) Dispatching of reading and other materials (Postage).

(*iii*) Conduct of examinations.

(*iv*) Development of software and procuring hardware to use mass media and the appointment of supporting staff.

(*v*) Establishment of Library-cum-study centers, organisation of contact programmes, counselling service etc.

The above are the main items of expenditure on distance higher education through open universities. However, considering the vastness of the country, effective use of a multi-media presentation of information, by printed word, taped lectures and video-taped demonstration for individual instruction will be necessary. The 'non-salary' component is likely to be bigger than the 'salary' component in total expenditure. The per student expenditure may be a little high in the initial stages, but this is bound to decline gradually as more and more students enrol themselves and by judicious use of available resources.

FINANCING DISTANCE EDUCATION

For meeting the items of expenditure given above, the main sources of income will be: (*i*) the Government (both Centre and State), and (*ii*) student fees (registration fee, tuition fee, examination fee etc.) A proper system of subsidisation needs to be developed based on certain norms of expenditure per student. The expenditure per student in some countries that have developed this new technique successfully, works out to about one-third of the expenditure in regular university system.

It is ideal to have a system in India under which the students finance at least 45-50 per cent of the recurring expenditure; the rest should be met by Central and State Governments. As the participants in the programme are likely to be mostly employed, this should not cause much of a burden. At present, in some schools directorates of correspondence course (attached to universities), nearly 45 per cent of the expenditure is being met by the students.

Distance higher education in the country has to be evolved according to a master plan, unlike as it happened in the case of conventional higher education. It is a good idea to have an open university for each State, but it should not be done in haste; care has to be taken to see that they have adequate support in the form of human and physical infrastructure and of course finance.

There has to be some kind of a centralised body of distance higher education to coordinate the working of the programme in the country. Also adequate funding should be ensured to maintain quality.

Government funds should not come from many agencies as is in the case of the existing higher education system wherein the need to manage and keep track of funds from so many different sources, subject to different rules and procedures, auditing and review, has created a lot of unmanageable problems.

FINANCIAL AUTONOMY NEEDED

There may be many difficulties besetting the growth of distance higher education. The size of the potential demand cannot be known initially, and the craze for conventional higher education is strong—people may resist change. But looking to the rapid and successful development of this system in many other countries, this new technique appears to be a feasible one. The use of multimedia instructional methods would no doubt mean building up of a new structure, and this would involve proper planning and implementation.

All these obstacles to develop distance education may however prove to be illusory, provided that the system can offer programmes of study of a kind which will attract large numbers. The large scale operation will enable the system to achieve economies of scale. If the programmes are just borrowed from conventional universities and/or a simplification of existing university courses, the system is not likely to be successful. To achieve this, planning and imagination of a higher order, and of an innovative and new kind, is absolutely essential.

The people to implement such a large scale system need not be large, but they have to be independent, enterprising and inventive and who know what they are doing. While recruiting the academic staff, one of the prime considerations should be the aptitude for producing reading materials. The reading materials produced (including books) by the Open University of the UK have become very popular even amongst those studying in conventional colleges/universities. The marketing of these materials has been entrusted there to a separate agency—the Open University Educational Enterprise Ltd.

This could be done by open universities in India too. Besides, modern printing technology has made publication of books, journals etc., easy and economical. By making use of these devices, our open universities can develop reading/learning materials of an innovative nature, in different languages.

These materials should be prepared in such a way that any normal student can study them in his home, and at his own pace. In short, every effort should be made to convince the public (and the employers) that the instruction imparted and degrees awarded by the open universities are as good as, or of equal status with, those offered by conventional colleges/universities

As far as the provision of finance for distance higher education is concerned, it is better to lay down certain norms for it in the beginning itself. The financial question should in fact come before the critical planning decision is made, and not after. The devising of appropriate methods of financing (that takes into account the social objectives) should not be treated as a 'second-order' problem as it happened in the past in the case of the existing regular system of higher education.

Proper attention has also to be paid to the down-to-earth problem of how to share the expenditure between the Government (i.e. the tax-payers) and the students. There has also to be a rational delineation of the respective roles of Central and State Governments as well as the beneficiaries of the new system, i.e. the students, with regard to the sharing of expenditure.

All this would call for a radical departure from earlier strategies relating to the growth and financing of conventional universities/colleges. If this is not recognised in the initial stage itself, many perplexities may arise later, which will affect the very character and efficiency of the new system. Because this had not been sufficiently examined well-in-advance in the case of conventional higher education, it is in the midst of a financial crisis.

Also considering the sheer size and complexity of the new system, its management will not be a simple administrative process amenable to the rigid rules of the Government, especially with regard to finances. The academic, financial and administrative autonomy of the open universities as well as their right to freedom to experiment should be guarded. There has to be a proper coordinating mechanism to reconcile such freedom with public provision of finance.

CONCLUSION

Although it has been established that distance education is less costly than conventional system of education, the cost factor should not be the sole determinant for the introduction of distance education. If distance education has been considered as an alternative to formal system, it should be able to stand on its own and not be a poor relation of the formal systems.

Distance education has to fill a void created by the ever-increasing demand for education and the incapacity of the formal system to meet it. In such a situation, the fact of its being less costly should not be the decisive element in its expansion.

Distance education should not be considered as a means of augmenting financial resources of the universities. In quite a few universities, it has been observed that correspondence courses are considered as the money-spinning devices. Students are admitted without due regard to the academic facilities that can be provided to them. The result is that there are inordinate delays in the preparation of academic materials and evaluation of response sheets from the students. Further, the personal contact programme and the library facilities are almost non-existent. It is no wonder then that such shabbily organised courses yield revenues disproportionate to the academic returns to the students.

Distance education programme should not be considered as a poor relation of the formal system with the universities dumping undesirable elements of the academic staff on these courses. Further a sizable proportion of the staff is on a part-time basis, which hampers the growth of organic relationship between them and their institutions.

In order to accord parity of prestige to the non-formal system, the academic staff should be on a full-time basis and be eligible for all the privileges available to the regular staff of the university. In order to attract and retain highly qualified persons, the staff may be given some special allowances. Furthermore, all promotional avenues should be open to them.

Universities should encourage researchers in the areas of cost-effectiveness and cost-efficiency of the distance education programmes. Moreover, the problems faced by the teachers and students under correspondence education should be subject to review so that prompt remedial action could be taken.

We may conclude that distance education has a vast potential for growth in a country like India. It is much more cost-effective than the traditional system. It has also the capacity to democratise the system of education, which has shown a tendency to be rigid, elitist and traditional. However, planning and implementation of distance education programmes is a challenging task. It requires considerable imagination, foresight and managerial skills. We may hope that our socio-political and academic systems will meet this challenge boldly.

17

Distance Education—A Boon for Neglected Sections of Society

ST, SC, BC, Physically Disabled, Women and Marginal Farmers etc.

INTRODUCTION

In a democratic social order every one must have proper education, therefore, distance education is seen as a popular and democratic appeal to the masses of the people who on any account are unable to attend classes of school, college and university campus. A large majority of our people, ST, SC, BC, physically disabled, marginal farmers etc, remain away from the functioning of our educational institutions, hence the concept of distance education provides them the most wanted opportunity for getting education.

It may be argued that the conceptual structure of Distance Education is nothing more than verbosity. It is the same old wine with new labels. The concepts of Correspondence Education, Mass Media in Teaching, Open University, Radio and Television lessons have all been included in the structure of Distance Education. The concept, therefore, has been comprehensive—a wide spectrum. Correspondence education is not a new experiment in the third world countries.

We are familiar with its limits and delimits. Despite the verbose nature of Distance Education let us examine some of its operational aspects to find out if it can be useful for our country in imparting education to the neglected sections of society.

We want to be certain about one thing. We have enough empirical data to support the hypothesis that so far our inputs in industry have gone in favour of the better off segments of society. A larger share of our investment in education at all its levels has been cornered by the people above the poverty line. We do not want this to be repeated any more. Let us be clear that this new movement of Distance Education does not end up by distributing all educational benefits to the non-poor segments of society.

The objective at present is to analyse the relevance of Distance Education for helping the backward classes of the country. Are the content and method of Distance Education compatible with the nature, temperament and problems of the backward classes?

This compatibility is the crux of the relevance of Distance Education. We make an attempt here to examine this relevance. We shall see how the backward classes looking to the new social order envisaged in our Constitution and government policies, namely, democratic-socialistic-secular, can meaningfully benefit through the programmes of Distance Education. If the contemplated benefits are larger, the concept has usefulness; if the benefits in the long or in the short run end up with the welfare of the non-poor, the concept is nothing short of a deceit, a farce.

INDIAN SOCIETAL PYRAMID

A view of the Indian societal pyramid reveals that the base of the pyramid is broad which indicates that the lower class, as represented by the masses, constitutes a large number. The middle and the upper classes that occupy the higher ranks of the pyramid, are numerically far inferior. The complex social stratification and a large number of people who are living below the poverty line, pose a challenge to the educational policy makers in terms of providing appropriate education.

It has been stated time and again that alternative education strategies have to be evolved for the weaker sections. The problem of educating rural children, drop-outs and non-starters has become a legend in our own time. Suffice it to say that the new educational policy has elaborately described the situation and has recommended diversified methodologies to compromise issues of equity, quality and quantity. In line with this ideology, India has been witnessing spectacular change sin its educational scenario.

Several institutes of correspondence education, including the Indira Gandhi National Open University have come into existence and are helping nearly three and a half lakh students in acquiring knowledge through non-conventional modes. It is estimated that five Open University and two Open School systems are also engaged in the sacred task of helping the adults to learn. However, it is observed that most of the Open University systems focus on conventional programmes and find it difficult to structure and deliver programmes that cater to the needs of the weaker sections.

NEGLECTED SECTIONS OF SOCIETY

A brief account of backward neglected sections of society in India is as follows:

The backward classes who are supposed to be the target groups of Distance Education are a large and mixed category of "Persons with boundaries that are both unclear and elastic. Together they comprise one third of the total population of the country. They are made up of three principle components, the scheduled tribes, the scheduled castes and the other backward classes.

The scheduled tribes and scheduled castes are well-defined categories comprising respectively about seven and a little more-than fifteen per cent of the population. The other backward classes are a residual category; their position is highly ambiguous; and it is impossible to give an exact statement of their number."

The scheduled tribes, characteristically are isolates. They have been living in forests and hills. Their habitation areas are found in pockets. The frontier tribes such as those residing in Mizoram, Nagaland, Arunachal Pradesh and parts of Assam have problems which are largely political and diplomatic. Their problems have sensitised the whole country. The tribal groups living in the heartland of the country have problems of illiteracy, backwardness and poverty. Their exploitation is colossal.

Distance education for them should mean a redress from this historical backwardness and isolation. They need to be functionally educated. At the outest one must say that our efforts of Distance Education should lie within the structural arena of these groups. Broadly, will the isolates characterised by the mass illiteracy, ignorance, least resources of income, poor holdings, benefits from the national or regional availability of the programmes of Distance education?

The scheduled castes are other constituent of the backward classes. The proportion of scheduled castes to total population in India, is about 18 per cent. Among states and union territories, Punjab occupies the first place having more than 26 per cent of scheduled castes to total population in 1981 followed by Himachal Pradesh. It must be observed in this connection that the scheduled tribes and scheduled castes are well-defined categories. The other backward classes are a residual category; their position is highly ambiguous; and it is impossible to give an exact statement of their number.

The backward classes have historically suffered for centuries from the operation and the high-handedness of the high caste Hindus. Their quality of life is very poor. Keeping in view their overall backwardness the Constitution has provided some securities and safeguards to these groups. It is believed that these constitutional privileges would enable them to come at par with the non-tribal groups of the country.

The broad objective of the Indian society is to attain democracy, socialism and secularism. The Constitution under the Directive Principles of State Policy lays down that the State shall strive to promote the welfare of the people by securing a social order based on special and political justice (Article 38).

The State shall endeavour to secure just and human condition of work, a living wage, a decent standard of living and social and cultural opportunities for all workers (Article 43). The State shall endeavour to raise the level of nutrition and standard of living and to improve public health (Article 47). The State shall direct its policy towards securing equitable distribution of material resources of the community and prevention of concentration of wealth and means of production (Article 39).

The marginal farmers, who may belong to any caste, are at the lowest rung of the economic ladder and need proper care in the agricultural development programmes. The present day radio and TV programmes in this regard mostly benefit the literate farmers.

BASIC PROBLEMS OF BACKWARD CLASSES

After having given a social profile of the backward classes and their place in the new social order we raise the basic question: What has Distance Education to offer to the backward classes keeping in view their attributes and traits which are historical to them?

The introduction of Distance Education for the backward classes regions of our country presupposes the existence of some functional requisites, for instance, if education is given through mass media, it assumes that the consumers possess radios, televisions, newspapers and other techniques and tools which are used for imparting knowledge.

Possession of all these articles cost the consumer. The cost varies at least from Rupees 500 to about 5000, if a transistor set or a television set is purchased. Owning equipment of Distance Education is not sufficient.

It also requires a regular service of electric supply and the services of mechanics for repairs etc. There are a number of other pre-requisites which are of trifling nature but are essential for the continuance of Distance Education. For instance, postal services, travel expenses for occasional contacts are the other necessities for maintaining the programmes of Distance Education.

The status of scheduled castes continues to remain more or less the same as it was in the past. They remain a marginal group in the village. Even if there is electricity in the village the lines are not drawn to the extent of fringes, for the funds of the Gram Panchayats are very limited to meet this sort of "luxury". The village electricity thus remains restricted to the habitation areas of the high castes Hindus. A TV set thus is denied to the scheduled castes members in the village.

Ownership of transistor can be within the reach of the scheduled castes. But then it would remain limited to the elites only. The masses of untouchables are by and large beyond the reach of a transistor. Our impressionistic but surely logical analysis of the situation of the scheduled castes also suggests that it is difficult for them to own meaningfully the equipment required for the consumption of the programmes of Distance Education.

We are afraid the weaker classes today do not have the infrastructure required for availing themselves of the benefits of Distance Education, and it does not require any debate, presupposes the availability and ownership of these tools of mass media. Correspondence course presuppose the existence of the three R's. And the members of weaker classes are beyond the purview of the three R's.

It all suggests that before we launch the programmes of Distance Education for weaker classes, we had better first prepare the infrastructure. Without that if we hasten to go with the Distance Education programme it would not benefit those who need it the most. The benefit on the other hand would be reaped by the high caste Hindus, the upper classes who are mobilising the masses to immediately start these programmes.

Our argument is that the demand for distance education programme is for the vested interests of the higher groups of the society at the cost of those who have been given promise by the Constitution to meet their educational needs on a priority basis.

Ground realities stated as problems of backward/neglected sections of society are lessening day by day with the establishment of 'Ambedkar Villages' and increasing social development of the people of these classes through various types of facilities given to them by the government, therefore, it is felt that persons of these classes would be able to make use of distance education.

ROLE OF COMMUNICATION IN DISTANCE DUCATION

Bordenave (1977), while describing the varied roles of communication, states that it can be important means for achieving conscientization, organization, politicization and technification. The prerequisite for achieving some of the goals outlined above is that there should be coherent communication philosophy and methodology acceptable to the beneficiaries.

Thus, the conviction is growing that the people should have more access to the communication media, not only as receivers but also as sources and actors. Bordenave, while reviewing the global situation of the role of communication in rural development, states that the adoption of this new approach to communication has produced several significant innovations in rural development communication which are as follow:

1. Media are becoming more accessible to the participation of rural population in various programmes.
2. Messages are originated among the rural population and government agents, technocrats and the elite who previously always acted as sources are now learning to become receivers.
3. The content of the message is more relevant to the rural people's problems and needs.
4. Rural people are learning to formulate and articulate their ideas and feelings about matters important to them.
5. The government is learning to communicate less patronizingly and with less authoritarianism, thus making a dialogue with the rural population possible.
6. New technologies, such as audio and videotape recording, are making it possible to receive messages and feed-back from all the parties thus facilitating mutual perception and understanding.

Most communication models still reveal a persuasive orientation and only a few attempts have been made to strengthen communication's role in facilitating the popular participation and action required for rural development (Schramma, 1973).

Very little research has been done so far on horizontal and participative communication areas and practically no research has been undertaken in developing countries to systematically analyse the impact of different media on adult learning, or statistically account for the overlapping variances arising because of the use of a variety of media.

Participatory Approach in Communication

The term "Participatory Communication" refers to the efforts along with several lines to develop communication involving the community who are the expected beneficiaries of the programme. The term deliberately focusses on involvement of those who are traditionally the message receivers, in formulation, in generating information as a source and in making the programmes.

Further, the success of the participatory communication rests, as Schramm (1959) states, on communication processes, which work both ways, i.e. the audience also affect the communicator. The messages sent are in part determined by the expected audience reactions. The audience or at least those audience about whom the communicator thinks, play more than a passive role in communication.

Media Approach

Developing countries utilize media such as radio, TV and print, for delivering developmental and educational messages. The media and the media forums have been generally effective in creating awareness, forming and changing attitudes and causing behavioural changes. But adequate scientific evidence as to how these media forums become effective, is rare.

There are three exceptions to this. They are Neurath's (1960, 1962) field experiments with the Indian Radio Forum, the SITE (Satellite Instructional Technology Experiment, 1974) which covered 8 states and involved agriculture telecasting for developing purposes and Jayagopal's (1981) participatory communication experiment with TV literacy programme in Madras and suburbs of Madras.

Dewal (1982) has stated that the resource constraints and the pressures of time, if not today, then certainly tomorrow, will compel us to focus on designing open education teaching structures. We have to have a selective thrust to concentrate on. As visualised by the Alberto Commission on Education Planning, it will not be necessary to establish any additional institutions of the conventional type.

One of the new systems that can be thought of is TV and radio schools. It is the only way by which the availability of Indian National Satellite (INSAT) can be optimally utilised. It is the only way by which elementary education, specially for the learners in the age group of 11-14 can be universalised. It is the only system which can be designed with the resources at our disposal.

The Department of Adult and Continuing Education has pioneered a number of distance education projects in South East Asia, specially intended for the weaker sections. Notable among them are the TV-literacy project (1981), the study of social impact of TV by Selvam (1981) and the multi-media project of the Department of Adult and Continuing Education (1984).

These projects have yielded valuable data by indicating that distance education can be a potential tool for education and training of the weaker sections, the prime condition being that the programmes should be structured and supported by proper educational technologies.

A description of the three typologies of distance education programmes mentioned earlier is provided below:

(1) TV Literacy Project of the Department of Adult and Continuing Education

The project, "Literacy through Television" (1981), is an attempt to reach the illiterate adults and to communicate with them effectively. The massive programme covered 1,500 adult illiterates in the districts of Chingleput, South Arcot and North Arcot which are within the radius of 90 km from Madras. In this programme, which commenced in 1978, all activities are designed to transmit knowledge and skills and create opportunities for self-fulfilment for those who have left formal educational institutions of the country. 'Life Education' is the title of the TV programme, which has three components, namely 1. Awareness, 2. Vocational skills, and 3. Literacy.

Each of the components is designed on the basis of the findings of a survey of 160 villages. The first component aims at providing information about various perplexing issues that one comes across in one's own family, community, etc. The second component deals with various occupational skills useful for improving the economic condition, while guiding them to utilize the time meaningfully. The third component aims at spreading literacy and numeracy.

With a view to evaluate the merits and demerits of the programme "Literacy through Television" and for getting feed-back from the receiving end, communications in the form of inland letters were sent to each centre every week, requesting the television animators to write their remarks about the programme, performance, the learners' interest and their willingness immediately after the weekly lessons were over. The main objectives of the programme were as follows:

1. To find out how far television has served as a tool for effective communication in rural areas.
2. To find out how far it could be converted into a participatory medium.
3. To find out the learner's interest and to identify whether a particular pattern of communication has emerged or not.
4. To find out the effects of one-way/two-way communication between the communicator and the receiver of the messages (animator and the learners).
5. To identify the reasons for high percentage of response during certain peak hours.
6. To find out the effectiveness of the training given to the animator by the communicators and the pattern of response after the training.

Results

The learner's interest increases when the communicator and the learner jointly take a decision to make communication effective. In the study at hand, it is clear that when the animators were sensitized through a training programme, and when they were made to articulate with the learners, the percentage of responses was high.

The percentage of responses was low when there was only one-way communication. The percentage of responses went up when there was a two-way communication, facilitated through an animator. In one-way communication system no feed-back could be obtained which made it difficult to improve the original programme according to the wishes and needs of the learners.

The percentage of response was high due to a favourable learning environment created through drama, the improved methods adopted in literacy teaching, the lean season, ultimately through establishment of the two-way communication process and the training imparted to the animator, who could communicate effectively with the source (communicator) and the receiver (animator and the learner).

The animator's role was crucial in the participatory process as he was able to bridge the gap between the source and the learner. Further, the animator had acted as a channel for pumping feed-back. The training programme helped to develop a good rapport with the learners for identifying their needs and interest.

(2) Social Impact of Television Programmes

Selvan (1981) studied "The Social Impact of the Telecast Programme: Education for Life" of the Madras Doordarshan Kendra on rural adults and has found out that television viewing played a positive role in enhancing the level of awareness, knowledge and adoption of experimental subjects.

(3) Multimedia Project of the Department of Adult and Continuing Education

An experiment on the "Study of the Impact of Multimedia Forum on Adult Learning and Attitude in some of the Selected Villages of Chingleput District in Tamil Nadu through Participatory Approach" was conducted Department of Adult and Continuing Education, University of Madras.

The experiment is conducted by the Department in collaboration with Madras All India Radio and Doordarshan Kendra was as a milestone in distance learning experiments in India, as it is to provide information on the design and objectives of the experiment to support the fact that distance learning can be a supporting strategy for achieving universalisation of elementary education and for developing programmes for weaker sections through open university and open school systems. The following were the broad objectives of the experiment:

1. To find out the impact of multimedia, i.e. TV, radio and animator on adult learning at some of the selected learning centres in the villages of Tamil Nadu.

2. To develop tools to measure the knowledge and attitudes of the adult learners.
3. To compare the knowledge and attitudes of learners educated through different media.
4. To identify the socio-economic background of the subjects involved in the experiment.
5. To measure the knowledge and attitude levels of adult learners, who are the subjects of this experiment, at the animator forum, TV forum and radio forum individually.
6. To measure the knowledge and attitude levels of the adult learners who are subjects of this experiment as per the combinations elaborated under "Design".
7. To study the changes in knowledge and attitude patterns and to conduct a baseline survey designed to provide information on knowledge and attitude levels.
8. To develop tools for measuring socio-economic status, knowledge and attitude levels of the subjects involved in this experiment.
9. To evolve typologies to describe the rural audience at the animator forum (A), the TV forum (B), and the radio forum (C).

Methodology

The study involved an experimental method for studying the impact of multimedia approach (TV, radio and articulation by animator which was an independent variable) on rural adult learners at selected Tamil Nadu villages, and followed a comparative approach to evaluate the outcome of the individual medium and the combination of different media in terms of learning.

The investigations referred to above throw light on the potentialities of selected media, such as TV and radio, for increasing the efficiency of educational programmes. The most important ones are as follows:

(*a*) Media, which is often neutral, can be converted into participatory media, through proper source-receiver linkages.

(*b*) Through proper training, we can increase the capabilities of the trainers/teachers to facilitate the maximum use of the media.

(*c*) By structuring the curricula as media-oriented the learners can be motivated.

(*d*) Media can be used effectively to raise the level of awareness and knowledge of the parents, thereby making it easier to mobilise the parents, who in turn will help their children participate in the elementary education programme (in the school or outside the school).

To summarise, media is a principal supporting system of distance learning that can cover a large area, reach the masses can be a motivating tool. Hence, organising distance learning programmes for weaker sections through Open University/School systems is possible, natural and urgent.

The experiments conducted at the Department of Adult and Continuing Education, University of Madras during the last ten years using media forums have bolstered the faith that through appropriate design and combination of media, we should be able to construct proper distance education programmes for the weaker sections.

18

Significance of Distance Education in Teacher Education

INTRODUCTION

Apart of teacher education (B.Ed. etc.) through distance learning, teachers need educational improvement and career enhancement on continuous basis, which is only possible through distance learning because new developments in education as well as in socio-political, socio-economic and politico-economic bring out social changes to light. These changes are of vital significance for a good teacher.

The programme of Action of the National Policy on Education 1986 aims at National Policy of Education improvement and career enhancement of teacher on a continuous basis through distance education which has following features:

(*i*) the large number to be created to,

(*ii*) the need to organise courses on a continuous basis in the career of a teacher, and

(*iii*) the unique potential of the distance mode of education to intervene without taking the teachers away from work, thus emerging as a better means of transferring knowledge, understanding and skills to them in their day-to-day practice.

Distance education has emerged as a new mode of teaching which is known as distance teaching. It is different from conventional mode of teaching. In distance teaching media of communication is most important factor whereas in conventional teaching method and techniques are essential for effective presentation. Thus, there should be two types of teacher education programmes for preparing teachers:

1. Teachers training for conventional teaching, and
2. Teachers training for distance teaching.

The conventional teachers training is organised through conventional teacher-education as well as through distance-education.

TEACHER EDUCATION FOR DISTANCE TEACHERS

Distance teaching has three dimensions, content, presentation and communication. The conventional teacher education programme prepares teachers for analysing content structure and effective presentation by employing appropriate methods and techniques of teaching.

The distance teachers training however, requires content, presentation and communication awareness and the practice for teaching. As distance teachers have to acquire teaching skills for the contact programme as supportive devices, distance teachers need different modes for preparing teachers.

NEED FOR DISTANCE TEACHER TRAINING

In distance education the learner is separated from the teacher. Multi-media strategies are followed. The preparation and presentation of materials is systematic. Student-support services are provided to make the system more effective. The design of the educational structure as a whole is much more advanced than the earlier correspondence or broadcasting education. The system is a deliberate effort to democratize education.

Distance education systems differ widely in their organisation, practices and objectives, as their target clientele, their scales of operation and their structural complexities differ. However, these systems are now a major force in educational development in many countries all over the world.

Today, a class distance educator is required to start new distance education institutions, to expand the range and number of student populations, to see what the community needs for its social and economic purposes, to revitalize the older institutions, to identify, describe and undertake new professional roles within the system to give new directions to the existing practices and to establish the system permanently.

People taking up key as well as subordinate positions in the distance education institutions were from other areas of education and face following two problems:

(*i*) They must adapt themselves to the new situation immediately,

(*ii*) They must contribute to the culture and vitality of distance education in positive terms for a long-term impact on the society in general and on education in particular.

The first of these problems is solved with the help of workshop's etc., but the second problem calls for professional training of a very high standard.

DISTANCE EDUCATION AS A CAREER

A statement made in 1987 in a UNESCO publication, considered pre-service training in distance education "only as a future prospect and scarcely yet a present reality" and suggested that "perhaps sometime in the future when distance learning systems and structure are an inevitable part of every general education system, distance teacher education may become an option in ordinary teacher education but that is not yet the case in the Asia-Pacific region."

It is suggested, that for some people involvement with distance education is a temporary phase in their career. Most people enter the system mid-career, and those who continue move from one work role to the other within the system, but there are hardly any who spend their entire working/professional lives in the same system.

The suggestion is superficially valid. Distance education institutions cannot claim to be older than two decades. It is premature to suggest that the personnel who enter the system or are not going to spend their professional lives in the system.

If what is indicated by the success of the courses given at Jordan Hill College, a more powerful and valid suggestion will be that the people are looking for pre-service training in distance education, which is not available presently except in a few rare cases.

A career of distance educator has not yet emerged. Distance education is 'an emergency system' which may attract talented and imaginative academics and non-academics as it provides outlets for their talents but may fail to retain them for long.

Success in such distance education experience may invite them back to the professions they originally came from and look for, explore and implement innovations in those professions. Such possibilities are open in fields like education, broadcasting, educational television, publishing and printing, educational communication etc.

However, most social reforms do appear on the scene as 'emergency system'. If found useful, they get established as parts of the overall social system. Though introduced as 'emergency systems' distance education system have come to stay. Of course, the period of transition has just begun in which the concerned population of academics and non-academics settle between their original professional interests and those offered by the systems of distance education. The fact that it has begun, is evidence enough to emphasis that distance education is emerging as a career.

Therefore, it needs to display a 'career' i.e., the various possible, or existing, stages of professional growth which follow one another successively providing the careerist ample opportunities for developing the career-system (distance education and his own personal career within the domain of distance education. This, by implication, is a question of asking whether or not 'distance education' is a discipline by itself.

It is to say here that any professional training in distance education worth its name should highlight "those progressive stages towards greater professionalism" which should enable it to be seen both as a career and a discipline. Providing fulfledged professional training in distance education is a positive and necessary step in this direction.

(*i*) Procedure for Training Distance Teachers

Many people are involved in the whole process of distance education. So far as the activities in a professional training programme for distance teachers are concerned, two major types of people, viz., those who are to be trained and those who will train them are engaged in the programme.

The first two sub-sections of this section are devoted to the two categories of trainees—the professionals and the non-professionals and the next two sub-sections will talk about those who will train the distance teachers.

(1) *The Professional Trainees*: Among the professionals, we may identify a few clearly definable categories of personnel, each category requiring a specific kind of training relevant to its needs and job requirements. These categories are:

(*a*) planners and administrators working at various levels of the system;

(*b*) surveyors, course planners, curriculum developers, course writers, editors, reviewers, course coordinators, tutors, counsellors, evaluators, and graphic artists;

(*c*) audio producers, script writers, evaluators, special effects personnel;

(*d*) video producers, script writers, designers, special effects personnel, evaluators;

(*e*) educational technologists, technical staff of various types, specialists in integrating the media-inputs; and

(*f*) facilitators of various services—librarians, laboratory staff etc.

(2) *The Non-professional Trainees*: Among the non-professionals, we list a host of people who may seemingly have nothing to do with distance education, but in reality may play a vital role in the success or failure of the system. We may categorise such people as follows:

(*a*) Politicians, policy/decision-makers who motivate the creation of distance education institutions, popularise the political statements in favour of such establishments and mobilise resources for them.

(*b*) The target learner populations of several types—school children, university students, professionals, old adults, housewives, drop-outs from the formal system of education etc.

These are the people whom the institution serves directly, and these people need to know how they may be serve maximally.

(*c*) Liaison agents of several types—social reformers, local community leaders/helpers, at places religious agents, parents of the learners, other professionals who can be used in local community situation etc.

The suggestion here is that for example, uninformed parents can do a lot of harm to their distance learning children, as it is the parents who are expected to create a learning environment (proper place, appropriate time etc.) for their children for which they need to be educated if they are not.

Similarly, the willing social reformers should know how they may arrange for self-help groups, pass on relevant information from time to time etc.

The above concept has been summarized in the following Table:

Table: Tasks and Training Needs of the Trainees

Role	*Tasks*	*Training Needs*
1	*2*	*3*
Policy maker	Makes decisions about establishing distance education systems; persuades policy making colleagues about advantages. Monitors progress of system; controls financial allocations.	'*Sensitisation*' to advantages of distance education. Knowledge of outline of systems and structures. Knowledge of cost benefit account of distance education.
Learners	Obtain study resources place, equipment, time, fees. Manage learning tasks. Decide courses, contribute to peer group activities, whenever possible.	Study skills, knowledge of local resources (persons, materials information sources). Knowledge of curriculum information about other distance learners.
Parents and family	Provide physical requirements (place of study and for keeping study materials, safe), writing, materials, light, heat, radio, TV, supervise learners, schedule of study, assignments etc. Adopt encouraging attitude. Provide information/ideas from own education if possible and from other sources. Monitor cultural/ethical/social appropriateness of material. Provide co-curricular needs.	Awareness of distance education. Knowledge of relevant local resources and support systems. Knowledge of outline curriculum requirements.

(*Contd.*)

(*Contd.*)

Role	*Tasks*	*Training Needs*
1	*2*	*3*
	Contact organisations, resource person on learners behalf.	
Other community resource persons (teachers at other levels, health workers)	Provide alternative study location. Provide study resources information and materials. Provide experience of practical situations. Adopt encouraging attitude. Contact logistic communication/ support systems.	Sensitivity/awareness of distance education. Awareness of relevant local resources. Knowledge of curriculum material. Knowledge of delivery systems.
Local community leaders	Encourage distance education as part of education system. Marshal local resources/ personnel to assist learners. Check and improve logistic/communication systems. Provide study resources information and materials and experiential/ practical situations.	Sensitivity/awareness of distance education. Knowledge of relevant local resources. Knowledge of delivery system.

(3) *The Sources of Staff Development*: Having identified the groups that need training of one or the other kind, we now turn to the question "who will train them?"

Hardly any pre-service training in distance education is available today, as such we need not look for qualified resource persons in distance teacher as trainers. In other words, like other teacher trainers, we do not have any full time trainers in the field of distance education. This fact needs to be noted carefully.

Obviously, today it is the 'distance educators' themselves who train others for distance education, and not the 'trainers' in the conventional sense of the expression. Thus 'distance education' have learnt their new skills and acquired the relevant knowledge about distance, education on their '*jobs*'. Most of them are fresh from their job experiences, as such they are themselves in the process of learning.

However, this fact need not prejudice us against them, for in most cases training in the various areas of distance education pertains to the early stages of its development, and the experts fresh from their job experiences have proved successful in such situations.

There is another factor too which helps this situation—mostly who join distance education institutions are trained and/or experienced teachers, administrators, technicians, and broadcasters. In many cases they have some information or even skills.

However vague or disorganised these skills etc., might be, they should help in the process of interaction between the finished product—the trained distance educator. A distance teacher-trainer should be:

(*a*) *Skilled*: The teaching materials (print, audio, video etc.) in distance education are more visible to greater numbers of people of various walks and levels of life. They have to be a very high standard for the credibility of the system and they have to be socially and pedagogically relevant for their social and pedagogic utility.

Such materials can be produced if the personnel employed to produce term are skilled people. A very high standard of academic and technical skills is, therefore, expected of the trainers.

(b) Cooperative: There are hardly any tasks and roles in the system of distance education which can be carried out in isolation from other tasks and roles. Most of these tasks and roles, however, dissimilar they may be and seem to be, are inter-linked and inter-related for purposes of making television finished product a success.

Co-operation is the corner stone of this success, and cooperation is not possible unless those involved in the tasks are cooperative, or have learnt to be so. Trainers, therefore, have themselves to be cooperative, for then alone can they promote this attribute among the prospective trainers (i.e., trainees).

(c) Flexibility: Rigidity of views and attitude is a major hurdle in making distance education a success. Flexibility helps the trainees to adapt themselves to the new situation and roles, and also to collaborate with others in effecting frequent readjustments of various kinds.

Only a flexible distance educator can take on such diverse roles as those of academicians, technicians, producers and administrators. To show its utility the trainers should be able to display this attribute in good measure.

(*d*) *Patience:* Some people believe that it is only at the early stages of the development of distance education institutions that the workers have to face anxieties, frustrations, delays and failures.

The fact, however, is that so long as the institution keeps on being innovative in terms of offering new courses, extending its reach to diverse sections of the society, reducing the costs of its products, and becoming increasingly trainer/distance educator and the trainee. Thus, the present responsibilities in the field of staff development for distance education are three-fold:

(*i*) to maintain the existing arrangements to meet the 'emergency type' needs,

(*ii*) also to build a system that will produce full time trainers, and

(*iii*) thus, achieve national/local self-sufficiency of training resources at the fastest possible rate.

As far as the resource personnel are concerned, we may depend on two sources:

(*i*) national or local, and

(*ii*) foreign, either from resource countries or from international agencies such as UNESCO.

Depending on local or national resources is advisable because the environmental factors pertaining to economic, social, industrial and educational development are shared and easily understood, common difficulties become tractable, and there is no scope for underhand exploitation.

If such local or national sources are not available, one has to depend on what may come from abroad. There too, it is better to depend on neighbour countries, or the countries that belong to a proximate region for similar reasons of shared environmental problems and understanding.

Personnel from abroad can be of great help, but only in a limited way. Their roles at best can be advisory in nature. They help in setting up systems or sub-systems, but the task of building the actual infrastructure will always be that of the local personnel. Besides, the personnel from abroads cannot be of any real help at the school and community level education or training needs.

The suggestion that is being made is that such personnel can be used as consultants who can present details about their systems, structures and the contexts wherein they were built, and suggest ways and means by which the hosts can adopt and adapt to those system and structure within the latter's contexts.

(4) *Qualities of Trainer of Distance Teacher:* Another point to be considered is what the attributes of the trainers should be. By implication, those very skills should be expected from responsive to social needs, the distance educators will continue to face frustrations, anxieties, etc.

Thus instead of making time for such difficulties to come to an end they should develop a work-culture which accepts these difficulties as routine episodes, and thus build confidence and optimism in and around their work. Basic to this attitude is the attribute of patience which the trainers will do good to display in their own approach to work.

(*e*) *Innovation:* Distance education is an innovation which survives on its ability to build one innovation on the other ranging from course design to course offerings, from cost efficiency to extended student services etc.

Innovation has to be the dominant factor in the '*personal profile*' of a distance educator. Through this attribute alone he can build a distinctive 'career profile', which may help '*distance education*' emerge as an autonomous discipline by itself.

THE 'CONTENT' OF DISTANCE TRAINING

The system of distance education consists of networks and chains of diverse tasks. Training in this field should provide expertise and practice to the personnel to carry out their own specific tasks and duties. The personnel should learn to function effectively along and within their role-chains and task-networks.

The training should provide them with understanding of and appreciation for inter-relation of their own work and tasks with those of others, and the means and ways of making the cooperative effort successful.

This training should provide for the building blocks of '*commitment*' on the part of trainees, who should get committed to distance education in their thoughts, words, and deeds. These are the underlying principles of the content of training.

Training should provide adequate and appropriate content in all the three domains: cognitive, curative and affective to build effective human resources for establishing, developing, maintaining and expanding the system of distance education.

IDENTIFYING TRAINING NEEDS

(*a*) Generalisation from the available literature on distance education in general, and on the roles of differing personnel categories in particular.

(*b*) Analysis of the tasks, the problems therein, anticipated tasks and the problems expected therein.

(*c*) Critical incident analysis i.e., an analysis of individual's behaviour in various situations, its consequences in terms of the productivity of the task concerned; exercise to identify problems which suggest training.

(*d*) Case studies of successful distance educators help in identifying those characteristics which contribute to their success. These characteristics may be pointed to and the trainees encouraged to develop them through training.

(*e*) Pooling the views and opinions of experienced people (about what they think and/or believe the training needs are) helps in preparing a long list of possible needs, wherefrom dependable training needs can be identified after further analysis.

IMPARTING THE TRAINING

'*Training once-in-a life-time*' is an obsolete concept in the present changing world. For serious professionalism, 'Training is a life time affair. The variety of the personnel to be trained is vast and they are at different stages of their careers—some in permanent positions and well established institutions, some in temporary positions, some working on projects, some on long-term assignments and all of them at differing levels of concern.

Those in permanent positions need revitalisation of their skills and practices so that they do not perpetuate those practice which have outlived their utility. Those in temporary positions will move to permanent positions. Those working on projects will go to long-term assignments. Those working on long-term assignments will step into permanent positions.

System and sub-systems within a known system of distance education undergo changes corresponding to the progressive upward mobility in the career prospects of a trainee. As communication technology is changing rapidly, educational concepts and learning theories are breaking new grounds.

An effective training programme will take care of all the changes and the corresponding activities which have been exemplified above.

STEPS IN SELECTION OF THE TRAINING PROGRAMME

(1) *Scaling the Scope of the Programme:* The trainers or the training institution must measure the scale and judge the scope of the programme for which training is to be arranged.

The training programme should suit that scale and scope. For a distance education project with a single specific objective, a training programme of two days may be enough to enable the personnel involved perform their tasks satisfactorily.

With the objective of achieving mltiplier effect through subsequent similar workshops conducted in participating countries through the personnel trained at the international workshop an international agency may conduct a workshop of eight to ten days' duration at a particular national centre involving trainees from a region.

(2) *Short and Long-term Advantages of the Programme*: The scale and scope of a training programme may impose limited objectives and activities on it.

Care should be taken that a programme of limited scope builds reasonable motivation for further work beyond what the programme provides. Conversely, a programme of vast scope should lay reasonable emphasis on immediate need and applications.

(3) *Catering both Institutional and Individual Needs:* Both the needs of the individual participants and those of the institute should be catered to. Though a training programme always aims at achieving an objective for an institution to reinforce an existing distance education system or modify and improve such a system, the building blocks of that reinforcement and/or changes are those who come forward for the training.

Though the overall objective continues to be the needs of the institute and/or the country the programme be successful should be satisfying for the individuals too.

(4) *Linking Past Activities/Events with Future:* Training should not be 'once-in-a-life-time affair. It should build links with the

training events that have gone before it. It should create scope for other training events that may be linked to it in the future. Each training programme must have to build evaluation mechanism which provide for follow-up changes modifications and extensions. As a result of such an approach the rewards of training turn to be cumulative.

(5) *Providing Models of Acceptable and Desirable Behaviour*: Training should modify the behaviour of the trainees by providing models of acceptable and desirable behaviour patterns expected of distance educators.

The objective can be achieved by practising what is preached about its characteristic features. It should be systematic, well planned, efficiently managed and well proportioned with regard to its components. To set living examples for the trainees the trainer should conduct himself admirably.

TASKS AND TRAINING-NEEDS

Table: Tasks and Training-Needs of Various Types of Personnel

Personnel	*Tasks*	*Training-needs*
1	*2*	*3*
1. Policy maker and planner	1. Within the framework of national priorities, needs, and constraints, etc., conceives, plans and guides, in the execution of distance education programmes.	1. Overview of distance education systems, its strength and weaknesses, its social need and economic viability. 2. Knowledge of developmental plains in other sectors so as to relate education to the overall development of the country.
2. Administrator	1. Overall manpower planning. 2. Institutional management. 3. Co-ordination and Supervision of institutional programmes.	1. Knowledge of Distance Education and its operation at grass-roots level. Knowledge of institutions.

(*Contd.*)

(*Contd.*)

Personnel	*Tasks*	*Training-needs*
1	2	3
	4. Popularising the distance education system. 5. Some other specific tasks related to service in the field as under: (*a*) Appoints tutors, allocates students to tutors. (*b*) Deals with students and tutors problems. (*c*) Responsible for efficient tutors functioning. (*d*) Arranges staff and equips study centres. 6. Schedules face-to-face sessions. 7. Arranges other uses of study centres. 8. Disseminates information to students. 9. Supplies feedback to institutions. 10. Collects marked assignments from tutors. 11. Sends samples for monitoring. 12. Conducts examinations, sends results to institutions. 13. Regional publicity. 14. Helps in admissions.	Programmes and procedures. 2. Knowledge of distance education. Institutions working within the country as well as abroad and communicate with them. 3. Student and tutor problems Training in Management and supervision of supporting staff. 4. Understanding of local conditions and problems. 5. Skills in establishing rapport with community at grassroots level. Skills in human relationships.
3. Researcher	1. Designs and carries out research in identified problems of distance education. 2. Analyses and interprets data.	1. Understanding of distance education and its strengths weaknesses and problems areas. 2. Orientation towards various educational research designs.

(*Contd.*)

(*Contd.*)

Personnel	*Tasks*	*Training-needs*
1	*2*	*3*
	3. Makes recommendations based on research findings.	3. Sampling techniques with reference to distance educations.
	4. Compiles final report.	4. Techniques of constructing instruments for data collection analysis of data.
	5. Disseminates research.	5. Report writing.
		6. Dissemination skills.

Table: Tasks Training of Personnel Related to Production of Materials

Personnel	*Tasks*	*Training needs*
1	2	*3*
1. Curriculum designer	1. Assesses distance learners needs. Situational analysis.	1. Overview of distance education system, its strengths and weaknesses etc.
	2. Conceptualises and designs appropriate need-based curriculum.	2. Understanding of needs, resources, constraints etc. of distance education in general and those of the institutions in particular.
	3. Co-ordinates with others.	3. Knowledge of target groups and their problems.
	4. Appreciates the role of media, face to face discussion and practical complements of the curriculum.	4. Knowledge of learning experience and activities etc.
	5. Prepares course outlines.	5. Knowledge of teaching strategies.

(*Contd.*)

(*Contd.*)

Personnel	*Tasks*	*Training needs*
1	2	3
	6. Suggests suitable learning experiences and activities.	6. Curriculum designing skills.
	7. Helps in the preparation of '*Learning outcomes*'.	7. Understanding the role of media in distance education.
	8. Helps in evaluation of curriculum.	8. Evaluation of curriculum skills.
2. Writer/ reviewer	1. Decides/adopts format.	1. Overview of the distance education system, its strengths and weaknesses etc.
	2. Organises material.	2. Knowledge of writing/reviewing skills.
	3. Develops detailed educational strategies.	3. Knowledge of target groups and their problems.
	4. Writes correspondence lessons, usually in close collaboration with other members of course team.	4. Knowledge of learning process and teaching strategy.
	5. Supplies ideas/drafts for illustrations.	5. Knowledge of content.
	6. Revises drafts.	6. Locating resources/materials etc.
	7. Works with reviewers, editors and illustrators until material is ready.	7. Knowledge of production of materials through course team.
	8. Tests, and evaluates material.	8. Testing and evaluation skills.
	9. Revise/reviews galley proofs from printers.	9. Some knowledge of design editing and printing processes.
	10. Prepares feedback, questionnaires, pre-tests and post-tests.	
3. Editor	1. Face-editing format, student-aids, layout, print get-up.	1. Overview of distance education system, its strengths and weakness.

(*Contd.*)

(*Contd.*)

Personnel	*Tasks*	*Training needs*
1	2	3
	2. In-depth text editing.	2. Knowledge of distance teaching techniques.
	3. Collaborates with authors to remove content ambiguities and confusions.	3. Editing skills.
	4. Language editing.	4. Presentation, layout skills.
	5. Checks readability, logical flow, sequencing and presentation of material.	5. Making-up Manuscript for printing.
	6. Checks suitability of illustrations, graph marking etc.	6. Proof-reading skills.
	7. Proof-reading.	7. Knowledge of different media and their role in teaching.
	8. Relates printed text with other media of the system.	8. Knowledge of printing stages.
	9. Contacts printers to get the materials printed.	
4. Course Co-ordinators	1. Schedules and arranges courses development, maintenance and renewal activities.	1. Orientation in philosophy of assistance education.
	2. Briefs external writers.	2. Writing skills.
	3. Co-ordiantes activities of courses team.	3. Co-ordination skills.
	4. Facilitates services to ensure smooth course production.	4. Sound knowledge of subject content and methodology.
	5. Collaborates with course team members.	5. Course production procedures.
	6. Prepares student and tutor guides and other supplementary materials such as	6. Scheduling communication.

(*Contd.*)

(*Contd.*)

Personnel	*Tasks*	*Training needs*
1	*2*	*3*
	assignments, tests, marketing guides etc. for mailing.	
	7. Arranges review and testing of materials.	7. Management skills.
	8. Communicates with students and tutors from time to time.	8. Testing and evaluation.
	9. Monitors/tutors marking of assignments.	
	10. Arranges workshop/practical components, if necessary.	
5. Tutor/ evaluators	1. Corresponds with students.	1. Know about distance education and its various aspects and tutors role in it.
	2. Holds face to face sessions.	2. Role of evaluator in distance content.
	3. Gives prompt accurate and constructive feedback to students on their progress.	3. Knowledge of the subject content.
	4. Marks assignments.	4. Knowledge of programmes, schedules, regional services, facilities.
	5. Sends in results.	5. Skills in communicating with students.
	6. Provides guidance and counselling to students.	6. Conselling skills.
	7. Provides feedback on students problems and procedural difficulties.	7. Human relations.

Table: Training-Needs: An Example

Personnel Tasks Category	*Training-needs*		
	Knowledge	*Attitudes*	*Skills*
Trainer/a Planning Administrators	1. Principles of need/problem identification.	Awareness of problems and difficulties faced by the country.	Skills in writing measurable objectives.
	2. Principles of measurable objectives formulation.	Appreciating need for prioritization of needs and problems.	Skills in designing project/ programme.
	3. Principle of generating alternative solutions.	Appreciation of need for systematic planning and evaluation of such plans.	Skills in control monitoring and follows up of project/ programme.
	4. Theories of research and evaluation		Skills in project/ programme evaluation.

The Programme at IGNOU

The diploma programme in Distance Education introduced by the Indira Gandhi National Open University, New Delhi, India is the third course being made available on the above lines, i.e., it is a pre-service training programme and assumes that distance education is a discipline in its own right. In our part of the world this is the first programme of its kind.

The following table presents briefly a view of the training programmes the world over.

Table: Training in Distance Education the World Over

Partial Training	Training in Separate components of Distance Education	Training in the Allied fields of Distance Education	Comprehensive Training in Distance Education	Coverage Strategies
UKOU (Course Development)	**	**	**	On-the-job learning
	UNESCO Programmes	**	**	Workshops etc.
**	**	Jordanhil Diploma and Survey Diploma	Australian Diploma and IGNOU Diploma	Regular Multi-Media Courses

DISTANCE EDUCATION FOR TEACHER

A Professional degree in education has always been obligatory for secondary school teachers. After independence about 46 per cent of teachers at the secondary stages were untrained. Due to the lack of enough trained graduates, untrained graduates had to be recruited all along.

Genuine concern about this situation led to the establishment of a number of teacher training colleges offering a one year training programme which was later restructured as the Bachelor of Education programme.

These institutions have been catering mostly to pre-service training. Enrolling only a small percentage from the category of working teachers as training in these institutions necessitates the working teachers to be away from work for a long period, which is not possible in most cases.

B.Ed. Programmes through Correspondence Education

In 1966 the Central Institute of Education (CIE), University of Delhi, started the B.Ed. programme through correspondence-cum-contact mode. The University of Bangalore and the Regional Colleges of F· cation under the NCERT followed suit.

The immediate objective of these programmes was to clear up the existing backlog of untrained secondary school teachers in the country. In 1968, the UGC sent a delegation to the USSR to ascertain the purposefulness of such a mode in the context of teacher training.

The delegation decided strongly in favour of teacher training programmes through the correspondence mode. Consequently there was a proliferation of B.Ed. programmes through the correspondence mode in the seventies and the eighties.

Today, there are fifteen institutes of correspondence (distance) education under the formal universities through the correspondence mode. State Open University (YCMOU) is launching the programme in Maharastra. Now many more universities offer such courses.

THE UGC AND THE NATIONAL COUNCIL OF TEACHER EDUCATION (NCTE)

The agencies which influence the policy and practice of teacher education in India include the State Ministries of Education, the Ministry of Human Resource Development, Government of India, the University Grants Commission, the National Council of Educational Research and Training and the National Council of Teacher Education.

Government of India have established a National University to run various courses/programmes through the distance mode and to promote and determine education institutions to make the system more responsive to social needs and more cost efficient. Substantial sums have been contributed by international bodies like the COL (Canada) for the promotion of distance education.

(*i*) Indian Government strongly believing in the effectiveness of distance education.

(*ii*) Indian Government is making all the efforts to promote it both nationally and internationally.

Government is determined to use this system to improve the existing state of educational affairs in the country. In their communications to the NCTE, the government has laid down the following:

(*a*) B.Ed. Correspondence programme should be made available to nursery and elementary school teachers who wish to improve their qualification and thereby career prospects.

(*b*) It would be helpful, if an up-to-date state of norms and guidelines could be evolved for B.Ed. correspondence courses keeping in view:

(*i*) the developments since 1980 (especially, the NPE and POA), and

(*ii*) the fact that at least for certain categories of candidates such course will have to be run for quite a few years to come.

(*c*) It is not clear what specific steps, NCTE or NCERT has taken so far to implement the Resolutions passed by NCTE from time to time for generally putting an end to correspondence courses by way of formally taking up the matter with UGC and Universities/State Governments concerned.

Thus the Government of India is keen to improve the lot of secondary school teachers as well as that the primary school teachers. They are concerned of about the efficient running of distance education courses. There is evidence that the Government favours the process of participatory decision-making.

Concerns of UGC and NCTE

Following in the statement of UGC with regard to distance/correspondence education is general.

"The Commission has been supporting the programmes of distance/correspondence courses with a view to providing a new stream of education to enable a large number of persons with necessary aptitude to acquire further knowledge and improve their professional competence."

In the eighties UGC shifted its point of view considerably basing it on the working of the correspondence courses and on the advice of the NCTE. In 1980 the NCTE appointed a committee to ascertain the quality of B.Ed. programmes offered through correspondence in several universities. After looking into the operational aspects of these programmes, especially the practice teaching component the committee recommended that it be confined to the respective states in which the universities concerned operate.

The programmes through correspondence-cum-contact mode should be offered only to clear the backlog of untrained secondary and primary teachers. The first degree in professional preparation of secondary school teachers should be obtained only through a formal course.

Out of the ten recommendations made by the committee, one recommends the correspondence mode (to remove the backlog), two propose to stop it altogether and seven recommend reforms to make the system effective. These seven reformative recommendations do not seem to have made any impact.

Concerned about the continuing deterioration in teacher education through correspondence mode, the August 87 meeting of the NCTE Standing Committee on Secondary and College Teacher Education coincided that B.Ed. through correspondence should be scrapped.

At the end of the meeting of Standing Committee in August, 1987, a delegation led by K.L. Srimali submitted a memorandum to the Ministry of HRD, GOI, demanding that the B.Ed. programmes offered through the correspondence mode be stopped forthwith.

Giving due consideration to the feeling among many educationists that the general deterioration of standards in secondary teacher education and the proliferation of B.Ed. programmes through correspondence are casually lined and also to the fact that recently impressive developments have taken place in the field of distance education, the NCTE appointed another committee to look into the relevant aspects of teacher education through correspondence and make recommendations on the use of distance education therein.

The Committee met on March 31, 1989 and then on June 8, 1989 and made five recommendations of which the major ones were as follows:

(*i*) The teacher education curricula demand a great deal of weightage for live classroom experiences and other forms of human interaction.

(*ii*) Teacher education through distance education modes, if suitably organised, can emerge as a trend setter in quality training for those working in face-to-face mode.

It recommended that clear and unambiguous guidelines should be arrived at incorporating new possibilities in distance education. It presented a set of seven well conceived guidelines that could be followed in order to organise effective training programmes through the distance mode. Recently in mid 1997 the Government put a stop on B.Ed. distance education, to clear the backlog of unemployed B.Ed. degree holders.

Indira Gandhi National Open University (IGNOU)

Organisation: According to the IGNOU Act (1985), IGNOU has been given the following dual mandate of functioning:

(*i*) As a university to provide opportunities for higher education to a large segment of the population and to promote the educational well-being of the community, and

(*ii*) As an apex body to encourage the Open University and distance education systems in the educational pattern of the country and to co-ordiante and determine the standards in such systems.

Keeping her objectives in view about the general quality of the teacher education programmes given through the distance mode, the views and commendations of the NCTE and the actions initiated by the UGC, IGNOU is expected to take appropriate steps with regard to teacher education programmes in anticipation of her assuming the role of co-ordination and determination of standards all over the country.

Deterioration of Quality: The quality of B.Ed. programmes through correspondence is inferior in many of the institutions. If practice teaching and other face-to-face components are to be parts of a programme they must be and are included without any hesitation.

Some institutions are concerned only with enrolling more and more students at the cost of the quality of programmes. It is the failure of the universities concerned and also of those who are expected to exercise control even then. The major reasons for the deterioration of quality are lack of restrictions on the size of enrolment and inferior organisation of the practice teaching component of the programmes. If a few universities give substandard degrees by subverting the system of distance education.

IGNOU was established to promote and maintain standards in Distance Education, that can cater to cognitive, psychomotor and affective domain of education successfully.

IGNOU launched a variety of teacher education courses at various levels of instructions as a continuing education programme. No prospective trainee will ever be admitted to programmes of B.Ed., M.Ed. etc. instead students will have to work through courses and only when they accumulate the required credits they will be awarded any certificates/diplomas/degree. During the entire experimental stage which may last for a few years on run, most of the IGNOU courses in this area will be open to inservice teachers only, except a few at lower levels which may suit parents as well.

19

The Truth About Distance Education

BRIEF PROFILE OF INDIRA GANDHI NATIONAL OPEN UNIVERSITY

It is true that in India there are some organisations, though not recognised by the University Grants Commission or by any state government, award, degrees and diplomas through correspondence courses. We have seen list of such institutions published by the UGC from time to time, therefore, by and large people feel that all correspondence courses are of the same class and degrees awarded through these courses are not at par with the degrees awarded by the universities following formal system of education, hence, this chapter is devoted to wipe out this and many more misunderstandings about distance education. Please ensure that the university/institution conducting distance learning courses is established/recognised by Government of India, State Government or UGC Hereunder, we are giving a brief profile of IGNOU for the good of the distance learners:

RECOGNITION

IGNOU is a Central University established by an Act of Parliament in 1985 (Act No. 50 of 1985) IGNOU Degrees/Diplomas/Certificates are recognised by all the members of the Association of Indian Universities (AIU) and are at par with Degrees/Diploma/Certificates of all Indian Universities/Deemed Universities/Institutions vide UGC Circular No. F1-8/92 (CPP) dated February 1992 & AIU Circular No. EV/(449)/94/176915-177115 dated January 1994.

UNIVERSITY GRANTS COMMISSION
BAHADUR SHAH ZAFAR MARG
NEW DELHI-110002

No. F.1-8/92(CPP) February, 1992

The Vice-Chancellor/Director's
of all the Indian Universities/
Deemed Universities/Institutions
of National Importance

Sub: Recognition of Degrees/Diplomas awarded by Indira Gandhi National Open University, New Delhi.

I am directed to say that Indira Gandhi National Open University, New Delhi has been established by sub-section (2) of Section (1) of the IGNOU Act, 1985 (50 of 1985) vide Notification No. F.13-12/85 Desk (U) dated 19.09.1985 issued by the Govt. of India, Ministry of Human Resource Development, (Department of Education), New Delhi and is competent to award its own degrees/diplomas. The Certificate, Diplomas and Degrees awarded by Indira Gandhi National Open University arc to be treated equivalent to the corresponding awards of the Universities in the country.

Yours faithfully
Sd/-
(GURCHARAN SINGH)
Under Secretary

ASSOCIATION OF INDIAN UNIVERSITIES
AIU HOUSE, 16 KOTLA MARG, NEW DELHI-110002

Phones: 3312305, 3313390
3310059 3312429

Gram: ASINGU
Telex: 31-66180 AIU IN
Fax: 011-3315105

No. EV/II (449)/94/176915-177115
January 14, 1994

The Registrar(s)
Member Universities.

Sub: Recognition of Degrees/Diplomas of Open Universities.

Dear Sir,

The Standing Committee at its 237th meeting held at Utkal University and the 68th Annual Session of the AIU and in December, 1993 at the University of Delhi have decided to in principle that the Degrees of the Open Universities be recognised in terms of the following resolutions:

"Resolved that the examinations of one University should be recognised by another on a reciprocal basis, provided that the entrance qualification, duration of course and the general standard of attainment are similar to those prescribed by the recognised university."

"Further resolved that in case of Degrees awarded by Open Universities, the conditions regarding entrance qualifications and duration of the course be relaxed provided that the general standard of attainment are similar to those prescribed by the recognised university."

The decision is brought to the notice of the Universities for favour of appropriate action in the matter. The additional information, if required in this behalf, may kindly be obtained from the Registrar of the Universities direct.

Thanking you,

Yours faithfully,
Sd/-
(K.C. Kalra)
Joint Secretary

BASIC FEATURES OF IGNOU

1. Introduction

The Indira Gandhi National Open University was established by an Act of Parliament in 1985 to achieve the following objectives:

- democratizing higher education by taking it to the doorsteps of the learners,

- providing access to high quality education to all those who seek it irrespective of age, region or formal qualifications,
- offering need-based academic programmes by giving professional and vocational orientation to the courses,
- promoting and developing distance education in India,
- setting and maintaining standards in distance education in the country as an apex body for the purpose.

2. Prominent Characteristics

- Relaxed entry regulations.
- Study according to your own pace and convenience.
- Flexibility in choosing the combination of courses from a wide range of disciplines.
- Study from your own chosen place (during the course of study you can change the opted study centre to any centre anywhere in India except for certain exceptional cases). You may sit for Term-end Examinations generally anywhere in India and some selected centres abroad.
- You may also pursue your study in any other university while being a learner of IGNOU.
- Cost effectiveness—Most of IGNOU study programmes are heavily subsidised by the Government of India.

3. Important Achievements

- Emergence of IGNOU as the largest Open University in the Commonwealth.
- Establishment of Distance Education Council (DEC) for the coordination and determination standards of Distance Education Systems in the country (1992).
- Recognition as Centre of Excellence in Distance Education by the Commonwealth of Learning (1993).
- Establishment of a Staff Training and Research Institute in Distance Education (STRIDE) with support from the Commonwealth of Learning (COL).
- Award of 100 Fellowships by COL as Rajiv Gandhi Fellowships to enable candidates from 19 countries in the Commonwealth to pursue IGNOU Programmes.
- Launching of an IGNOU-ISRO joint channel for organising a one-way video, two-way audio teleconferencing (1993-94).
- Taking IGNOU programmes to West Asian countries, Maldives, Mauritius, Nepal and Seychelles.

- Award of Excellence for Distance Education materials by Commonwealth of Learning (1999).
- Launch of an Educational Channel 'Gyan Darshan'. IGNOU is the nodal agency for 'Gyan Darshan' and regular transmissions are done from the studios at the EMPC, IGNOU (2000).

4. The Schools of Studies

With a view to develop interdisciplinary studies, the University operates through Schools of Studies. Each School is headed by a Director who arranges to plan, supervise, develop and organise its academic programmes and courses in coordination with the 'School staff and the different academic, administrative and service wings of the University. The emphasis is on providing a wide choice of courses at different levels. The Schools of Studies currently in operation are as follows:

- School of Computer & Information Sciences
- School of Continuing Education
- School of Education
- School of Engineering & Technology
- School of Health Sciences
- School of Humanities
- School of Management Studies
- School of Science
- School of Social Sciences

5. Academic Programmes

The University offers both short-term and long-term programmes leading to Certificates, Diplomas or Degrees, which are conventional as well as innovative. Most of these programmes have been developed after an initial survey of the demand for such studies. They are launched with a view to fulfil the learner's needs for:

- Certification,
- improvement of skills,
- acquisition of professional qualifications,
- continuing education and professional development at work place,
- self-enrichment,
- diversification of knowledge.

6. Course Preparation

Learning material is specially prepared by teams of experts drawn from different Universities/Institutions all over the country as well as in-house faculty. This material is scrutinized by the content experts supervised by the instructors/unit designers and edited by the language experts at IGNOU before they are finally sent for printing. Similarly, audio and video cassettes are produced in consultation with the course writers, in-house faculty and producers. The material is previewed and reviewed by the faculty as well as outside media experts and edited or modified, wherever necessary, before they are finally dispatched to the Study Centres and Doordarshan.

7. Credit System

The University follows the 'Credit System' for most of its programmes. Each credit in our system is equivalent to 30 hours of student study comprising all learning activities (i.e. reading and comprehending the print material, listening to audio, watching video, attending counselling sessions, teleconference and writing assignment responses). Thus, a four credit course involves 120 hours of study. This helps the learner to understand the academic effort one has to put in, to successfully complete a course. Completion of an academic programme (Degree, Diploma or Certificate) requires successful clearing of both the assignments and the term-end examination of each course in a programme.

8. Support Services

In order to provide individualized support to its learners, the University has large number of Study Centres throughout the country. These are co-ordinated by 29 Regional Centres and 17 Recognised Regional Centres as on date. At the Study Centres, the learners interact with the Academic Counsellor and the other learners, refer to books in the library, watch/listen to video/audio cassettes and interact with the Coordinator on administrative and academic matters. The list of Regional and Study Centres is given in this handbook (Section 4). Support services are also provided through Work Centre: Programmed Specific Centres and Skill Development Centres and Special Study Centres.

9. Programme Delivery

The methodology of instruction in this University is different from that of the conventional Universities. The open university system is more learner-oriented and the learner is an active participant in the teaching and learning process. Most of the instructions are imparted through distance education methodology rather than face-to-face communication.

The University follows a multimedia approach for instruction. It comprises:

(*a*) *Self Instructional Written Material:* The printed study material (written in self-instruction style) for both theory and practical components of the programmes is supplied to the learners in batches of blocks for every course (on an average 1 block per credit). A block which comes in the form of a booklet usually comprises 3 to 5 units.

(*b*) *Audio-Visual Material Aids*: The learning package contains audio and video cassettes which have been produced by the University for better clarification and enhancement understanding of the course material given to the learner. A video programme is normally 25-30 minutes duration. The audio tapes are run and video cassettes are screened at the study centres during specific sessions which are duly notified.

The video programmes are telecast on National Network of Doordarshan. Some of the selected stations of All India Radio are also broadcasting the audio programmes. Learners can confirm the dates for the programme from their study centres. The information is also provided through the National Newspapers and IGNOU Newsletters sent to the learners periodically.

(*c*) *Counselling Sessions*: Normally counselling sessions are held as per schedule drawn by the Study Centre. These are mostly held during the non-working hours of the host institutions of the study centres.

(*d*) *Teleconferences*: Live sessions are conducted via satellite through Training and Development Communication Channel (TDCC) the schedule of which is made available at the study centres. The learner will have to go to the nearest reception centre at the scheduled time for taking the benefit of this facility.

(*e*) *Practicals/Project Work*: Some Programmes have practical/ project components. Practicals are held at designated institutions for which schedule is provided by the Study Centres. Attendance at practicals is compulsory. Keeping in tune with the flexibility as regards choice of time for study one way skip practicals during a year but for doing it in a subsequent year or in order to have a repeat exercise additional fee determined by the University has to be paid. For project work, study centres will provide the necessary guidance but the learner will have to manage his/her own resources.

(*f*) *Gyan Darshan Educational Channel*: A collaboration between MHRD, Doordarshan, IGNOU and other organisations has resulted in DD Gyan Darshan, the Educational Channel of India. In a significant gesture, EMPC has been identified as the coordinating and transmitting agency. Regular transmission of Educational Programmes from the EMPC studios started on January 10, 2000. The Channel is providing Educational Programme on a variety of subjects for 19 hours a day to enhance the learning process. Steps are being taken to relay the Gyan Darshan Channel through different Cable Operators in the Country for wider outreach.

(*g*) *Gyan Vani*: IGNOU has been offered one FM Channel in 40 cities and town for education and development. EMPC will be the nodal agency for implementing the project. The first station will come into operation soon. EMPC is also studying an experimental proposal global Gyan Vani.

(*h*) *Interactive Radio-Counselling*: Interactive Radio-Counselling is a recent concept in distance learning in India. Live counselling is provided on radio by invited experts. Students can ask questions right from their homes on telephone. These sessions are conducted for an hour on Sundays from 189 radio stations of the country.

10. Evaluation System

The system of evaluation in IGNOU is also different from that of conventional universities. IGNOU has a three tier system of evaluation.

1. Self-assessment exercise within each unit of study.
2. Continuous evaluation mainly through assignments which are either tutor-marked or computer-marked, practical assignments and seminar/workshops.
3. The term-end examinations/projects work.

The evaluation of learners depends upon various instructional activities undertaken by them. A learner has to write assignment responses compulsorily before taking term-end examination from time to time to complete an academic programme. A learner has to send tutor marked assignment responses to the concerned Coordinator of the Study Centre to which s'he is attached. Computer marked assignments containing multiple-choice questions are evaluated at the SR&E Division at the headquarters. A learner should keep duplicate copies of assignment responses of Computer-marked assignments that may be required to produce at SR&E Division, on demand. The marks weightage given to assignments, seminars/practicals varies from 25 per cent to 50 per cent of the maximum possible score.

IGNOU uses two types of assignments tutor-marked assignment (TMA) and computer-marked assignment (CMA). At present CMAs constitute nearly one-third of the total number of assignments in most courses. In some courses both TMAs and CMAs are used and some courses have only TMAs. Evaluation of assignments is called continuous assessment (CA). Besides CA, a learner has to sit for term-end examinations (TEEs) (carrying 70% to 75% weightage) conducted at various examination centres all over the country in June and December.

IGNOU uses the system of "Grading" for evaluating learners' achievement (assignment responses, project work, etc.) on a five-point scale using letter grade A, B, C, D, E. The notional correlates of the letter grades are as follows:

Letter Grade	*Qualitative Level*	*Point Grade*
A	Excellent	5
B	Very Good	4
C	Good	3
D	Satisfactory	2
E	Unsatisfactory	1

For some of the programmes (like the BDP, CFN, BCA, MCA, BTCM, BTWRE, BTS, BLISc, MLIsc etc.) the system of numerical marking is followed, and the marks secured in assignments, TEEs, etc. are later converted into grades as per the five-point grading scale given above.

In each course except BTCM and BTWRE wherever grading is adopted a learner is required to score at least a 'D' grade in each of the components-continuous assessment, practical assignment, seminar, workshops and term-end examination. However, in the overall computation, s/he must have a 'C' grade in each course to claim a degree/diploma. In the courses, where numerical marking scheme has been adopted the learner is required to secure minimum 35 per cent to 50 per cent qualifying marks as per programme curriculum in each component of evaluation.

For BTCM and BTWRE programmes a learner is required to score atleast 45 per cent marks in each of the continuous evaluation component (CEC) and Term-end examination (TEE) separately. However, to clear a course, students must score 50 per cent marks in CEC and TEE taken together. The details of the same have been presented in Programme Guide prepared by School of Engineering & Technology which will be supplied to you along with the first despatch of the study materials.

To facilitate our learners to obtain due recognition from other academic institutions and employment agencies, the University has converted the grade system into 'conventional' marks for the B.A./ B.Com./B.Sc./BLI.Sc. Degrees, etc. and the learners are placed in I, II or Pass Division on the following criteria:

BLIS/MLIS

I Division	60% or more marks
II Division	50% or more but less than 60% marks
Pass	40% or more but less than 50% marks

./B.Com./B.Sc.

I Division	60% or more marks
II Division	50% or more but less than 60% marks
Pass	40% or more but less than 50% marks

BCA

I Division with Distinction	75% and above
I Division	60% or more but less than 75%
II Division	50% or more but less than 60%
Unsuccessful	Less than 50%

THE STRUCTURE OF IGNOU'S DISTANCE LEARNING PROGRAMMES

In our day-to-day life we come across with persons who say that the structure of programmes offered for distance learning is not at par with formal system of education. This view is most unfortunate and most damaging. We also come across with persons who when asked by others to suggest that in view of their resources they should go for distance learning of their children but they themselves prefer formal system of education, though they too are not better in financial resources, therefore, this chapter is devoted to emphasise that distance learning programmes of most distance learning universities and institutions are at part with each other and which are offered by the formal system of education. Apart from it facilities of distance learning are available in all cities and major terms in India as listed in the last chapter. Hereunder structure of programmes offered by IGNOU for distance learning at doorsteps are given, which will enable the common people to compare it with the structure of programmes offered by formal system of education so that they are able to benefit from this alternative system of education at much lower cost without being away from home and while earning and looking after their family.

STRUCTURE OF IGNOU PROGRAMMES

The structure of the academic programmes already launched, are outlined below. It may be noted here that each programme consists of a few courses, each course consists of a few blocks, and each block consists of a few units. Each programme is modular in nature and consists of a definite number of credits which have to be acquired to complete the programme. Eligibility, age, duration and medium of instruction are all given in the table wherein basic information for all the programmes has been mentioned, therefore, it has not been repeated here in the list of University Programmes.

1. Master of Arts in Distance Education (MADE)

This Programme has been designed to develop human resources in various specialized areas of Distance Education. Obviously, the inputs made in this Programme go beyond those made in the Diploma Programme. The details of the Programme are as follows:

The programme comprises the following four courses and a Project:

Course Code	*Title of the Course*	*Credits*
ES-315	Research for Distance Education	6
ES-316	Curriculum Development for Distance Education	6
ES-317	Distance Education: Economic Perspective	6
ES-319	Staff Development in Distance Education	6
ES-320	Project Work	6
Total	Five Courses	30

The medium of instruction is English

2. Master in Computer Applications (MCA)

Objective: The objective of this programme is to meet the manpower requirement of the fast developing software industry and the requirement of the institutions of higher learning for capable teachers.

Lateral entry to MCA III semester is allowed to the candidates who have already successfully completed:

(*i*) PGDCA or ADIT or its equivalent programme from recognised University and deemed Universities.

(*ii*) 'A' level examination of DOE, after graduation.

Those desirous of taking admission in MCA III semester – lateral entry, have to clear all the papers of MCA I & II semesters (of IGNOU) through examinations to be conducted in June and December every year.

Those who have not studied Mathematics at the 10+2 level will be required successfully complete the Preparatory Programme in Computing (PPC) concurrently with the 1st/2nd semester and such candidates are also required to pay an additional fee of Rs. 500/- along with the admission form. The details of PPC are as follows:

The Preparatory Programme in Computing is divided into five blocks, namely—(*i*) Some basic concepts, (*ii*) Elementary Algebra, (*iii*) Geometry and Trignometry, (*iv*) Equations and Matrices and (*v*) Calculus and Statistics.

The student will indicate this when submitting the acceptance of the offer of admission and there will be separate item for this purpose in the acceptance form.

Programme Structure of the MCA Programme

	I-SEMESTER			*II-SEMESTER*	
Course Code	*Course Title*	*Credits*	*Course Code*	*Course Title*	*Credits*
CS-02	Introduction to Software	6	CS-01	Computer Fundamentals	6
CS-04	Data Structure through 'C' and 'PASCAL'	6	CS-03	File Structure and Programming in COBOL	4
CS-05	Elements of System Analysis and Design	6	CS-06	Database Management Systems	4
	III-SEMESTER			*IV-SEMESTER*	
CS-08	Numerical and Statistical Computing	6	CS-07	Discrete Mathematics	6
CS-09	Data Communication and Networks	6	CS-10	Software Engineering	6
CS-51	Operations Research	4	CS-54	Accounting and Finance on Computers	4
	V-SEMESTER			*VI-SEMESTER*	
CS-12	Computer Architecture	4	CS-13	Operating Systems	4
CS-16	Object Oriented Systems	4	CS-14	Intelligent Systems	4
CS-17	Project (Part I)	8	CS-15	Relational Database Management Systems	4
			CS-17	Project (Part II)	4

Admission to MCA programme will be made on the basis of region-wise Merit List or Entrance Test depending on the number of seats available in a given region.

3. Master in Library and Information Science (MLIS)

The general objective of this programme is to contribute to building of professional human resources to meet the varied demands for information handling in libraries and information centres in the country.

The medium of instruction of MLIS programme for the time being is only English.

Course Code	*Title of the Course*	*Credits*
MLIS-01	Information, Communication and Society	4
MLIS-02	Information Sources, Systems and Programmes	4
MLIS-03	Information Processing and Retrieval	4
MLIS-04	Information Institutions, Products and Services	4
MLIS-05	Management of Library and Information Centres	4
MLIS-06	Application of Information Technology	4

Elective: (Out of following four electives, a learner has to opt for any two).

Course Code	*Title of the Course*	*Credits*
MLIS-E1	Preservation and Conservation of Library Materials	4
MLIS-E2	Research Methodology	4
MLIS-E3	Academic Library System	4
MLIS-E4	Technical Writing	4

4. Master in Tourism Management (MTM)

The MTM is designed for those students who are interested in pursuing a career in tourism at managerial level. This is for aspiring entrepreneurs of those running their own tourism agencies. The programme consists of four semesters.

All students seeking admission under Category 2 will have to pass the following four courses during their period of study.

Course Code	*Title of the Course*	*Credits*
TS-01	Foundation Course in Tourism	8
TS-02	Tourism Development: Operations and Case Studies	8
TS-03	Management in Tourism	8
TS-06	Tourism Marketing	8
		Total: 32 Credits

Course Code	*Title of the Course*	*Credits*
I Semester		
MTM-01	Management Functions and Behaviour in Tourism	4
MTM-02	Human Resource Development and Planning in Tourism	4
MTM-03	Managing Personnel in Tourism	4
MTM-04	Information Management and Information Systems in Tourism	4
II Semester		
MTM-05	Accounting, Finance and Working Capital for Tourism Managers	4
MTM-06	Marketing for Tourism Managers	4
MTM-07	Sales and Advertising Management in Tourism	4
MTM-08	Managing Small Scale enterprises in Tourism	4
III Semester		
MTM-09	Understanding Tourism Markets	4
MTM-10	Tourism Products: Design and Development	4
MTM-11	Tourism Impacts	4
MTM-12	Tourism Planning and Development	4
IV Semester		
MTM-13	Tourism Operations	4
MTM-14	Tourist Transport Operations (Road Transport)	4
MTM-15	Meetings, Incentives, Conferences and Events (MICE)	4
MTM-16	Dissertation	8
		Total: 68 Credits

5. Master's Degree in English (MEG)

The aim of the Master's Degree in English (MEG) programme is to give the learners a sound base in language besides giving them an intensive exposure to a wide range of literatures, with options, for specialisation in a particular area of interest. The learners would thus hopefully acquire linguistic competence, critical abilities and analytical skills.

The Programme comprises the following courses:

I Year Course		
MEG-01	British Poetry	Compulsory
MEG-02	British Drama	
MEG-03	British Novel	
MEG-04	Aspects of Language	
II Year Courses		
MEG-05	Literary Criticism and Theory	Compulsory
MEG-06	American Literature	Optional
MEG-07	Indian English Literature	
MEG-08	New Literatures in English	
MEG-09	Australian Literature	
MEG-10	English Studies in India	

6. एम.ए. हिन्दी (एम.एच.डी.)

इस पाठ्यक्रम का उद्देश्य विद्यार्थियों को हिन्दी भाषा और साहित्य के क्षेत्र में विस्तृत जानकारी और विशेषज्ञ ज्ञान प्रदान करना है जिससे वे साहित्य के आस्वादन और विश्लेषण-मूल्यांकन में दक्षता का विकास भी कर सकें।

प्रथम वर्ष के पाठ्क्रम (8 क्रेडिट के):

1. एम.एच.डी.-2: आधुनिक हिन्दी कविता
2. एम.एच.डी.-3 उपन्यास एवं कहानियाँ
3. एम.एच.डी.-4 नाटक एवं अन्य गद्य विद्याएँ
4. एम.एच.डी.-6 हिन्दी साहित्य एवं भाषा का इतिहास

दूसरे वर्ष में साहित्य, भाषा और संप्रेषण की धाराओं में विशेष अध्ययन के 32 क्रेडिट के पाठ्यक्रम उपलब्ध होंगे, जिनकी सूचना उचित समय पर दी जाएगी।

7. Bachelor Degree Programmes (BDP)

Entry to Bachelor Degree Programme is through two means: the non-formal and the formal. The non-formal is through BPP and the formal is after passing 10+2 or its equivalent examination.

BACHELOR PREPARATORY PROGRAMME (BPP)

Learners who are admitted to the BPP must opt for two of the following three courses. After six months, there is a qualifying examination in June and December by which time the learner should have submitted his/her assignments as well.

(*a*) Preparatory Course in General Mathematics (Compulsory for all)—PMT

(*b*) Preparatory Course in Social Sciences (those wishing to go for B.A.)—PSS

OR

Preparatory Course in Commerce (Those wishing to go for B.Com.)—PCO

Those who do not have the formal educational qualification, but have attained the age of 18 years or more on 1st January/1st July of the academic year can apply for admission to the Bachelor's Preparatory Programme (BPP).

BPP Programme is available in English as well as Hindi medium.

(1) Bachelor Degree Programme (BDP)

(*a*) B.A., Bcom Programme for 10+2 and BPP Promotees, and

(*b*) B.Sc. Programme for 10+2 with Science subjects.

The University offers a Bachelor Degree Programme leading to a B.A./B.Com./B.Sc. Degree both in English as well as in Hindi. A minimum period of three years is required for completing the Bachelor Degree Programme. However, if the learner wants, a maximum of 8 years is allowed. The University follows the credit system in organising this programme. Credit weightage is given against each course. A learner will be eligible to get a B.A./B. com./ B.Sc. Degree when she/he earns 96 credits as given under:

Programme	*Foundation Courses*	*Elective Courses*	*Application Oriented Courses*
B.A.	24 Credits	64 or 56 Credits	8 or 16 Credits
B. Com.	24 Credits	64 or 56 Credits (not less than 48 Credits from Commerce)	8 or 16 Credits
B. Sc.	24 Credits	64 or 56 Credits (al least 25% of the total credits in Physics, Chemistry or Life Sciences have to be obtained from Laboratory Courses)	8 or 16 Credits

(2) Foundation Courses—common to all B.A./B.Com./B.Sc.

(Compulsory 24 Credits (Ist Year 16 credits, II year 8 credits)

The following are the Foundation Courses which are compulsory:

Course Code	*Title of the Course*	*Credits*
FHS-1	Foundation Course in Humanities & Social Sciences	8
FST-1	Foundation Course in Science & Technology	8
FEG-1	Foundation Course in English-1	4
	OR	
FHD-2	Foundation Course in Hindi-2	4

Modern Indian Languages

A Foundation Course in any one of the following Modern Indian Languages is to be opted:

Course Code	*Title of the Course*	*Credits*
FAS-1	Assamese	4
FBG-1	Bengali	4
FEG-2	English	4
FGT-1	Gujarati	4
FHD-1	Hindi	4
FKD-1	Kannada	4
FML-1	Malayalam	4
FMT-1	Marathi	4
FOR-1	Oriya	4
FPB-1	Punjabi	4
FTM-1	Tamil	4
FTG-1	Telugu	4
FUD-1	Urdu	4

(3) Elective Courses-B.A.

Following are the Elective Courses:

Discipline	*Course Code*	*Title of the Elective Courses*	*Credits*
Hindi			
	EHD-1	Hindi Gadya	8
	EHD-2	Hindi Kavya	8
	EHD-3	Hindi Sahitya ka Itihas evam Sahitya Parichya	8

(Contd.)

Discipline	*Course Code*	*Title of the Elective Courses*	*Credits*
	EHD-4	Madhya Kaleen Bhartiya Sahitya: Samaj aur Sanskriti	8
	EHD-5	Adhunik Bhartiya Sahitya Rashtriya Chetna aur Navjagran	8
	EHD-6	Hindi Bhasha: Itihas aur Vartman	8
	EHD-7	Hindi Samrachna	8
	EHD-8	Prayojan Moolak Hindi	8
English			
	EEG-1	Language through Literature	8
	EEG-2	The Structure of Modern English	8
	EEG-3	Communication Skills in English	8
	EEG-4	English for Practical Purposes	8
	EEG-5	Understanding Prose	8
	EEG-6	Understanding Poetry	8
	EEG-7	Understanding Drama	8
	EEG-8	Reading the Novel	8
Political Science			
	EPS-1	Introduction to Political Theory and Institutions	8
	EPS-2	Government & Politics in India	8
	EPS-3	Modern Indian Political Thought	8
	EPS-5	Government and Politics in South Asia	8
	EPS-6	Government and Politics in East and South East Asia	8
	EPS-7	International Relations	8
	EPS-8	Government and Politics in Australia	8
History			
	EHI-1	Modern India, 1857-1964	8
	EHI-2	India: Earliest Times to the 8th Century A.D.	8
	EHI-3	India from 8th Century to 15th Century A.D.	8
	EHI-4	India from 16th to Mid-18th Century	8
	EHI-5	India: From Mid-18th to Mid-19th Century	8
	EHI-6	History of China and Japan: 1840-1949	8
	EHI-7	Modern Europe: Mid Eighteenth To Mid Twentieth Century	8
Economics			
	EEC-1	Fundamental of Economics	8
	EEC-2	Indian Economic Development Since Independence	8

(Contd.)

Discipline	*Course Code*	*Title of the Elective Courses*	*Credits*
	EEC-3	Elementary Statistical Methods and Survey Techniques	8
	EEC-4	Agricultural Development in India	8
	EEC-5	Elementary Mathematical Methods in Economics.	4
	EEC-6	Patterns of Economics Development: A Comparative Study.	8
	EEC-9	Economic Concepts and Politics	4
Public Administration			
	EPA-1	Administrative Theory	8
	EPA-2	Indian Administration	8
	EPA-3	Development Administration	8
	EPA-4	Personnel Administration	8
	EPA-5	Financial Administration	8
	EPA-6	Public Policy	8
Sociology			
	ESO-1	The Study of Society	8
	ESO-2	Society in India	8
	ESO-3	Sociological Thought	8
	ESO-4	Social Stratification	8
	ESO-5	Society and Religion	8
	ESO-6	Social Problems in India	8
Rural Development			
	ERD-1	Rural Development in India	8

(Learners who successfully complete 48 credits in any one discipline will be given a Major in B.A. degree after completion of 26 credits whereas others will be awarded B.A. General Degree).

Commerce			
	ECO- 1	Business Organisation	4
	ECO- 2	Accountancy-1	4
	ECO- 3	Management Theory	4
	ECO- 5	Mercantile Law	4
	ECO- 6	Economic Theory	4
	ECO- 7	Elements of Statistics	4
	ECO- 8	Company Law	4
	ECO- 9	Money, Banking & Financial Institutions	4
	ECO-10	Elements of Costing	4
	ECO-11	Elements of Income Tax	4
	ECO-12	Elements of Auditing	4

(Contd.)

Discipline	*Course Code*	*Title of the Elective Courses*	*Credits*	
	ECO-13	Business Environment	4	
	ECO-14	Accountancy-II	4	
Mathematics				
	MTE-1	Calculus	4	
	MTE-2	Linear Algebra	4	
	MTE-4	Elementary Albebra	2	To be taken together
	MTE-5	Analytical Geometry	2	
	MTE-6	Abstract Algebra	4	
	MTE-7	Advanced Calculus	4	
	MTE-8	Differential Equations	4	
	MTE-9	Real Analysis	4	
	MTE-10	Numerical Analysis	4	
	MTE-11	Probability and Statistics	4	
	MTE-12	Linear Programming	4	
	MTE-13	Discrete Mathematics	4	
	MTE-14	Mathematical Modelling	4	
Physics				
	PHE-1	Elementary Mechanics	2	To be taken together
	PHE-2	Oscillations and Waves	2	
	PHE-3(L)	Physics Laboratory-I	4	
	PHE-4	Mathematical Methods in Physics-I	2	To be taken together
	PHE-5	Mathematical Methods in Physics-II	2	
	PHE-6	Thermodynamics and Statistical Mechanics	4	
	PHE-7	Electric and Magnetic Phenomena	4	
	PHE-8(L)	Physics Laboratory-II	4	
	PHE-9	Optics (Physical & Lasers)	4	
	PHE-10	Electrical Circuits and Electronics	4	
	PHE-11	Modern Physics	4	
	PHE-12(L)	Physics Laboratory-III	4	
	PHE-13	Physics of Solids	4	
	PHE-14	Mathematical Methods in Physics-III	4	

(*Contd.*)

Discipline	*Course Code*	*Title of the Elective Courses*	*Credits*	
Chemistry				
	CHE-1	Atoms and Molecules	2	
	CHE-3(L)	Chemistry Laboratory-I	2	
	CHE-2	Inorganic Chemistry	4	
	CHE-4	Physical Chemistry	4	
	CHE-5	Organic Chemistry	4	
	CHE-6	Organic Reaction Mechanism	4	
	CHE-7(L)	Chemistry Laboratory-II	2	To be taken together
	CHE-8(L)	Chemistry Laboratory-III	2	
	CHE-9	Biochemistry	4	
	CHE-10	Spectroscopy	4	
	CHE-11(L)	Chemistry Laboratory-IV	4	
	CHE-12(L)	Chemistry Laboratory-V	4	
	MTE-3	Mathematical Methods	4	
Life Sciences				
	LSE-1	Cell Biology	4	
	LSE-2	Ecology	4	
	LSE-3	Genetics	4	
	LSE-4(L)	Laboratory Course-I	4	
	LSE-5	Physiology	4	
	LSE-6	Developmental Biology	4	
	LSE-7	Taxonomy and Evolution	4	
	LSE-8(L)	Laboratory Course-II	4	
	LSE-09	Animal Diversity-I	6	To be taken together
	LSE-10	Animal Diversity-II	6	
	LSE-11(L)	Animal Diversity Laboratory	4	
	LSE-12	Plant Diversity-I	6	To be taken together
	LSE-13	Plant Diversity-II	6	
	LSE-14(L)	Plant Diversity Laboratory	4	

Note: MTE-1 is a prerequisite for MTE-7 to MTE-10
MTE-7 is a prerequisite for MTE-11
MTE-7 is a prerequisite for MTE-8
CHE-1 is a prerequisite for CHE 5 and CHE-10, CHE-4, is also co-requisite for CHE-2.
CHE-5 is a co-requisite for CHE-6& pre-requisite for CHE-9 & 10.
CHE-4 and 5 are prerequisite for CHE-9.
MTE-3 credits will not be given to any student who opts for any mathematics electives.

LSE-1 is a prerequisite for LSE-3, 5 and 6
CHE-1 is a co-requisite for CHE-2
CHE-2 is a prerequisite for CHE-10
PHE-2 is a prerequisite for PHE-09
PHE-4 and PHE-5 are pre-requisite for PHE-14
PHE-7 is a prerequisite for PHE-10

Co-requisite and prerequisite courses refer to the courses which the learners are strongly advised to register for and complete, so that the related courses could be followed easily. Otherwise, it is not a compulsory directive.

(4) Application Oriented Courses Common to all B.A./B.Com./B.Sc.

AFW(E)-1	Feature Writing (English)	4
AWR(E)-1	Writing for Radio (English)	4
AFW(H)-1	Feature Lekhan (Hindi)	4
AWR(H)-1	Radio Lekhan (Hindi)	4
ATR-1	Translation (English 4+Hindi 4 Credits)	8
ACC-1	Organising Child Care Services	8
ANC-1	Nutrition for the Community	8
AHE-1	Human Environment	8
AMK-1	Marketing	4
AED-1	Export Procedure and Documentation	4
AOM-1	Office Organisation and Management	4
ASP-1	Secretarial Practice	4
*AMT-1	Teaching of Primary School Mathematics	8
ACS-1	Consumer Studies	8
CTE-3	Teaching Strategies	4
CTE-4	Teaching English—Elementary School	4
CTE-5	Teaching English-Secondary School	4

* (This course is also on offer under Associate Studentship Scheme. See 1, 11, p.a.)

SCHEME OF STUDY

In order to enable you to complete Bachelor's Degree Programme within the minimum period of three years, you are allowed to take 32 credits worth of courses in each year. In the first year of study you should take 16 credits in Foundation Courses (FHS-1, FEG-1 or FHD-2 and FEG-2 or any one of MILS), and 16 credits in Elective Courses. In the second year you should take 8 credits of Foundation Course (FST-1) and 24 credits of Elective Courses. In the third year you should take 24 credits in Elective Courses and 8 credits in Application-Oriented courses; alternatively, you can take 16 credits in Elective Courses and 16 in Application-Oriented Courses.

How to Choose Courses for B.A./B.Com./B.Sc.?

B.A.

We have already explained the number of credits to be obtained in various categories of courses, viz. Foundation, Elective and Application-Oriented Courses. We discuss below the choices available in all these groups.

Foundation Courses: In this category of courses you have to choose from the following:

FEG-1 or FHD-2

FEG-2 or FHD-1 or any one of the listed Modern Indian Languages.

FHS-1 Foundation Course in Humanities and Social Sciences, FST-1 Foundation Course in Science and Technology are compulsory.

Elective Courses: The main task to select elective courses. Please remember that as a learner in an Open University you have this unique opportunity of free choice of courses. You must have noticed that the list of elective courses is very big and you have to choose courses worth 64 or 56 credits from this group. There can be two ways of selecting these courses.

1. If you want to go for in-depth study of one particular discipline to obtain B.A. Major or you want to pursue the same discipline for your postgraduate studies you can select courses worth 48 credits from that discipline. Rest you should take from other disciplines. For your convenience we have grouped courses belonging to one discipline at one place in the list given in this guide.
2. If you do not intend to specialise in one discipline you can choose courses from various disciplines. Here you will have to be careful. If you choose from many disciplines you might end up doing one course from each discipline which might not give you enough knowledge in any of the discipline. You should try to select courses of your choice from 2 or 3 disciplines.

These courses would be available to you in a phased manner i.e. some would be available in the first year. A few more would be available in the second year and the remaining in the third year. This phasing has been done for the convenience of counselling and examination. In this scheme all the elective courses have been divided into 6 groups.

Only Group 1 and 2 courses are available in the first year. Rest of the Elective Courses would be offered in second and third year.

Group 1	EHD-1, EHD-5, EEG-1, EPS-1, EHI-1, EEC-1, EPA-1, ESO-1, MTE-1, MTE-4, MTE-5, ECO-1, ECO-2, EHI-7
Group 2	EHD-2, EHE-8, EEG-2, EPS-2, EHI-2, EEC-2, EPA-2, ESO-2, MTE-2, MTE-6, ERD-1

In first year you have to choose courses worth 16 credits only. Select 8 Credits from each group.

You should offer elective courses in such a way that overlapping is avoided i.e. You should offer courses of 8 credits from Group 1 and 8 credits from Group 2.

Application-Oriented Course: In the third year you have to take courses worth 8 or 16 credits from this group. Wile selecting these courses take care that they are of use to you in the profession, you are working in or intend to take up in future.

B.Com.

In order to enable you to complete B.Com. Programme within the minimum period of three years, you are allowed to take 32 credits worth of courses in each year. In the first year you should take 16 credits in Foundation Courses (FHS-1, FEG-1 or FHD-2 and FEG-2 or any one of the MILs), 8 credits of Elective Courses in Commerce (ECO-1 and ECO-2) and 8 credits of Elective Courses in other Disciplines either from Group 1 and 2. In the second year you should take 8 credits of Foundation Courses (FST) and 24 credits of Elective Courses in Commerce (ECO-3, ECO-5, ECO-6 or ECO-13, ECO-7, ECO-12 and ECO-14). In the third year you should take 16 credits of Elective Courses in Commerce (ECO-8, ECO-9, ECO-10 and ECO-11), and 8 or 16 credits in Application-Oriented Courses. In case you take only 8 credits in Application Oriented courses, you should take 8 credits in elective courses in Other Disciplines. It shall be noted that the Commerce based Application Oriented courses are AMK-1, AED-1, AOM-1 and ASP-1.

B.Sc.

In order to enable you to complete the Bachelor's Degree Programme in Science within the minimum period of three years, you are allowed to take 32 credits worth of courses in each year. Elective courses worth of minimum of 8 credits and a maximum of 48 credits in any one of the four Science disciplines can be opted. You can choose 56 to 64 credits of elective courses from a minimum of two disciplines and a maximum of four disciplines. Of the total credits opted in elective courses in Physics, Chemistry and Life Sciences Disciplines, at least 25 per cent must be from the laboratory courses. The year-wise scheme of study is shown in the following table.

Year-wise Scheme of Study

Year of Study	*Foundation Courses*	*Elective Courses*	*Application Oriented Courses*	*Total Credits*
First Year	**16 Credits as under** 1. FST-1 8 Credits 2. FEG-1 or FHD-2 4 Credits 3. FEG-2 or 4 Credits FHD-1 or any one of the MILs	**16 Credits** (From PHE-01, 02, 03(L) 04, 05, 06 Che-01, 02, 03(L) 05 07(L), 08(L) LSE-01, 02, 03, 04(L) MTE-01, 02, 03, 04, 05 (06)	—	**32 Credits**
Second Year	**8 Credits** (FHS-1) 8 Credits	**24 Credits** (From PHE-01, 02, 03(L) 04, 05, 06, 07, 08 (L), 09, 10 CHE-01, 02, 03(L), 04, 05, 06, 07(L), 08 (L), 09, 11(L) LSE-01, 02, 03, 04(L) 05, 06, 07, 08(L) MTE-01, 02, 03*, 04, 05, 06, 07, 08, 09, 10	—	**32 Credits**
Third Year		**16 Credits or 24 Credits** (From PHE-01, 02, 03(L), 04, 05, 06, 07, 08(L), 09, 10, 11, 12(L), 13, 14 CHE-01, 02, 03(L), 04, 05, 06, 07 (L), 08(L), 09, 10, 11(L), 12(L) LSE-01, 02, 03, 04(L), 05, 06, 07, 08 (L), 09,	**16 Credits or 8 Credits**	**32 Credits**

(Contd.)

Year of Study	*Foundation Courses*	*Elective Courses*	*Application Oriented Courses*	*Total Credits*
•		10, 11(L), 12, 13, 14(L), MTE-01, 02, 03, 04, 05, 06, 07, 08, 09, 10, 11, 12, 13, 14)		
Total Credits	**24 Credits**	**56/64 Credits**	**8/16 Credits**	**96 Credits**

Note: *MTE-03 credits will not count towards mathematics electives.

As per the above table, in the first year of study, you should take 16 credits in Foundation Courses (FST-1, FEG-1 or FHD-2 and FEG-2 or FHD-1 or any one of the MILs) and 16 credits in Elective Courses. In the second year, you should take 8 credits of Foundation Course in Humanities and Social Sciences (FHS-1) and 24 credits of Elective Courses: In the third year, you can take 24 credits in Elective Courses and 8 credits in Application-Oriented Courses; alternatively, you can take 16 credits in Elective Courses and 16 Credits in Application-Oriented Courses.

B.Sc.(Major)

For **B.Sc. (Major) in Botany,** Elective Courses worth 48 credits in Life Sciences (LSE-01, to LSE-08(L) worth 32 credits and a package of courses (LSE-12, 13, 14(L) worth 16 credit(s) should be taken.

For obtaining **B.Sc. (Major) Degree in Chemistry,** Elective Courses in Chemistry worth 40 credits (CHE-01 to CHE-12(L) should be completed.

For **B.Sc. (Major) Degree in Mathematics.** Elective Courses worth 40 credits in Mathematics (MTE-01, 02, 04 to 14) should be completed. Of these 40 credits, 28 credits worth of courses viz. MTE-01, 02, 04 to 09 are compulsory.

For **B.Sc. (Major) Degree in Physics,** Elective Courses worth 48 credits (PHE-01 to PHE-14) should be completed.

For **B.Sc. (Major) Degree in Zoology,** Elective Courses, worth 48 credits in Life Sciences (LSE-01, to LSE-08(L) worth 32 credits and a package of courses (LSE-09, 10, 11(L) worth 16 credits) should be completed.

Note: Package of Course LSE 9, 10 and 11(L) or LSE 12, 13, 14(L) are to be taken together.

In case you do not complete the courses above prescribed for various B.Sc. (Major) degree and complete any other combination of courses of Sciences Electives, you will be awarded a B.Sc. (General) degree. **At least 25 per cent of elective credits in non-mathematics science courses, i.e. Physics, Chemistry & Life Sciences must be from laboratory courses.**

Year of Study	*Foundation Courses*	*Elective Courses*	*Application Oriented Courses*	*Total Credits*
First Year	16 Credits	16 Credits	—	32 Credits
Second Year	8 Credits	24 Credits	—	32 Credits
Third Year	—	16 Credits OR 24 Credits	16 Credits OR 8 Credits	32 Credits
Total Credits	**24 Credits**	**56/64 Credits**	**8/16 Credits**	**96 Credits**

8. Bachelor in Computer Applications (BCA)

Objective: The basic objectives of this programme are to open a channel of admission for Computer Courses for students who have done the 10+2 and are interested in taking up Computer as a career. After acquiring the Bachelor's degree at IGNOU, there is a further educational opportunity to go for an MCA at IGNOU or Master's Programme at another University.

The development of the course structure for the BCA programme has kept in mind the current trends of encouraging students at the Bachelor degree level to have exposure in some areas beyond their immediate specialisation. The curriculum of BCA includes foundation/introductory courses in English for computing. Humanities, Social Sciences and Sciences and Technology. It is expected that with this background of foundation courses in a somewhat broad range of areas, a student would be in a better position to make effective use of the technical knowledge and skills that he acquires in the courses which are specifically related to computer topics. Some of the computer science related courses covered in BCA include topics like Computer Fundamentals, Problem solving. Data Structure using 'C'. Graphical User Interface, Data Base Management Systems and Computer Organisation.

Another feature of the BCA programme is the addressing of the current topics such as Windows, Multi-Media, Object-Oriented Programming, Internet and Internet related topics. It is expected that a student pursuing the BCA programme would find himself exposed to a broad based education expected at the undergraduate level, together with a reasonable employment potential in the emerging job markets of the future.

Note: Candidates not having mathematics at 10+2 level will have to complete (PPC) with the first year course by paying Rs. 500/- additional along with admission form: Please refer to MCA main Test Clause for PPC details.

Programme Structure

The basic structure of IGNOU's Bachelor in Computer Applications Programmes is as follows:

	I Semester			*II Semester*		
Year	*Course Code*	*Course Title*	*Credits*	*Course Code*	*Course Title*	*Credits*
I	CS-610	Foundation Course in English for Computing	4	CS-612	PC, Software Application skills	4
	FHS-01	Foundation Course in Humanities and Social Sciences	8	CS-60	Foundation Course in Mathematics in Computing	8
	CS-611	Computer Fundamentais	4	CS-62	'C' Programming & Data Structure	4
II	FST	Foundation Course in Science & Technology	8	CS-06	Introduction to DMS	4
	CS-63	Introduction to System Software	4	CS-64	Introduction to Computer Organisation	4
	CS-05	Elements of System Analysis and Design	4	CS-65	Window Programming	2 2
				CS-66	Multimedia	4
				CS-67	RDBMS Lab	
III	CS-68	Computer Network	4	CS-72	C++ and Object Oriented Programming	4
	CS-69	TCP/IP Programming	4	CS-73	Theory of Computer Science	4 4
	CS-70	Introduction to Software Engineering	4	CS-74	INTRODUCTION TO INTERNET PROGRAMMING (JAVA ACTIVE X)	2
	CS-71	Computer Oriented Numerical Techniques	4	CS-75	Intranet Admini-	2
				CS-76	stration Project	4

Note: Admission to BCA programme will be made on the basis of region-wise Merit List or Entrance Test depending on the number of seats available in a given region.

9. Bachelor in Library and Information Science (BLIS)

The Bachelor's Degree in Library and Information Science Programme comprises nine courses; of these seven courses deal with theoretical aspects of this discipline, while courses are meant to provide practical exercises to the learners. Out of seven courses on theoretical aspects, one course (BLIS-07) also includes practical components. Medium of instructions for this programme is English. However, students are allowed to write their assignments and the term and examinations in Hindi.

Course Code	*Title of the Course*	*Credits*
BLIS-01	Library and Society	4
BLIS-02	Library Management	4
BLIS-03	Library Classification Theory	4
BLIS-03P	Library Classification Practices	4
BLIS-04	Library Cataloguing Theory	4
BLIS-04(P)	Library Cataloguing Practice	4
BLIS-05	Reference and Information Sources	4
BLIS-06	Information Services	4
BLIS-07	Information Technology: Basics	4
	Total	32

10. Bachelor of Science in Nursing (B.Sc. Nursing)

The programme is intended to provide an opportunity to a large segment of in service nurses to upgrade their knowledge and skills to respond to the changing health needs of society, to motivate nurses to maintain clinical competence, to provide quality care, to develop teaching, administrative and research skills and to promote personal and professional growth for better promotional opportunities. It is a 3-year programme of 80 credits. It comprises 10 courses in Theory and 8 courses in Practical as under:

Course Code	*Title of the Course*	*Credits*
First Year Theory		
HS1T1	Primary Health Nursing	4
HS1T2	Applied Sciences (Physics,	4
Course Code	*Title of the Course*	*Credits*
	Chemistry, Microbiology, Nutrition and Dietetics)	
HS1T4	English	4

(Contd.)

(*Contd.*)

Course Code	*Title of the Course*	*Credits*
Second Year Theory		
HS2T1	Medical Surgical Nursing	4
HS2T2	Community Health Nursing	4
HS2T3	Behavioural Sciences (General Psychology, Educational Psychology, Sociology, Economics)	4
Third Year Theory		
HS3T1	Paediatric Nursing	2
HS3T2	Mental Health Nursing	2
HS3T3	Nursing Administration	4
HS3T4	Nursing Education and Research	4
	Total	36
First Year Practical		
HS1P1	Primary Health Nursing	8
HS1P2	Applied Sciences (Physics	4
	Chemistry, Microbiology, Nutrition and Dietetics)	4
Second Year Practical		
HS2P1	Medical Surgical Nursing	8
HS2P2	Community Health Nursing	
Third Year Practical		
HS3P1	Paediatric Nursing	6
HS3P2	Mental Health Nursing	6
HS3P3	Nursing Administration	2
HS3P4	Nursing Education and Research	2
	Total	44

Selection Criteria: Selection for B.Sc. Nursing programme is by merit. The merit is worked out on the basis of giving 80 per cent weightage to the total marks obtained in General Nursing and Midwifery (RNRM) and one mark for each year of experience in nursing over and above the years of experience required for eligibility for admission subject to a maximum of 20 years.

Eligible candidates for B.Sc. Nursing must fill up Form 'A' also and submit it along with Application Form for Admission, Experience Certificate and Category Certificate.

11. B.Tech. Civil (Construction Management)—(BTCM)

The B.Tech. Civil (Construction Management) programme has been designed to impart training and continuing professional education to upgrade diploma level manpower engaged in managing construction task. The design of programme structure provides in-built modularity and flexibility. The successful completion of first two modules (First and Second years) make you eligible for the award of Advanced Diploma in Construction Management (ADCM). In this way, a learner then has a flexibility to study either only for the award of ADCM and exit from the system or to move further to complete B.Tech. degree.

Year-wise Course Registration Plan for BTCM

Course Code	*Title of the Course*		*Credits*
First Module			32
	ET-101A	Mathematics-I	3
	ET-101B	Mathematics-II	3
	ET-105A	Physics	4
	ET-105B	Chemistry	4
	ET-202A	Engineering Mechanics	2
	ET-202B	Principles of Electrical Science	4
	ET-301A	Systems Methods	2
	ET-301B	Computer Applications	2
	ET-204A	Materials Sciences	2
	ET-204B	Engineering Materials	2
	ET-501A	Soil Mechanics	2
	ET-501B	Foundation Engineering	2
Second Module			
	ET-521A	Planning and Construction of Building	2
	ET-521B	Building Architecture	2
	ET-521C	Design Detailing	2
	ET-521D	Quantity Surveying & Valuation	2
	ET-523A	Construction Works Supervision	2
	ET-523B	Operation and Maintenance of Const. Equipment	3
	ET-523C	Repair and Maintenance of Buildings	
	ET-524A	Principles of Engg. Management & Economics	3
	ET-524B	Construction Management-1	

(Contd.)

Course Code	*Title of the Course*		*Credits*
	ET-522	Concrete Technology &	4
		Construction Techniques	4
	ET-581A	Testing for Quality Control	2
	ET-581F	Mechanical Equipment in Construction	2
	ET-571	Laboratory-1 (ADCM)	2
Third Module			32
	ET-102	Mathematics-III	4
	ET-201A	Mechanics of Fluid	4
	ET-201B	Engineering Thermodynamics	4
	ET-540B	Flow in Open Channel	2
	ET-302A	Computer Programming & Numerical Methods	3
	ET-302B	Technical Writing	1
	ET-502A	Strength of Materials	4
	ET-502B	Structural Analysis	4
	ET-500	Project	6
Fourth Module			32
	ET-508A	Structural Design-I	4
	ET-508B	Structural Design-II	2
	ET-507A	Pollutants and Water Supply	4
	ET-535A	Elementary Hydrology	2
	ET-535B	Hydraulic Structures	4
	ET-525	Construction Management-II	6
	ET-505	Transportation and Traffic Engineering	4
	ET-581B	Inventory and Stores Management	2
	ET-581C	Building Services	2
	ET-574	Laboratory-II	2

12. B.Tech. Civil (Water Resources Engineering)-(BTWRE)

B.Tech. Civil (Water Resources Engineering) is a continuing education programme for the working polytechnic diploma holders engaged in water resources sector. It is a 4 year degree programme which offers in-built flexibility in terms of intermediate award of Advanced Diploma in Water Resource Engineering (ADWRE) after successful completion of first two modules (First and Second years). The students also have option to discontinue after obtaining ADWRE and take up the study at a later date to complete the degree programme.

Year-wise Course Registration Plan for BTWRE

Course Code		*Title of the Course*	*Credits*
First Module			32
	ET-101A	Mathematics-I	3
	ET-101B	Mathematics-II	3
	ET-105A	Physics	4
	ET-105B	Chemistry	4
	ET-201A	Mechanics of Fluids	4
	ET-201B	Engineering Thermodynamics	4
	ET-531A	Earth & its Environment	3
	ET-531B	Soil Sciences	3
	ET-501A	Soil Mechanics	2
	ET-501B	Foundation Engineering	2
Second Module			31
	ET-532A	Hydrology	4
	ET-532B	Ground Water Development	2
	ET-533A	Irrigation Engineering	4
	ET-533B	Open Channel Flow	4
	ET-502A	Strength of Materials	4
	ET-502B	Structural Analysis	4
	ET-534A	Principles of Engineering Management & Economics	3
	ET-534B	System Methods	2
	ET-534C	Water Resources Planning	3
	ET-573	Laboratory-I (ADWRE)	1
Third Module			32
	ET-102	Mathematics-III	4
	ET-302A	Computer Programming and Numerical Methods	3
	ET-302B	Technical Writing.	
	ET-536A	Hydraulic Structures-I	4
	ET-536B	Hydraulic Structures-II	4
	ET-202A	Engineering Mechanics	2
	ET-202B	Principles of Electrical Science	4
	ET-505	Transportation and Traffic Engineering	4
	ET-500	Project	6
Fourth Module			31
	ET-537A	Soil Conservation & Agronomy	4
	ET-537B	Agricultural Legislation & Management	4
	ET-204B	Engineering Materials	2
	ET-524B	Construction Management-I	3
	ET-508A	Structural Design-I	4
	ET-508B	Structural Design-II	2

(Contd.)

Course Code	Title of the Course	Credits
ET-507A	Pollutants and Water Supply	4
ET-507B	Waste Water Treatment	4
ET-581F	Mechanical Equipment in Construction	2
ET-574	Laboratory-II	2

13. Bachelor in Tourism Studies (BTS)

BTS is a 3 year Programme. Total programme will be of 96 credits and in each year—a student can offer 32 credits.

Course Code		Title of the Course	Credits
First Year			32
	TS-1	Foundation Course in Tourism	8
	TS-2	Tourism Development: Products Operations and Case Studies	8
	FHS-1	Foundation Course in Humanities & Social Sciences	8
	FEG-1	Foundation Course in English	4
		OR	
	FHD-2	Foundation Course in Hindi	4
		Modern Indian Language (any one of the following)	4
	FEG-2	Foundation Course in English-2	
	FAS-1	Foundation Course in Assamese	
	FBG-1	Foundation Course in Bengali	
	FGT-1	Foundation Course in Gujarati	
	FHD-1	Foundation Course in Hindi	
	FKD-1	Foundation Course in Kannada	
	FML-1	Foundation Course in Malayam	
	FMT-1	Foundation Course in Marathi	
	FOR-1	Foundation Course in Oriya	
	FPB-11	Foundation Course in Punjabi	
	FTM-1	Foundation Course in Tamil	
	FTG-1	Foundation Course in Telugu	
	FUD-1	Foundation Course in Urdu	
Second Year			32
	TS-4	Indian Culture: Perspective for Tourism	8
	TS-5	Ecology, Environment and Tourism	8
	FST-1	Foundation Course in Science and Technology	8
	PTS-4	Project in Indian Culture: Perspective for Tourism	4

(Contd.)

Course Code	*Title of the Course*	*Credits*
PTS-5	Project in Ecology, Environment and Tourism	4
Third Year		32
TS-3	Management in Tourism	8
TS-6	Tourism Marketing	8
PTS-6	Project in Tourism Marketing	4
Anyone of the following		
AFW-1	Feature Writing	
AWR-1	Writing for Radio	
AOM-1	Office Organisation Management	
ASP-1	Secretarial Practice	
Anyone of the following		8
AHE-1	Human Environment	
EHI-1	Modern India 1857-1964	
EHI-2	India: Earliest Time to 8th Century AD	
EHI-3	India from 8th to 15th Century A.D.	
EHI-4	India from 16th to Mid 18th Century A.D.	
ESO-5	Society and Religion	
EEG-3	Communications Skills in English	

14. Advanced Diploma in Construction Management (ADCM)

Objective

To train the polytechnic diploma holders engaged in construction industry & to provide them opportunity of pursuing continuing education with up-gradation in their professional knowledge.

Programme Structure

Advanced Diploma in Construction Management—Modules I & II

Course Code	*Title of the Course*	*Credits*
ET 101A	Mathematics-I	3
ET 101B	Mathematics-II	3
ET 105A	Physics	4
ET 105B	Chemistry	4
ET 202A	Engineering Mechanics	2
ET 202B	Principles of Electrical Sciences	4
ET 301A	Systems Methods	2
ET 301B	Computer Applications	2
ET 204A	Materials Science	2
ET 204B	Engineering Materials	2
ET 501A	Soil Mechanics	2

(*Contd.*)

Course Code	*Title of the Course*	*Credits*
ET 501B	Foundation Engineering	2
ET 521A	Planning & Construction of Buildings	2
ET 521B	Building Architecture	2
ET 521C	Design Detailing	2
ET 521D	Quality Surveying & Valuation	2
ET 523A	Construction Works Supervision	2
ET 523B	Operation Maintenance of Construction Equipment	3
ET 523C	Repair and Maintenance of Buildings	3
ET 524A	Principles of Engineering Management & Economics	3
ET 524B	Construction Management-I	3
ET 522	Concrete Technology & Construction Techniques	4
ET 581A	Testing for Quality Control (Elective-I)	2
ET 581F	Mechanical Equipment in Construction (Elective-I)	2
ET 571	Laboratory-I (ADCM)	2
	Total	64

15. Advanced Diploma in Water Resources Engineering (ADWRE)

Objectives

To train the polytechnic diploma holders engaged in water resources sector & to provide them opportunity of pursuing continuing education with up-gradation in their professional knowledge.

Programme Structure

Advanced Diploma in Water Resources Engineering—Modules I & II

Course Code	*Course Title*	*Credits*
ET 101A	Mathematics-I	3
ET 101B	Mathematics-II	3
ET 105A	Physics	4
ET 105B	Chemistry	4
ET 201A	Mechanics of Fluids	4
ET 201B	Engineering Thermodynamics	4
ET 531A	Earth & Its Environment	3

(*Contd.*)

Course Code	*Course Title*	*Credits*
ET 531B	Soil Science	3
ET 501A	Soil Mechanics	2
ET 501B	Foundation Engineering	2
ET 532A	Hydrology	4
ET 532B	Ground Water Development	2
ET 533A	Irrigation Engineering	4
ET 533B	Open Channel Flow	4
ET 502A	Strength of Materials	4
ET 502B	Structural Analysis	4
ET 534A	Principles of Engineering Management & Economics	3
ET 534B	System Methods	2
ET 534C	Water Resources Planning	3
ET 573	Laboratory-I (ADWRE)	1
	Total	63

16. Postgraduate Diploma in Distance Education (PGDDE)

The Postgraduate Diploma in Distance Education (PGDDE) programme is the first of this kind in the Commonwealth. It has been designed to provide essential knowledge how, skills and professional knowledge for the staff involved in developing and maintaining distance education programmes for higher levels of instruction and also for those who want to join distance education institute in future as professional. The programme consists of five courses.

Course Code	*Title of the Course*	*Credits*
ES-311	Growth and Philosophy of Distance Education	6
ES-312	Design & Development for Self-Learning Print Materials	6
ES-313	Learner Support Services	6
ES-314	Management of Distance Education	6
ES-318	Communication Technology for Distance Education	6
Total	**Five Courses**	30

The programme is of one year duration. The medium of instruction is English with provision to write assignments and Term-end-Examinations in Hindi as well. The University Grants Commission (UGC) has recognised "The PGDDE of IGNOU as equivalent to the two refresher courses for Teachers of Distance Education in various universities." Vide circular No. FI-6190 (ASC) dated September, 1993.

17. Postgraduate Diploma in Higher Education (PGDHE)

The Programme has been visualised and developed in response to the recommendations of the National Policy of Education (1986) with a view to provide necessary knowledge, understanding and skills pertaining to higher education for university and college teachers. The UGC has recognised the PGDHE as being equivalent to two refresher courses in Education and orientation course for disciplines other than Education. The Programme is meant for:

(*i*) regular teachers in universities, colleges and other institutions of higher learning.

(*ii*) those having a postgraduate degree in any subject with at least IInd Division.

(*iii*) professional degree holders in areas such as engineering, medicine and agricultural science.

The Programme consists of four theory courses, Practical Component of Contact Programme and a Project. They are:

Course Code	*Title of the Course*	*Credits*
ES-301	Higher Education: Its Context and Linkages	6
ES-302	Instruction in Higher Education	6
ES-303	Higher Education: The Social Psychological Field	6
ES-304	Planning and Management of Higher Education	6
ES-305	Project Work	6
ES-306	Extended Contact Programme	4
	Total	34

18. Postgraduate Diploma in Maternal & Child Health (PGDMCH)

The programme is intended to provide an opportunity to medical personnel and private practitioners for upgrading their knowledge and skills in Maternal and Child Health (MCH) for providing better quality of MCH services.

The programme covers the concepts, practices and application for knowledge in the field of MCH services and aims at improving the knowledge and skills of medical personnel working both in the governmental health care delivery system and the private sector.

Objectives

After completion of the PGDMCH programme, a student should be able to achieve the following objectives:

1. Acquire comprehensive knowledge on ongoing Maternal and Child Health Programmes, I.E.C. and ability for the day-to-day management of Health Care Services at different institutional levels;
2. Provide antenatal care including those of high risk pregnancy, conduct normal delivery and identify referral situations, handle common emergency care related to pregnancy and its outcome;
3. Manage common gynaecological morbidities and provide family planning services;
4. Provide new born care, identify high risk babies, diagnose and manage common childhood morbidities including emergencies.
5. Acquire knowledge on nutritional needs, assess growth and development of children and manage their respective problems; and
6. Tackle the disease out-breaks and effectively manage the National Health Programmes specially in relation to MCH services.

PGDMCH is a multimedia package which includes audio-video material, besides print material. It has six courses involving three broad disciplines of conventional medical education system. Course I and VI are grouped under the discipline of Preventive and Social Medicine (PSM), course II and III are grouped under Obstetrics & Gynaecology (O & G) and course IV and V are grouped under Paediatrics discipline. Here the issues related to programme implementation are dealt in the light of these three broad groupings though each course is considered as a separate entity by itself.

Course Code	*Title of the Course*	*Credits*	
		Theory	*Practical*
I	Preventive MCH	4	2
II	Maternal Health	4	3
III	Reproductive Health	2	1
IV	Child Health	4	4
V	Growth and Nutrition	2	2
VI	Planning & Management	2	2
	Total	18	14

Selection Criteria

Selection will be made on the basis of merit. A separate merit list will be prepared for each Regional Centre on the basis of the total score of applicants. Separate merit lists will be prepared for different categories as per Central Govt. rules.

The scores will be calculated by considering two criteria:

- Total percentages of marks secured in all MBBS Examinations.
- Total years of experience (Period from the date of completion of internship up to the date of beginning of session.)
- Additional weightage will be given to the candidates sponsored by State/Central Government (i.e. by Department of Health & FW or by Directorate of Health Services).

Programme Implementation

The students will be compulsorily required to attend three spells of seven days each at allotted medical college in addition to carrying out practical activities at district hospitals. At present there are 24 medical colleges acting as PSC which have been listed in the prospectus regional centrewise. However, additional centres are likely to be activated in Maharashtra, Andhra Pradesh, Jammu, Haryana, Uttar Pradesh, West Bengal and in north-east region. The activities of these centres is subject to the approval of respective State Governments. There are 30 seats at each Programme Study Centre.

Please note that students must send their forms to the Regional Centre as per their address of correspondence (refer the operational area of Regional Centres). The programme Study Centre (PSC) once allotted will not be changed.

19. Post-Graduate Diploma in Hospital and Health Management (PGDHHM)

Objective

The programme fulfils specified needs of a middle level administrators in hospital or health care departments. This comprehensive programme will provide a professional qualification and an insight in managerial functional for those serving graduates who wish to take up hospital and health administration as a career. It will also be of immediate benefit to those currently engaged in hospital administration at senior levels.

Eligibility Requirements

Eligibility criteria are as under:

(*a*) Medical/Dental graduates from a Medical Dental Institute of India or other countries recognised by Medical Council of India (MC) or Dental Council and should have two years experience after registration with MCI/Dental Council.

(*b*) Graduates in Indian system of medicine and homeopathy, recognized by the respective Council with five years experience after Registration.

(*c*) Candidates holding MBA degree of PG Diploma in Financial, Material or Personnel Management with five years hospital experience.

(*d*) Graduates in nursing and pharmacy with at least five years hospital experience.

(*e*) Graduate in Engineering and or Architecture associated with hospital for five years.

Preference will be given to applicants working in a hospital/ health care institution and holding administrative responsibilities.

Selection Procedure

Those satisfying the eligibility requirements will be selected on the basis of the criteria laid down by the School of Health Sciences, IGNOU. The criteria for selection will be developed taking into account hospital experience, years of service and educational qualification. Selection will be made on regional centres/PSC basis. In each PSC a minimum of 30 students will be admitted. In case number of students is less than 30 then they will be given option to opportunity for nearby Regional Centre/PSC at the following places: Bangalore, Belgaum, Calcutta, Chandigarh, Chennai, Cochin, Delhi, Goa, Guwahati, Hyderabad, Jaipur, Jammu, Kanpur, Lucknow, Mumbai, Nagpur, Patna, Pune, Srinagar and Trivendrum.

Fee Schedule

(*a*) Rs. 10,100/- which inludes Registration & Programme fee to be paid through Bank Demand Draft drawn in favour of IGNOU payable at the city where the concerned Regional Centre is located.

(*b*) Rs. 3,000/- for three training-cum-contact programmes of seven days duration to be paid through Bank Draft drawn in favour of Academy of Hospital Administration payable at New Delhi.

Programme Design

PGDHHM is a multimedia package which includes General Management. Management of Human Resources, Finance, Logistics and Equipment in Hospitals; also include Organisation and Management of Hospital and Planning. Organisation and Management of all type of services provided in a hospital; further it includes health system management including epidemiology and biostatistics. Each course is considered as a separate entity by itself, although interrelated when conceptually comprehended as issues of the hospital system.

Course Code	*Name of the Course*	*No. of Credits*	
		Theory	*Practical*
I	Introduction to Management-I	3	2
II	Introduction to Management-II	3	2
III	Organisation and Management of Hospital	3	2
IV	Clinical, Diagnostic and Therapeutic Service	3	2
V	Support and Utility Services and Risk Management	3	2
VI	Health System Management	3	2
	Project Work		2
	Total	18	14

Admission & Conduction

Students will be admitted at identified Programme Study Centres (PSCs). 30-35 students will be admitted at each PSC. These PSCs would be located at the selected medical colleges/hospitals/ management institutes in above mentioned places. On admission, each student will be attached to a PSC where he/she will be attending counselling sessions to clear their doubts related to theory component. The local counsellor will also act as a guide for project study to be undertaken by each student during the programme. In addition, three contact programmes of seven days duration each for practical activities will be held in the PSC, as per dates to be notified by the PSC incharge concerned.

Attendance to these contact programmes is mandatory to qualify for the final examination.

20. Postgraduate Diploma in Rural Development (PGDRD)

The Post Graduate Diploma in Rural Development provides comprehensive knowledge of socio-economic factors affecting the transformation of rural society. The contents are designed to impart an integrated understanding to learners about the crucial dimensions of rural development. It aims at enabling the learners to acquire skills related to planning, formulation, monitoring and evaluation of rural development projects and programmes. The Diploma Programme also introduces the learner to the basic aspects of research and project-work. The Project Work provides its learners an opportunity to study rural development problems, which enables them to develop necessary skills to undertake research work in rural development. The programme consists of the following five courses:

Course Code	*Title of the Course*	*Credits*
RDD-1	Rural Development: Indian Context	6
RDD-2	Rural Development Programmes	6
RDD-3	Rural Development: Planning and Management	6
RDD-4	Rural Social Development	6
RDD-5	Research and Project Work	6
	Total	30

21. Post-Graduate Diploma in Translation (PGDT)

Post Graduate Diploma in Translation (PGDT) aims to teach Translation from English to Hindi and vice-versa. Translation is a major professional area in our country and plays an important role in our understanding of the diversity of Indian culture and society. PG Diploma in Translation is designed to develop the translation skills of the learners. Besides imparting the knowledge of the theory and practice of translation, it will help the students to understand the socio-cultural dimensions of translation. The programme consists of 4 Courses and a Project comprising Practical Translation.

Course Code	*Title of the Course*	*Credits*
PGDT-01	Anuvad: Sidhant Aur Pravidhi	6
PGDT-02	Anuvad Ka Bhashik Aur Samajik Paksh	6
PGDT-03	Vyavaharik Anuvad Ke Vivid Star Aur Kshetra	6
PGDT-04	Prashasnik Anuvad	6
PGDT-05	Anuvad Pariyojna	6
	Total	30

22. P.G. Diploma in Journalism and Mass Communication (PGJMC)

The Postgraduate Diploma Programme in Journalism and Mass Communication has been designed and structured to provide basic knowledge to the learners on Journalism and Mass Communication. It aims to sharpen the basic skills needed to function effectively in a media organisation. The programme consists of four courses.

Course Code	*Title of the Course*	*Credits*
JMC-01	Introduction to Journalism and Mass Communication	8
JMC-02	Mass Media and Society	8
JMC-03	Reporting, Writing and Editing	8
JMC-04	Public Relations	8
	Total	32

23. P.G. Diploma in International Business Operations (PGDIBO)

School of Management Studies, the biggest business school in Open Learning System in the world has developed an innovative programme in the area of International Business. The main objective of this programme is to equip the students with necessary conceptual, entrepreneurial and analytical skills required for handling the International Business Operations. The curriculum focusses on the applied aspects of International Business.

The salient features of this programme are as follows:

- Focus on operational areas of International Business
- Courses designed and prepared by top notch academia in the field of international business
- Students, centred multimedia learning materials

- Strong Students Support Services
- Regular Teleconferencing
- Opportunity to interact with the leading experts through the teleconferencing.

Programme Structure

PGDIBO is a one year Post Graduate Diploma Programme, comprising of the following six courses of 6 credit each. All the following six courses are compulsory.

Course Code	*Title of the Course*
IBO-01	International Business Environment
IBO-02	International Marketing
IBO-03	India's Foreign Trade
IBO-04	Export-Import Procedures and Documentation
IBO-05	International Marketing Logistics
IBO-06	International Business Finance

24. Diploma in Creative Writing in English (DCE)

The Programme provides understanding, skills and professional knowledge about the art of imaginative writing to help develop the creative ability of those interested in taking up careers as professional or freelance writers. Applicants for this programme are expected to have a flair for writing. The Programme consists of two compulsory courses and four elective courses.

(*i*) Compulsory Courses

DCE-1	General Principles of Writing
DCE-6	Guided Project Work

(*ii*) Elective Courses (any three to be opted)

DCE-2	Feature Writing
DCE-3	Short Story
DCE-4	Writing for Media: Radio and Television
DCE-5	Writing Poetry

25. Diploma in Creative Writing in Hindi (DCH)

The objective of the Diploma Programme in Creative Writing in Hindi is to provide guidance to those who are interested in taking up career as professional or freelance writers. It aims to provide understanding, skill and professional knowledge about the art of writing and to develop the learner's creative potential. During the Programme learners are encouraged to get their writing published. This Programme comprises six courses and a project, as given below:

Course Code	*Title of the Course*	*Credits*
(*i*) Compulsory Courses		
DCH-1	Srijanatmak Lekhan Ke Siddhant	4
DCH-7	A writing project: Each learner is required to write short stories, a play, a novella, essays of features approved by Hindi Faculty.	4
(*ii*) Elective Courses (any three to be opted)		
DCH-2	Feature Lekhan	4
DCH-3	Gadya Lekhan	4
DCH-4	Radio Lekhan	4
DCH-5	Vibhinna Samajik Vargon Ke Liye Lekhan	4
DCH-6	Kavita Lekhan	4

26. Diploma in Early Childhood Care and Education (DECE)

The Diploma in Early Childhood Care and Education is a unique holistic package that aims to help the learners develop the knowledge, attitudes and skills necessary for working with young children (i.e. children from 0 to 6 years of age) and equip them to organize and manage child care centres like crèches, pre-schools and day care centres. The programme provides in-depth theoretical and practical knowledge related to Early Childhood Care and Education. The project work and practicals that form a major component of the programme would help the learners develop the requisite attitudes and skills necessary for working effectively as early childhood educators. The Diploma Programme is very specifically vocational in nature, opening avenues for employment as well as self-employment.

Course Code	*Title of the Course*	*Credits*
DECE-1	Organizing Child Care Services	8
DECE-2	Child Health and Nutrition	8
DECE-3	Services and Programmes for Children	8
DECE-4	Project Work: Working with Young Children in a Child Care Setting	8
	Total	32

Project Work: For the Project Work, the learner is placed in a nursery school identified by IGNOU for 30 to 45 working days (depending upon the pace and schedule of the work of the learner). The learner is required to carry out play activities with the children there. The play activities have to be planned and carried out by the learner based on the broad parameters indicated in the Project Manual. For the duration of the Project Work, the learner will be attached to a Guide, who will be a pre-school educator from the nursery school where the learner has been placed for the Project Work. The Guide will guide, supervise as well as evaluate the learner. The Project Work has been designed to give the learners hands-on experience. Learning in the actual field situation under the guidance of a judiciously selected professional (pre-school educator) is expected to help the learner in imbibing and developing the requisite skills, leading to a better understanding of how the theoretical concepts may be translated into practice and make a major contribution to the development of the learner's competence.

27. Diploma in Nutrition & Health Education (DNHE)

The Diploma Programme is a holistic package which provides opportunities to the learner to gain knowledge about nutrition and public health. It also enables the learners to develop skills in communicating nutrition and health related information to community. The aim of the programme is to develop a knowledge base in areas of nutrition and public health, promote awareness about concepts and principles in communication and their application in nutrition and health education and develop skill in playing the role of nutrition/health educators in the community.

Learners with basic 10+2 qualification, and an interest in community work will find the Diploma very useful. It is a professional training programme. People working with both governmental and non-governmental sectors in the role of community workers would also benefit from this Programme. The Diploma will provide an additional qualification helping them to improve their professional competence and promotion chances. The Diploma in Nutrition and Health Education is a 32 credit programme consisting of four courses.

Course Code	Title of the Course	Credits
DNHE-1	Nutrition for the Community	8
DNHE-2	Public Health and Hygiene	8
DNHE-3	Nutrition and Health Education	8
DNHE-4	Project Work: Nutrition and Health Education	8
	Total	32

Practicals: Practical Manuals are to accompany the course material.

Project Work is a vital component of the DNHE programme. Through the project work, the learner will be able to experience the "feel" of working as a nutrition and health educator in community setting. Such an interaction would provide good insight into the problems and possible solutions in community work. The Project will equip the learner to plan and conduct nutrition/health education campaigns and programmes in community settings.

28. Diploma in Tourism Studies (DTS)

The Programme consists of 36 Credits only.

Course Code	Title of the Course	Credits
(*i*) Compulsory Courses		
TS-1	Foundation Course in Tourism	8
TS-2	Tourism Development: Products, Operations and Case Studies	8
TS-3	Management in Tourism	8
(*ii*) Any one of the following groups of Electives		
TS-4	Indian Culture-A Perspective for Tourism	8
PTS-4	Project	4
	OR	
TS-5	Ecology, Environment and Tourism	8
PTS-5	Project	4
	OR	
TS-6	Tourism Marketing	8
PTS-6	Project	4

29. PG Certificate in Radio Writing (PGCR)

This programme is designed to enhance the writing skills of the learners who are interested in taking up career as professional and freelance writer in the field of Writing for Radio. Any Graduate can opt for this programme. This programme is available in Hindi medium. This programme is comprised of 4 courses including a Project, as given below:

Course Code	*Title of the Course*
WRT-01	A General Study of Mass Communication
WRT-02	Writing for Radio-I
WRT-03	Writing for Radio-II
WRT-04	Radio Writing Project

30. Certificate in Disaster Management (CDM)

The Certificate in Disaster Management Programme aims at providing knowledge to the learners in the areas of disaster preparedness, prevention, mitigation, relief, reconstruction and rehabilitation. The programme is of use to NGO functionaries and volunteers; military, para-military, police, home guards, civil defence personnel; professionals such as Geologists, Scientists, Meterologists. Engineers, Foresters, Fire-Service personnel, Administrators, Government and Public Sector Undertakings officials.

Rural Development Functionaries, Urban Government Officials; Primary Health Centres Functionaries; etc. The Programme consists of 16 credits.

Course Code	*Title of the Course*	*Credits*
CDM-01	Foundation Course in Disaster Management	8
CDM-02	Disaster Management: Methods & Techniques	8
	Total	16

31. Certificate in Environmental Studies (CES)

The programme is of use to general public; at every age and at all levels of formal and non-formal education, Professional; such as ecologists, hydrologists, foresters, landscape architects. Occupational or Social Groups; for instance, administrators and planners, engineers, industrialists, agriculturists, etc. The NGOs with their dissemination capabilities shall find it very useful.

Course Code	*Title of the Course*	*Credits*
AHE-01	Human Environment	6
TS-5	Ecology, Environment and Tourism	8
PES-01	Project in Environmental Studies	4
	Total	18

32. Certificate in Foods and Nutrition (CFN)

The Certificate in Foods and Nutrition is basically a Post-Literacy level awareness programme meant for people with basic reading and writing skills. The Programme aims to acquaint the learner with the role of food in ensuring healthy living for the individual, family and community. It includes features like food section and preparation, nutrition from infancy to old age, economics of food, kitchen gardening, food adulteration, consumer rights, safety and education, etc. The programme lays primary emphasis on Nutrition with relevance to present day scenario, cost effectiveness, environment friendly approaches that reaches to almost the entire nation, hence making the learners responsible and aware citizens of tomorrow.

Course Code	*Title of the Course*	*Credits*
CFN-1	Your and Your Food	6
CFN-2	Your Food and its Utilisation	6
CFN-3	Economics of Food	4
	Total	16

This Certificate Programme is a Multi-lingual Programme. The Telugu & Urdu version is run by Dr. B.R. Ambedkar Open University, Hyderabad.

33. Certificate in Human Rights (CHR)

Know them	Promote them	Defend Them	Protect Them

Certificate in Human Rights Programme is an innovative learning package of 16 credits spread over 3 courses, designed specifically to sensitize and educate professionals and workers who, as a part of their duty interact with masses of people daily. Besides general students, specific target groups include law enforcement personnel (police, army, paramilitary forces) and functionaries of the lower judiciary and administrative officers, primary school teachers and NGO functionaries. In preparing the course material, special care has been taken to address the concerns raised by the UN High Commissioner for Human Rights at the time of launching of the UN Decade for Human Rights Education.

The Programme is open to all persons with 10+2 or equivalent qualifications. Students doing any other degree/diploma/certificate course from any University/institution can also do this Certificate Programme simultaneously. Those who do not possess 10+2 or equivalent qualification can pursue this programme after completing BPP (Bachelors Preparatory Programme) of Indira Gandhi National Open University.

The Programme is recommended for all categories of professionals regardless of their educational qualifications; it has been called a Certificate Programme only to make sure that the entrant has a 10+2 level of learning in the minimum.

Programme Structure

The Programme consists of a Work Book designed for promoting sansitization through practice-based learning. The courses are:

Course Code	*Title of the Course*	*Credits*
CHR-1	Human Rights—Society and Development	6
CHR-2	Human Rights and India	6
CHR-3	Human Rights in Everyday life: What we can do?	4
	Total	16

34. Certificate in Computing (CIC)

Objectives

This programme is aimed to fulfilling the need of an opportunity in the nature of an "adult computer literacy" programme which could meet the large demand of people who are interested in at least some computer education. It is a short programme which almost every future graduate including those from IGNOU can take. This programme is of some use as a means to assess the student's potential for taking up computer education in a distance mode. It is therefore relied upon by IGNOU to determine the suitability for admission to the BCA and MCA programmes of IGNOU depending upon his/her qualification.

Programme Structure

Course Code	*Title of the Course*	*Credits*
CIC-I	The Context	4
CIC-2	The Technology	4
CIC-4	The Applications	4
CIC-5	MS-Office	4
	Total	16

35. Certificate in Guidance (CIG)

The Certificate in Guidance Programme is a joint project of Indira Gandhi National Open University and the National Council of Educational Research and Training (NCERT). This programme would enable the participants to:

(*a*) develop an understanding of child development and individual differer.ces in the context of the educational processes.

(*b*) develop an understanding of the concepts and processes involved in guiding elementary school children for learning and socio-emotional development.

(*c*) Identify children with special needs and problems, and

(*d*) suggest intervention strategic for parents, teachers, teachers and other adults to facilitate all round development of children.

The Programme is essentially for a target group comprising teachers, parents, social workers, personnel from voluntary agencies or any individual who is interested in understanding and guiding children. The Programme consists of four courses of four Credits each.

Course Code	*Title of the Course*	*Credits*
ES-101	Understanding the Elementary School Child	4
ES-102	Facilitating Growth and Development	4
ES-103	Guiding Children's Learning	4
ES-104	Guiding Socio-emotional Development of Children	4
	Total	16

36. Certificate in Labour Development (CLD)

When a view to provide educational empowerment labourers in general and unorganised workers in particular, the Economics Discipline of School of Social Sciences has developed a new programme "Certificate Programme in Labour in Development". The programme intends to widen and deepen the process of creation of awareness among labourers in general and unorganised workers in particular through educating the rural educators and trainers, NGO functionaries, trade union functionaries, social activists. The Certificate Programme consists of the following four courses each of 4 credits:

Course Code	*Title of the Course*	*Credits*
CLD-01	Political Economy of Labour in India	4
CLD-02	Organising the Unorganised	4
CLD-03	Child and Bonded Labour	4
CLD-04	Migrant and Female Workers	4
	Total	16

Note: CLD-01 and CLD-02 are compulsory while CLD-03 and CLD-04 are optional. The learners has two options.

1. To offer one out of the two optional courses (course 3 and course 4) and attend one rural labour camp.
   Or
2. To offer both the optional courses.

37. Certificate in Nutrition and Child Care (CNCC)

This Programme of study would be of tremendous relevance and use to all those who need to have the knowledge, understanding and skills, both with regard to Nutrition and Child Development. The Certificate in Nutrition and Child Care is specifically vocational in nature, opening avenues for employment as well as self employment. Doing a programme of this nature, combining knowledge and skill development in the areas of Nutrition and Early Childhood Care and Education would make the learner uniquely qualified to take up jobs as functionaries with Government and Non-Government organisations working for women and children.

Course Code	Title of the Course	Credits
CNCC-1	Nutrition for the Community	8
CNCC-2	Organizing Child Care Services	8
	Total	16

38. Certificate in Participatory Forest Management (CPFM)

General objective of the Certificate Programme is to develop an approach to integration of forest dependent communities into forest management. The specific objective is to build the bridges of understanding between foresters and forest communities. Our long-term aim is to build the mechanisms of collective action by user groups, for protecting the already existing natural forests and regenerating degraded forests. The professional certificate programme to those learners who want to understand social and cultural issues in forestry. This understanding is necessary to develop sustainable systems of forest management. The interactive nature of the Certificate in Participatory Forest Management Programme is to generate this sensitivity among all stakeholders in forest resources, and qualify the learners to improve services in the forestry sector.

The Certificate in Participatory Forest Management Programme consists of a total of 16 credits with four courses of 4 credits each, that is:

Course Code	Title of the Course	Credits
PFM-1	Forest Resources and Use Practice	4
PFM-2	Foresters' Views of Forest Management	4
PFM-3	Forest Dwellers' Perceptions & Responses	4
PFM-4	Implications of Joint Forest Management	4
	Total	16

39. Certificate in Consumer Protection (CCP)

A 16 Credit Programme on Consumer Protection is open to candidates with 10+2 qualifications. The Programme aims at creating an overall awareness and training on consumer affairs with special emphasis on Consumer Protection. After going through this Certificate Programme the students can be consumer activists, work in industries, NGOs and government departments on consumer affairs. They can file and plead cases in Consumer Protection Courts. The programme consists of three elective courses as per details below:

Course Code	*Title of the Course*	*Credits*
ACS-01	Application Oriented Courses in Consumer Studies	8
CPI	Consumer Protection Issues and Acts	4
CCP	Project Work in Consumer Protection	4
	Total	16

40. Certificate in Rural Development (CRD)

This programme in Rural Development provides a comprehensive knowledge of socio-economic factors affecting the transformation of rural society. The contents are designed to impart the integrated understanding about the crucial dimensions of rural development. It is primarily meant for those learners who, because of the limitations of time and resources are unable to take up Post Graduate Diploma in Rural Development but see still interested to have a comprehensive orientation in rural development within a short period of time.

Course Code	*Title of the Course*	*Credits*
RDD-1	Rural Development: Indian Context	6
RDD-2	Rural Development: Programmes	6
RDD-3	Rural Development: Planning and Management	6
	Total	18

41. Certificate in the Teaching of English as a Second Language (CTE)

This Programme is based on the communicative approach to language teaching and is designed to enhance the teachers understanding of the learners, the learning process, and the nature and structure of the English Language. It will also help the teacher to innovate strategies for teaching the skills of listening, speaking, reading and writing.

Students will need to study four courses in all three compulsory and one optional.

Course Code	*Title of the Course*	*Credits*
(*i*) Compulsory Courses		
CTE-1	The Language Learner	4
CTE-2	The Structure of English	4
CTE-3	Teaching Strategies	4
(*ii*) Optional Courses (Select any one)		
CTE-4	Teaching English-Elementary School	4
CTE-5	Teaching English-Secondary School	4
	Total	16

42. Certificate in Tourism Studies (CTS)

The programme is aimed at familiarising you with varied aspects of Tourism, creating awareness about Tourism, imparting basic training in organising Tourism services, opening career opportunities. It consists of two courses of eight credits each.

Course Code	*Title of the Course*	*Credits*
TS-1	Foundation Course in Tourism	8
TS-2	Tourism Development: Products Operation and Case Studies	8
	Total	16

43. Certificate in Empowering Women through Self-Help Groups (CWDL)

Indian women are often segregated-deprived of education, employment and awareness of their rights. This denies women access to a holistic understanding of their needs and expectations from the mainstream life necessities. "Empowering Women through Self-Help Groups" is a certificate programme designed to provide systematic communication for women, with the aid of hardware support to deliver information relevant to women's social context. The programme aims to enhance women's confidence, improve their interpersonal relations/leadership qualities/general management abilities and also help them to acquire access to credit and resources. Learners who clear the certificate programme from IGNOU will be equipped as resource persons to train other change agents similarly situated in their regions/work sphere. The process will help promote formation and sustainability of SHGs as well. The objective of this certificate programme is two fold.

(1) *At the training level*

- Strengthen ongoing efforts to train master trainers of SHGs, thereby also evolving an effective resource pool of such trainers.
- Empower change agents to function more effectively as trainers/community organinsers in addressing gender issues.

(2) *At the system level, the programme will help to*

- Assess the effectiveness of a development oriented satellite based broadcast cum interactive network system to support continuing education and development;
- Evaluate the impact of such a system in programme development; and
- Provides insights into organisational, managerial and other aspects required to run such a system on a permanent basis.

The programme comprises of four courses:

Course Code	*Title of the Course*	*Credits*
CWDL-01	Women's Empowerment Perspective and Approaches	4
CWDL-02	Application Oriented Courses in Consumer Studies	4
CWDL-03	Consumer Protection Issues and Act	4
CWDL-04	Project Work in Consumer Protection	4
	Total	16

44. Certificate in Women's Empowerment and Development (CWED)

In the recent years there has been a growing concern both at the national and international levels on the subjugated and the disadvantaged position of women in the society. In India the development functionaries of various government departments, numerous women's groups, voluntary organisations and international agencies are endeavouring to espouse the cause of women as a part of their development initiatives. However, there exists a gap between the social realities pertaining to women's questions on the one hand and the popular perceptions on this issue, on the other. As against this backdrop, this programme aims to:

(*a*) sensitise the students in general and the development workers in particulars on the gender related questions.

(*b*) Provide the necessary expertise to function as specialist on women's issues.

(c) Help generating a social environment, through the intervention of Distance Education, free from inequalities disfavouring women.

This education package focuses on understanding on the issues pertaining to social development and empowerment of women in the context of historical and contemporary socio-economic and political realities of India. Within the given scenario of the society gender issues are examine to highlight the strategies for women's empowerment and development.

Programme Structure

Course Code	*Title of the Course*	*Credits*
FEW-01	Foundation Course in Women's Empowerment and Development	4
WED-01	Women in Indian Society: Socio-Historical Contexts	4
WED-02	Constitutional and Legislative Foundations for Gender Equality	4
WED-03	Women and Economy	4
	Total	16

45. Certificate in Participatory Project Planning (SAVINI)

A 16 credit Certificate programme in SAVINI is open to NGO functionaries. The programme aims at capacity building of development workers to effectively carry out their projects in rural areas. The programme comprises the following four courses of four credits each and is available in Hindi at selected Programme Centres in Rajasthan, Madhya Pradesh and Uttar Pradesh, Chhatisgarh and Uttaranchal.

Course Code	*Title of the Course*	*Credits*
SAVINI-1	What is Development?	4
SAVINI-2	Working with Groups	4
SAVINI-3	Participatory Planning	4
SAVINI-4	Field Project	4
	Total	16

46. Certificate in Teaching of Primary School Mathematics (CTPM)

This awareness level practical-oriented programme provides some strategies for teaching mathematics to children in a way that will make them feel positive about it. The programme is aimed at preprimary and primary school teachers, as well as parents of young children. Its basic objectives are to help primary school teachers to critically look at their mathematics teaching strategies and after them to suit their students' background; to refresh teachers about the acquisition and learning process in the context of mathematics learning; and to make a discourse of mathematics teaching available to a wider section of society by exposing them to the need for giving a meaning and context while learning or teaching mathematical concepts, processes and skills.

The programme consists of two courses as detailed below:

Course Code	*Title of the Course*	*Credits*
AMT-01	Teaching of Primary School Mathematics	8
LMT-01	Learning Mathematics	8
	Total	16

47. Certificate in Laboratory Techniques (CPLT)

This programme is intended for persons employed as or aspiring for employment as laboratory technicians in school or college laboratories. This programme is designed to train the learners to provide effective and efficient services to the faculty and students by familiarising them with the basic facilities available in a school/ college science laboratory; imparting; knowledge on the basics of organisation and management of science laboratories; training in handling and maintaining simple instruments. Due emphasis has been laid on the procurement procedures and storage of laboratory related materials, equipment etc. It is expected that after doing this programme, lab technicians will be able to contribute significantly in improving the delivery of science educators.

The programme consists of 4 courses listed below:

Course Code	*Course Title*	*No. of Credits*		*No. of Days of Practical Work**
		Theory	*Practical*	
LT-1	Good Laboratory Practices	4	2	7
LT-2	Laboratory Techniques in Biology	2	2	7
LT-3	Laboratory Techniques in Chemistry	2	2	7
LT-4	Laboratory Techniques in Physics	2	2	7
	Total	18		

* Those working as regular employees in the laboratories of senior secondary schools/colleges/universities will have the option to carry

out 12 days of practical work at their work place under the supervision of a local teacher. However, 16 days of practical work and presence will necessarily be required at identified study centres.

48. Certificate in Health and Environment (CHE)

Target Group

The target group for this programme would include Health Professionals, Paramedical Staff, NGO Workers, Teachers of Schools, Colleges and Institutions, Industrial Workers, Creative Writers, Senior Citizens, Sanitary Inspectors, Nursing Home Administrators and other interested group with a minimum of 10+2 qualification with Science.

Aims and Objectives of the Programme

The Programme of Certificate in Health and Environment has been developed to provide comprehensive knowledge about the environment, its present state and the reasons for its degradation. It also acquaints the learner with basic principles of health and attempts to describe inter-relationship between health and environment. After completion of this Programme, the learner should be able to:

- Comprehend the principles of environment, health and their relationship.
- Develop skills to diagnose the problems generated as a result of environmental degradation.
- Acquire competency to apply the knowledge, understanding and skills of health and environment for personal and social health and well being as related to environment.

Implementation

Students allotted to the programme study centre/study centre have to attend a contact period spell of nine days duration. This will include two days of theory counselling, five days of practical work in laboratory one day of field visit and one day practical term-end examination.

All assignments for this programme are to be computer marked.

Programme Design

The Programme consists of 3 courses. Courses 1 and 2 are theory courses. Course-3 has two practical manual and one project guide.

The course wise credit distribution of theory and practical courses is shown below:

Course Code	*Name of Course*	*Credit*
CHET-001	Our Environment	6
CHET-002	Promoting Health	4
CHET-003	Practical Aspects of Environment	4
	Total	14

Proposed Programme Study Centres/Study Centres

In each regional centre it is proposed to have at least one programme study centre/study centre for a maximum of 20 students. The proposed centre have been indicated in the common list of study centres. Regional Centres not having indicating any proposed centre in the list are in the process of finalising the centres.

Selection of the students would be done on the basis of following criteria:

Sl.No.	*Criteria*	*Score*
1.	10+2 Marks	Percentage of marks
2.	Year of experience after 10+2	1 mark for each year of experience to a maximum of 20 years.

49. Certificate in HIV and Family Education (CAFE)

The Certificate in HIV and Family Education provides comprehensive knowledge of the what, why and how of HIV/AIDS, family life education, facts of life and substance abuse. The contents are designed to impart an integrated understanding to the learners about the issues involved in HIV/AIDS and behaviour modification. The target learners include School teachers, NGO functionaries, paramedical parents of adolescents and those interested in acquiring knowledge on the subject. The Certificate programme has the following courses of 4 credits each. A learner has to choose the 2 compulsory courses and any two options from the 5 electives.

Course Code	*Title of the Course*	*Status*	*Credits*	*Credits Required*
AFE-01	Basics of HIV/AIDS	Compulsory	4	
AFE-02	Elective on HIV/AIDS	Elective	4	
AFE-03	Basics of Family Education	Compulsory	4	
AFE-04	Elective on Family Education	Elective	4	
AFE-05	Alcohol, Drugs & HIV	Elective	4	
AFE-06	Communication & Counselling in HIV		4	
AFE-07	Project Work	Elective	4	
	Total		28	16

Note: IGNOU is most innovative developing and expanding university. It is trying to start more and more study centres. In addition to above mentioned programmes it has many more programmes for distance learners. There are many more universities and institutions established and recognised by the state governments and UGC and their programmes in most cases are equally good and useful, hence it is suggested that each one of us must have the benefit of distance learning as per one's, need, ability and resources for one's own good and social and national good.

20

Future Scenario of Distance Education in India

INTRODUCTION

Future of Distance Education (DE) can be projected keeping in view different parameters like present trend of the system, technological development in future, social anticipation, and policies of education at institutional level as well as at national level. Moreover, the prospects and constraints existing inside and outside the functioning of DE system can be the bases of projecting plausible futures of the system.

Indian system of DE has acquired a sound base at university stage for almost three decades. Research experiences on functioning of this system can be linked with growing educational aspiration of society and technological development in educational system. Establishing such a link can be useful in building future scenario of DE in India.

GENERAL SCENARIO OF DISTANCE EDUCATION

Distance education has been perceived as a means of democratization of educational system. Almost all countries look forward providing higher learning facilities to a large chunk of under privileged members of society through DE. Such deprived groups of learners who are capable enough to pursue higher studies but could not do so through regular courses because of several reasons.

At higher education stage while different countries have specific reasons for establishment of such system, all of them agree upon the reason for democratisation of education through DE. The Indian system of higher education has been encouraging DE with a view to meet genuine demands for higher education through different flexible means.

Expansion of DE in India depends on increasing pressure of aspirants of higher education in general. In spite of fast rate of growth of higher education upto 2000 not even ten per cent of learners of age group of 17 to 23 have been brought into the fold of higher education.

This rate of participation in India is very much lower than that of America and European countries. In these countries 27 to 35 per cent of total population of the age cohort of higher education join different higher education courses.

As pointed out by the new policy of education (1986) and its programme of action the future emphasis of education would rest on expansion of DE. There has been a positive response for establishment of full fledged DE institutions like Indira Gandhi National Open University (IGNOU) and other state level open universities in the states of Andhra Pradesh, Rajasthan, Maharashtra and Bihar. There has been proposals for establishment of open universities in other states like Gujarat, Karnataka, Madhya Pradesh, Orissa, Punjab, Tamil Nadu, Uttar Pradesh, and West Bengal. The emergence of open university system may or may not come in the way of traditional system of correspondence courses offered by universities of respective states.

For instance, on the one hand, the creation of Kota Open University brought a closure of traditional set ups of correspondence courses in two of the teaching universities of Rajasthan state. On the other hand, the Dr. B.R. Ambedkar Open University is coexistent of further expanding traditional correspondence courses in Andhra Pradesh. While emergence of open university system has brought boosts to DE in the country the traditional correspondence courses have been striving for development of DE inside university structure.

Whatever may be the forms of DE in the country the futures of DE depend upon the interaction of several educational and social factors in future. A study conducted by Satpathy (1989) indicated that following the major events in social and educational spheres would take place in the following forms:

- Further expansion of DE in terms of establishment of new institutions, course structure and enrolment;
- Innovations inside distance education system;
- Expansion of science and technology;
- Further expansion of education of weaker sections of society;

- Decrease of student participation in campus based politics;
- Increase of educated unemployment;
- Progress of inservice and continuing education.

Taking into consideration the results of cross impact analysis of above forecasted events and other relevant references the following scenario can be generated about DE in India.

Major developments which would take place in DE in future is emergence of improved educational technology. The DE shall have better scope to exploit the available instructional media including mass communications and other electronic gadgets. The rapid emergence of behavioural science and especially the area of specialization of instructional technology would be useful for the production of softwares and appropriate management and evaluation of the system.

As pointed out by UNESCO (1985), "The emergence of instructional design techniques for analysing the structure of subject matter, assessing the critical learning attributes of students, specifying clearly required learning outcomes, selecting appropriate learning experiences in a carefully delineated sequence and designing appropriate assessment instruments with associated diagnostic-remedial support systems has created the potential for a significant improvement in the quality of teaching and learning. The administrators of new system of distance education have the opportunity to create a new organisational infrastructure, capable of supporting the production of instructional materials of the highest quality.".

Unlike traditional academic structure where major emphasis is given to course content DE would emphasise on efficacy of Instructional processes through use of modern edcuational technology. This would require systematic integration of research inputs with instructional system of DE. The potentials and effective use of sophisticated educational technology in the forms of softwares and hardwares, student support services and evaluation process would evolve new system of instruction through DE in future. The expansion of DE would accommodate new discoveries of different modes of communication, provision of instructional facilities, development and production of materials, monitoring and evaluation.

Because of popularisation of science and technology in the forms of radio, TV, computers, mailing services, information storage facilities, satellite networks etc., DE will make use of such facilities for its expansion as well as effectiveness. Alternative channels of DE can be available to distance learners.

Because of fast changes in the field of knowledge and skills the masses would be motivated to pursue DE courses. DE will be used as a means of popularising science and technology in different walks of life.

Because of media exposure the common masses have access to changes taking place in different aspects of social life. The expansion of DE would compliment informal and formal agencies of education, especially for the weaker sections of the society. More demand for DE would come from such sections since there is every possibility of first growth of literacy rate in future.

The limitations of formal education in terms of its expensive nature, compulsory attendance, urbanised orientation would force the ruralites, women, SC and ST groups etc. to opt for DE courses enmass.

Whether it is a positive or negative indicator of democratic life DE will come on the way of campus based student policies. Lack of chances to gather in the campus, more involvement in self instruction and other activities at home and working places may not motivate students to participate in politics as seen in the present day educational institutions. In general hindrances of educational management through students politics will be reduced to a large extent since a large chunk of student of higher education will be diverted to DE system.

One of the major problems, the country has been facing since independence, is increasing rate of educated unemployment. Further expansion of higher education and growing aspirations of masses for education have been adding more figures to the existing educated unemployment.

It is forecasted that while educated unemployment problem will intensify further in future, the demand for DE will increase to a large extent. Increasing rate of unemployment would demotivate students to join formal courses because of their expensive nature. In future, the provision of competitive and job oriented experiences would be available in open forms through DE.

This would divert the job aspirants to join DE while searching for jobs. The competitive life situation in future would encourage inservice and continuing education programme for personnel involved in different areas of modern occupations. New discoveries of science and technology would motivate the skilled workers to

In future if DE is to play its academic and socio-economic roles successfully, planning for DE should base on the identification of social, economic and individual objectives in the Indian context. Unfortunately, so far, DE has not specified its objectives outside the preview of regular courses at university stage. As a result the DE has remained subservient to the regular system.

The course structure, nature of courses, admission policies and evaluation system followed the foot prints of regular courses. The limitations of regular courses with regard to their potentials in development of needed manpower have been identified in similar forms in DE system. The limited scope of DE has been found in relation to satisfaction of economic requirement of employment sector.

With a view to make DE accessible to the existing heterogeneous groups of learners of different occupational background and the freshers aspiring for employment positions there is a need to reorganise the courses of DE. The discipline oriented studies must be diverted towards problem based and work force oriented areas.

This situation needs planning of DE in terms of study of needs of relative youth population specially residing in rural areas, existing language differences in population, remoteness of location of students, present position of university graduates, needed manpower on short-term and long-term basis from the point of view of technological development, etc.

This will pave ways for creation of pragmatic and flexible studies for target group learners of DE. It must take into account cost-benefit nature of instruction while being consistent with national needs.

Place of Distance Education in Traditional University System

Growing popularity of DE in the forms of correspondence courses is one of the indicators of stability of this system in the country. It has been found that in spite of large number of dropouts thousands of students continue with studies till course completion. These students possessed high positive attitude towards DE system (Khan, 1982; Sahoo and Bhat, 1986). In comparison to the attitude of men students towards DE the women students had shown more positive attitude towards the system. The employed students had expressed more positive attitude towards DE that that of their unemployed counterparts.

However, the teaching faculties did not show much commitment towards the system. In this context, the UGC (1986) study revealed that correspondence education was perceived as a kind of social service mechanism giving second chance to the disadvantaged section of society. Most of the faculty members of traditional DE did not favour the idea of total autonomy for DE. They opined that DE can achieve comparability with regular system qualitatively provided it adopts flexibility, openness, adoption of electronic media and provision of research facilities in instructional system.

Most of the teachers were of the opinion that in addition to parity in required qualification of teachers of both regular and DE streams, DE staff should possess additional training on DE instructional system and positive attitude towards DE. Most of the teachers favoured the idea of mobility of teachers between different DE institutions and the teaching departments of parent universities. The extent to which the faculty members of regular courses appreciate this idea would reveal the equal status of DE with regular courses.

This has been observed that even though in the initial stages most of the correspondence study institutions had not maintained parity between teaching faculties of both the streams, currently as per UGC norms improvements have been made in almost all the cases in this context.

However, the teachers of correspondence studies have a longing for getting more facilities for teaching regular courses, guiding PG and doctoral level projects and working on independent research projects.

Most of them are curious to participate in orientation and training programmes on DE. They demand for due representation in academic and policy making bodies of parent universities.

Of course, wherever they got such opportunities they perceived that they were outnumbered by the regular course faculty members who had hostility towards innovations in DE (Sahoo, 1985).

The UGC (1986) study, also, revealed that the Vice-Chancellors of universities having correspondence courses perceived DE as secondary channel of higher education. To them DE is not as good as regular education. While some of them perceived it as a medium of extension education, some of them viewed it as second choice institution for deprived students.

As a whole, the correspondence education has been treated as income generation institution for a sizable number of Indian universities. In most of the cases where participation is sought from regular course faculty staff DE is perceived as a source of additional income for their involvement in instructional activities of DE.

While some of the institutions of DE have been recognised with the status of a separate faculty or institutions of concerned universities in most of the cases the institutions of DE possess conspicuous position since their status in the university statutes is undefined. Therefore, many directors and faculty members of DE demand clear-cut statutory position of DE in university acts. They demand separate identities of DE in terms of academic bodies of their own.

The above facts reflect on undermining positions of DE inside the structure of traditional universities. This problem creates a serious concern for further progress of DE inside traditional university system. No longer DE can be treated as a tail of traditional system of higher education if it intends to achieve socio-economic and academic goals.

The forecast on future position of DE in university structure indicates alternative pictures. One, there will be a shift of traditional DE institutions from its present status to autonomous college status. Two, there will be a deviation from existing structure of traditional DE giving rise to creation of large number of open universities giving due emphasis to regional demands of higher education.

Three, there is every possibility that existing structure of traditional universities would appreciate the distance media based teaching programmes by integrating their campus based teaching with them. They would make use of distance media programmes available through Educational Media Research Centres (EMRC), Audio Visual Research Centres (AVRC), Satellite TV programmes, telephone networks, etc.

An alternative may emerge that almost all the continuing education and in-service programmes of traditional universities would be offered by DE institutions of concerned universities.

Instructional System of Distance Education

Educational Technology has significant contributions towards instructional system of DE in the forms of hardware and software, management technology, and evaluation strategies. Usually the instructional system of DE has three major components:

- Print based course materials and supplementary reading materials;
- Student support services through tutor contacts and assignment system;
- Mass communication and electronic media based programmes.

The traditional institutions of DE have been extending instructional programmes mostly through the first component and partially through the second component. The open university system intends to cover all possible activities under three components systematically. Keeping in view the existing system of instruction of DE and its problems in general some meaningful observations can be made about functions of these components with futuristic perspectives.

Print Based Materials

The research studies on use of print based materials reveal that a wide range of materials are used as correspondence texts of distance education courses of Indian universities. Institutions differ from each cther with regard to formats of such texts.

While a large number of institutions use modified text book type materials some institutions make use of modular and semi modular programmed texts, traditional programmed learning materials, etc. This has been found that a large segment of students population (81 to 91 per cent) depend solely on use of correspondence texts for completing their studies (Anand, 1979; Khan, 1982; Sahoo, 1985; and Tyagi, 1990). All the studies conducted so far have reported about usefulness of printed course materials in one or other ways.

On the basis of research experiences it can be suggested that since print based materials are treated as key components of DE in India, systematic efforts are to be made for preparation of effective written materials, their production and delivery system. The UGC has been giving guidelines for these activities from time to time.

Besides these guidelines the concerned institutions must pay attention to the suggestions rendered by the participants of DE system. First, the print based instructional materials should be based on sound principles of instructional technology. They must have potentials to achieve specific objectives and be learner oriented. The validity and relevance of materials are to be judged against the following criteria:

- specific objectives of concerned courses;
- updated knowledge in the concerned field;
- breadth and depth of knowledge required for the course;
- learnability of materials in terms of students' academic background, interest, motivation, understanding level, language comprehension level, and their local specific environment.

There must be clear-cut mechanisms for integrating the contributions of subject experts and educational technologists in the process of development of materials. While financial incentives act as an influential factor in motivating experts to participate in course development process, academic and professional incentives play vital role in this process.

There is a need for regular scrutiny of instructional materials on the basis of empirical evidences. There must be expert committees for each course in a DE institution for academic decision-making purpose. There must be provisions for seminars, orientations, workshops, and refresher programmes for course writers and editors.

Self-instructional training packages in modular forms for resource persons as suggested by UNESCO (1990) can be used as necessary input of course development programmes. Major emphasis is to be given on tackling the problems of involvement of outside experts in development of course materials.

DE institutions must create their independent bases for printing of materials and scheduling of production keeping in view timely preparation and revision of materials, course schedules and storage system. Appropriate coordination between preparation of materials and production of materials must be ensured for timely supply of materials to DE learners.

Research studies indicate that while appropriate measures are to be taken for quality control of instructional materials, equal emphasis is to be given on management of development of materials, production of materials and sound delivery system.

Besides print based course materials other support materials like relevant excerpts from text books already published, journals and newspapers cuttings and experimental handbooks are in great demand by DE learners. As per suggestions of students and products of DE the institutions must make appropriate arrangements for availability of these materials along with the course texts.

This provision may be encouraged by charging additional contributions from students, supplying materials on credit basis, regional level libraries in study centres and mobile library system. In this context DE institutions will have to reorganise their academic and management set up for each course in specific.

Student Support Services

Instructional processes in DE get strengthened through necessary student support services. The Indian system of DE especially correspondence courses have provisions of assignment and contact programme activities varying from institution to institution in form and nature. No doubt such provisions have strengthened the functioning of DE to some extent.

Studies conducted on usefulness of existing facilities of student support services revealed moderately encouraging responses about the system.

It was also revealed that those students who received evaluated response sheets in time from DE institutions found the assignment system useful to some extent (Sahoo, 1985; UGC, 1986). In the case of IGNOU, comments given by tutors on assignments were found useful by almost 77 per cent students (Tyagi, 1990). It was revealed that there was lack of seriousness in correspondence courses in clarifying students' doubts (Nagaraju, 1982; Sahoo, 1985). Students expressed their demands for detailed comments on assignments, and appropriate evaluation of their performances.

Barring a few cases, because of limited time available for correction of assignments, lack of guidelines given to evaluators and insufficient remuneration, proper steps could not be taken by evaluators for checking the response sheets (Biswal, 1979; Sahoo, 1985). Appropriate distribution of workload of faculty members of correspondence courses was also demanded by the teachers for improvement of evaluation of response sheets.

Lack of proper time management in despatch system of evaluated assignments was marked in most of the institutions (Sahoo, 1985; Bala Subramaniam, 1986; UGC, 1986).

Along with assignment system PCPs are common features of correspondence courses (Dutt, 1976; Biswal, 1979). There are some

DE institutions which insist on compulsory attendance in PCPs in the case of professional courses. In most of the institutions attendance in PCP is kept optional. It was found that in the case of compulsory provision of attendance 70 to 80 per cent students turned up for PCPs. In the case of voluntary attendance around 33 per cent students participated in the PCPs (Sahoo, 1985).

The creation of IGNOU has set an ideal for strengthening student support services through creation of study centres in students' localities, use of local library facilities, use of local laboratory facilities, and tutor student contacts. As presented above traditional system of correspondence courses gave emphasis on assignment and PCP activities. Improvement in these systems draw special attention of academics and managers of these institutions.

Assignment system is to be strengthened with a view to encourage two way interaction between students and tutors. Unfortunately the value of this system has not been perceived with right perspective by the students as well as DE institutions. Improvement of assignment system is carried out in terms of the nature of tasks included under the system and evaluation mechanism adopted therein.

One of the ways of improvement of the nature of assignment is to make it instruction oriented with a coverage of tasks on each and every topic. It should be integrated with study of learning materials having problem solving questions. Of course, the questions can be of objective type as well as essay type along with model answers for self checking.

With a view to minimise the workload of evaluators computerised evaluation system must be incorporated in DE. Questions seeking short answer and long answer responses can be evaluated with the help of model answers supplied to evaluators.

The evaluators must be acquainted with the entire instructional system along with appropriate information about students' background. Since the instructional system is examination oriented most of the learners of DE system expected the weightages for assignment marks in award of examination results (Sahoo, 1985). In this context there has been problems regarding evaluation of copied answers from lesson scripts and text books. Such problems can be avoided by incorporating improved quality questions in assignments.

Responsibility of assignment evaluation can be given to tutors at regional study centre level where regular interaction can be developed through occasional visits of students and tutors on fixed schedules. This can be encouraged along with postal and telephone interactions. Moreover, complete individual record system is to be maintained for each learner indicating his bio-data and present academic growth. The role of computerised filing system can be of great significance in this regard.

Personal contact programmes should not be confined to classroom lectures neglecting group interaction oriented activities. Major emphasis of such programmes should concentrate on clarification of doubts of students' which might have been faced during self study activities. In this context teachers must have thorough knowledge about the instructional inputs given to students and their background.

Teaching activities during contact programmes should highlight solution of students' problems through interaction between teacher and students and students and students. Small group activities, project works and supervised learning exercise must be incorporated in the process of contact programme activities.

Besides these frameworks, the management should take care of due orientation of expert teachers involved in PCP activities, provision of appropriate facilities for generating group interaction environment, and motivation of learners for attending PCPs regularly. Considerations for identification of venues of PCPs, appropriate physical facilities for boarding and lodging, time scheduling etc., are to be made keeping in view learners' requirement and problems.

As mentioned above study centre activities have been encouraged in open university set up. Success of such activities depend upon collaboration between available facilities in students' localities/central places in terms of both manpower and physical resources.

It is a gigantic responsibility on the part of DE institution to identify and motivate local level tutors, training of local tutors, monitoring their activities, and providing appropriate institutional facilities for meeting queries of learners and sustaining motivation of learners for regular participation in study centre activities.

Electronic Media Based Instruction

This has been emphasised in New Policy on Education (1986) that mass media system including radio, TV and computer will be given higher priorities in different levels of education. DE system must exploit such facilities for efficient and cost effective instruction. The studies conducted so far on this aspect project a gloomy picture about the use of electronic media programmes in DE.

This has been revealed by UGC (1986) study that in general there were little support of radio programmes for DE. Even though All India Radio station of Tamil Nadu broadcast educational programmes for correspondence courses, all the DE institutions of the concerned region did not make full use of such facilities. Radio talks to supplement lesson scripts were introduced by only two institutions. Audio cassettes were used to correct pronunciation and delivery in the teaching of languages.

Currently the IGNOU has made provisions for audio and video assisted instructions in study centres. Tyagi (1990) found that around 54 per cent of students of IGNOU of Indore region attending study centres made use of such facilities. Beyond study centre activities such media facilities were not exploited by learners. It was noticed that almost 49 per cent students of IGNOU of this zone did not know about the TV programmes available for students of higher education.

Morever around 45 per cent students did not know about the availability of video cassette programmes for different courses. These facts reflected on passive placement of electronic media in DE system at present.

In spite of present limitations in use of electronic media in DE system, it is forecasted that modern media based programmes will be popular in DE system in future. Research based experiences show that well co-ordinated audio-video system with print based materials can achieve instructional objectives more effectively than the uses of any single medium.

Especially in DE where learner remains away from the formal interaction situation, multimedia package of instruction including video tapes and audio tapes, radio broadcast, TV telecast, computer assisted learning, interactive video programmes and talk back system cab be integrated with instructional system of DE in future.

With a view to develop and produce suitable multi media packages DE institutions must have technological and academic expertise. Collaborations with EMRCs and AVRCs for production and validation of suitable audio and video materials can strengthen this effort. Of course, for TV and radio broadcast of independent programmes of DE there must be proper understanding at concerned departmental levels. The production of appropriate software while keeping in view the course requirement will be a challenging task for DE institutions.

Mere delivery of electronic media based instructional materials will not enable students to make use of such facilities for self studies. Certain considerations like accessibility of hardwares and receiving equipments, suitable time table for broadcast programmes, coverage of programmes in students' regions and programmes in local specific languages are to be kept in mind while planning multi media programmes of instruction. Application of popular communication technologies in DE system with appropriate planning and research support can bring anticipated futures for higher education in the coming century.

Bibliography

Association of Indian Universities, Delhi, *Utilisation of INSAT1B for Higher Education*, New Delhi, 1984.

Association of Indian Universities, *Handbook of Correspondence Courses*, New Delhi, 1984.

Association of India Universities, *Handbook of Distance Education*, New Delhi, 1986.

Baath, J. and Flink, R., *Two-way Communication in Correspondence Education*, Sweden, University of Lund, 1973.

Baath, J.A., *Correspondence Education in the light of a number of Contemporary Teaching Models*, Malmo: Liber Hermods, 1979.

Balasubramaniam, S., *"The Status of Correspondence courses in India"*, University News, Vol. XXIV, No. 42, Nov. 8, 1976.

Bates, A.W. (ed.), *The Role of Technology in Distance Education*, London, Croom Helm, 1984.

Birch, D.W. and Cnthbert, R.E., *Costing Open Learning in Further Education*, London, Council for Educational Technology, 1981.

British Broadcasting Corporation, London, *BBC and the Open University: An Introduction*, London, Author, 1974.

Chang, T.M. *et al.*, *Distance Learning: On the design of an Open University*, Boston, Kluwer-Nijhoff Publishing, 1983.

Chib, S.S., *Teaching by Correspondence in India*, New Delhi, Light & Life, 1977.

Chittibabu, S.V., *Open University and the University of the Air*, Madurai, Madurai University, 1976.

Council of Europe, Council for Cultural Co-operation, *Combined use of Radio and TV and Correspondence Courses in Higher Education*, Strasbourg, Author, 1979.

Crooks, S.B., *Open University of the United Kingdom*, Paris, UNESCO, IIEP, 1976.

Childs, O.D. (1971), *Recent Research Developments in Correspondence Education*, In Mackene and Chistansen (eds.): *The Changing*

World Correspondence Study: International Readings, Pennsylvania State University Press.

Datt, Ruddar, *"Planning and Development of Distance Education"*, Journal of Higher Education 9(3); Spring 1984, *"Role of Distance Education"*, University News 24(13), 1 April, 1986.

Deshmukh, K.G., *"Distance Education and its Future Through Communication Technologies"*, University News 24(47), 16 Dec., 1985.

Dodda, T., *Administration of Distance Teaching Institutions: A Manual,* Cambridge: International Extension College, 1983.

Edwards, E.G., *Higher Education for Everyone,* Nottingham, U.K., Spokesman, 1982.

El-Bushara, J., *Correspondence Teaching at University,* Cambridge, International Extension College, 1973.

Erdos, R.F., *Teaching by Correspondence,* London, Longman, 1967.

Eurich, Nell, *Great Britain's Open University: First Chance, Second Chance or last Chance?* New York: Academy for Educational Development, 1971.

Ewing, J.L., *Correspondence Courses in the Training of Teachers: A Survey of Current Practice in the Commonwealth,* London, H.M.S.O., 1966.

Faure, E., *et al., Learning to Be, The World of Education—Today and Tomorrow,* Paris, UNESCO, 1972.

Ferguson, John, *Open University from Within,* London, University Press, 1975.

Flink, R., *The Telephone as an Instructional aid in Distance Education,* Sweden: University of Lund, 1975.

Flink, R., *The Telephone used in an experiment of Distance Education at University Level,* Sweden, University of Lund, 1976.

Flink, R., *Correspondence Education, Combined with Systematic Telephone Tutoring,* Malmo, Hermods, 1978.

Freire, P., *Pedagogy of the Oppressed,* London, Sheed and Ward, 1970.

Friedman, H.Z., *Case Study in Distance Learning System: Universidad Nacionral Abierta of Venezuela (UNA),* Milton Keynes, Open University, Centre for International Corporation and Services, 1978.

Garrison, D.R., *Understanding Distance Education: A Framework for Future,* London, Routledge, 1989.

Glatter, R., and Wedell, E.G., *Study by Correspondence,* London, Longman, 1971.

Goodenough, Stephanie, *The Free University of Iran: Case Study in Distance Learning Systems,* Milton Keynes: Open University, 1978.

Govt. of India, Ministry of Human Resource Development, *National Policy on Education,* New Delhi, 1986.

Govt. of India, Ministry of Human Resource Development, *National Policy on Education, Programme of Action,* New Delhi, 1986.

Gupta, A.K. (1982): *Status of Correspondence Education in India: A Survey,* in J.S. Deniel *et al.* (eds.), *Learning at a Distance: A World Perspective,* Athabasca University.

Gupta, M.L., *Indian Economy and Higher Education with reference to Correspondence Education,* Jaipur, Aalekha Publi., 1985.

Halperin, S., *Any home a Campus: Everyman's University of Israel,* Washington, D.C., The Institute for Educational Leadership, Inc., 1984.

Harris, W.J.A., *The Distant Tutor,* London, University of Manchester, 1975.

Harry, K., *Case Study in Distance Learning System: University of Lagos Correspondence and Open Studies Unit,* Milton Keynes, Open University, Centre for International Cooperation and Services, 1978.

Holmberg, B., *On the Methods of Teaching by Correspondence,* Sweden, University of Lund, 1960.

Holmberg, B., *Correspondence Education,* Malmo, Hermods-Nkl, 1967.

Holmberg, B., *Distance Education: A Short Handbook,* Malmo, Hermods, 1974.

Holmberg, B., *Distance Education: A Survey and Bibliography,* London, Kogan Page, 1977.

Holmberg, B., *Trends and Status of Distance Education,* London, Kogan Page, 1981.

Holmberg, B., *Status and Trends of Distance Edcuation,* Lund, Lektor Publishing, 1985.

Holmberg, B., *Theory and Practice of Distance Education,* London, Routledge and Kegan Paul, 1989.

Houle, C.O., *The External Degree,* San Franscisco, Jossey—Bass, 1974.

Illich, I.D., *De schooling Society,* New York, Harper and Row, 1971.

Indian University Association for continuing Education, *Correspondence Education,* New Delhi, 1976.

Inter University Board of India, New Delhi, *University Handbook*, 1973.

Johansen, R., *Teleconferencing and Beyond*, New York, Mc Graw-Hill, 1984.

Kabwasa, A. and Kaunda, M.M., (ed.), *Correspondence Education in Africa*, London, Raultledge and Kegan Paul, 1973.

Kailley, G.S., *Distance Teaching at the UPNG: An Evaluation Report of the Matriculation Studies, 1978-79*, New Guinea: University of Papaua, 1960.

Kakemulder, J.R., *Distance Education for Development: Report of International Seminar Addis Ababa, 1979*, Bonn, German Foundation for International Development, 1979.

Kaulshrestha, P.K., *Marek Fisz Probability and Mathematical Statistics*, Delhi, S. Chand & Co., 1961.

Kaye, A.R., *The Sri Lanka Institute of Distance Education: Case study in Distance Learning Systems*, Milton Keynes: Open University, Centre for International Co-operation and Services, 1979.

Kaye, A.R. and Rumble, G., *Distance Teaching for Higher and Adult Education*, London: Croom Helm, 1981.

Keegan, D., *The Foundations of Distance Education*, London, Croom Helm, 1986.

Khan, I., *Suitability of Teaching English through Correspondence*, New Delhi, Ashis, 1985.

Knyanjui, Peter E., *Teaching through Correspondence and Radio: Kenya's Experience*, Nairobi, Ministry of Education, 1972.

Koul, B.N. Singh, B. and Ansari, M.M. (ed.), *Studies in Distance Education*, New Delhi, Association of Indian Universities and Indira Gandhi National Open University, 1988.

Kumar, K., *et al.*, *Motivation of B.Ed. Correspondence Course Students*. Unpublished report, NCERT, New Delhi, 1985.

Mackenzie, O., Postgate, R. and Scupham, J.(eds.), *Open Learning: Systems and Problems in Post-secondary Education*, Paris, UNESCO, 1975.

Mason, J., *Correspondence Programme of the University of Waterloo*, Ontario, Canada, Milton Keynes, Open University Centre for International Co-operation and Services, 1963.

Mason, Robin and Kaye, Anthony, *Mindweave: Communication, Computers and Distance Education*, Oxford, Pergamon, 1989.

Mathur, V.S., *Personal Contact Programmes—A Study in Utility*, Mimiograph, DCC, Panjab University, Chandigarh, 1979.

Menon, M.B., *Multi-media Instructional Strategy at Post-graduate Level: An Experience*, International Conference on New Technologies in Higher Education, Delhi, November, 28-30, 1985.

Ministry of Education and Social Welfare, Govt. of India, *Education in India*, New Delhi, 1950-51.

Ministry of Education and Social Welfare, Govt. of India, *Education in India*, New Delhi, 1955-56.

Ministry of Education and Social Welfare, Govt. of India, *Education in India*, New Delhi 1960-61.

Ministry of Education, Govt. of India, *The Report of the University Education, Commission, 1948-49.*, vol. I, New Delhi, 1962.

Ministry of Education and Culture, Govt. of India, *Expert Committee on Correspondence Courses and Evening Colleges, 1961: Report*, Publication Division, Delhi, 1963.

Ministry of Education, Govt. of India, *Education and National Development, Report of the Education Commission, 1964-66*, New Delhi, 1966.

Ministry of Education, Govt. of India, *Challenge of Education, A Policy Perspective*, New Delhi, 1985.

Ministry of Human Resource Development, Govt. of India, *National Policy on Education*, New Delhi, 1986.

Moore, M.G., *On a Theory of Independent Study*, Hagen, Fern Univeritat, 1977.

Naik, J.P., *The Education Commission and After*, New Delhi, Allied Publishers, 1982.

Neil, M., *Education of Adults at a Distance*, London, Kogan Page, 1981.

National Policy of Education , Programme of Action, Ministry of Human Resource Development, Government of India, August, 1986.

Nagaraju, C.S., *Evaluation of Radio-Correspondence-cum-Contact-In Service Teacher Training Programmes in Kerala*, Unpublished Report, ISEC, Bangalore, 1982.

Ortmeier, A., *External Studies in Australia*, Armidale, Institute of Higher Education, 1982.

Panchmukhi, P.R. "The Open University in a developing Country: A critique", New Quest, Nov.-Dec. 1985.

Parmaji, S., *Distance Education*, Delhi, Sterling Publication, 1984.

Perry, W., *Open University*, London, Open University Press, 1976.

Planning Commission, Govt. of India, *'First Five Year Plan'*, New Delhi, Publication Division, 1953.

Planning Commission, Govt. of India, *'Second Five Year Plan'*, New Delhi, Publication Division, 1956.

Planning Commission, *'Third Five Year Plan'*, New Delhi, Publication Division, 1961.

Planning Commission, Govt. of India, *'Draft Fourth Five Year Plan'*, New Delhi, Publication Division, 1966.

Planning Commission, Govt. of India, *'Fourth Five Year Plan'*, New Delhi, Publication Division, 1970.

Pogrow, Stanley, *Education in the Computer Age*, London, Sage, 1983.

Rao, K.S. (ed.), *Open Learning System*, New Delhi, Lancer, 1989.

Rao, V.K.R.V., *Education and Human Resource Development*, New Delhi, Allied Publishers, 1966.

Reddy, G.R., (ed.) *Open Universities: The Ivory Towers thrown Open*, New Delhi, Sterling, 1988.

Rogers, V.R., and Church, B. (ed.), *Open Education: Critique and Assessment*, Washington: Association for Supervision and Curriculum Development, 1975.

Rumble, G. and Harry, K. (ed.), *Distance Teaching Universities*, London: Croom Helm, 1982.

Rumble, G., *Costing Distance Education*, London, The Commonwealth Secretariat, 1986.

Rumble, G., *Planning and Management of Distance Education*, London, Croom Helm, 1986.

Schramm, W., *Big Media, Little Media: Tools and Technologies for Instruction*, Beverly Hills, Calif.: Sage, 1977.

Sewart, David *et al.*, *Distance Education: International Perspective*, London: Croom Helm, 1983.

Sharma, Shashi Prabha, *Teacher Education—Principles, Theories and Practices*, Kanishka Publishers, Distributors, New Delhi-110002, 2003.

——, *Career Guidance and Counselling—Principels and Techniques*, Kanishka Publishers, Distributors, New Delhi-110002, 2005.

Sharma, Y.K., *Fundamental Aspects of Educational Technology*, Kanishka Publishers, Distributors, New Delhi-110002, 2002.

——, *Textbook of Educational Psychology*, Kanishka Publishers, Distributors, New Delhi-110002, (2004).

——, Principles of Educational and Vocational Guidance (2005).

——, *Population Education—Concepts, Principles and Approaches,* Kanishka Publishers, Distributors, New Delhi-110002, 2005.

Singh, B., *Correspondence Education in India,* National Council of Correspondence Education, India, 1979.

Singh, B., *Correspondence Education in India,* Patiala: National Council for Correspondence Education, 1979.

Singh, M., *Teaching by Correspondence,* Patiala, Punjabi University Press, 1976.

Singh, R.K., *Building a University,* H.P. University, Simla, 1972.

Status and Trends of Distance Education: A Survey and Bibliography, London, Kogan Page, 1981.

Swaminathan, D., *"Utilization of INSAT Facility for Higher Education in India,"* Paper presented at the International Conference on "New Technologies in Higher Education, Nov. 28-29, 1985, New Delhi.

Taylor, H., *Students Without Teachers—The Crisis in the University,* New York, McGraw Hill, 1969.

Tunstall, J. (ed.), *The Open University Opens,* London, Routledge, 1974.

Tyagi, P., *A. Study of Socio-Economic and Academic Background of Students of IGNOU and their Perception of Multimedia Instructional System,* Unpublished M.Ed. Dissertation, D.A. University, Indore, 1990.

UNESCO, Research materials used in distance teaching by higher education institutions. Bangkok, UNESCO Regional Office for Education in Asia and the Pacific, 1984. (Regional Co-operative Programme in Higher Education for Development).

University Grants Commission, *Standards of University Education,* New Delhi, 1963.

Wagner, L., *The Economics of Educational Media,* London, The Macmillan Press, 1982.

Wentworth, R.B., (ed.), *11th ICCE Conference Papers I,* London, Tuitian House, 1978.

Willen, B., *Distance Education at Swedish Universities,* Uppsala: Almgvist & Wiksell International, 1981.

Woodley, A., *The Open University of the United Kingdom,* Amsterdam: European Cultural Foundation, Institute of Education, 1981.

Young, M., Perraton, H., Jenkins, J. and Dodds, *Distance Teaching for the Third World: The Lion and The Clockwork Mouse,* London, Routledge and Kegan Paul, 1980.

Index